Understanding Technological Politics

A Decision-Making Approach

Patrick W. Hamlett
North Carolina State University

PRENTICE HALL, Englewood Cliffs, New Jersey 07632

Library of Congress Cataloging-in-Publication Data

Hamlett, Patrick W.
    Understanding technological politics : a decision-making approach
    Patrick W. Hamlett.
       p.   cm.
    Includes index.
    ISBN 0-13-947094-8
    1. Technology and state--United States.   2. Science and state-
-United States.   3. Decision-making--United States.   I. Title.
    T21.H36   1991
    338.97306--dc20   91-21780
                                                                  CIP

Acquisitions editor: Karen Horton
Production editor: Elaine Lynch
Copy editor: Mary Louise Byrd
Cover design: Ben Santora
Editorial assistant: Dolores Mars
Prepress buyer: Kelly Behr
Manufacturing buyer: Mary Ann Gloriande

 © 1992 by Prentice-Hall, Inc.
A Simon & Schuster Company
Englewood Cliffs, New Jersey 07632

Printed in the United States of America
10 9 8 7 6 5 4 3 2 1

ISBN 0-13-947094-8

Prentice-Hall International (UK) Limited, *London*
Prentice-Hall of Australia Pty. Limited, *Sydney*
Prentice-Hall Canada Inc., *Toronto*
Prentice-Hall Hispanoamericana, S.A., *Mexico*
Prentice-Hall of India Private Limited, *New Delhi*
Prentice-Hall of Japan, Inc., *Tokyo*
Simon & Schuster Asia Pte. Ltd., *Singapore*
Editora Prentice-Hall do Brasil, Ltda., *Rio de Janeiro*

Contents

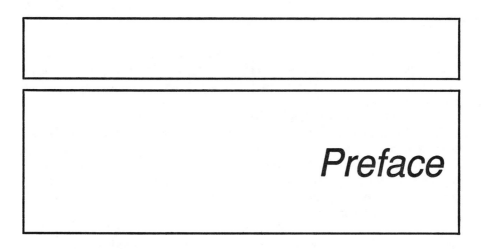

Preface

This book deals with political decision makers and decision making about modern science and technology. Our goal is to provide a useful theoretical framework for understanding how decision makers reach the kinds of decisions they do concerning a wide array of scientific and technological issues. Unlike much of the general literature about the social and political consequences of science and technology, and about the impact of science and technology on contemporary politics, in this book we will avoid the esoteric abstractions often found elsewhere. Our goal here is to examine real decisions made by real decision makers facing very real problems. Only by beginning our investigations at the most objective level can we hope ever to evaluate the larger theoretical importance of the phenomena we study.

There can be no doubt that both science and technology have dramatically changed how we live, work, spend leisure time, and understand the natural world around us. It is the awareness of how powerful these two phenomena are that leads many people to hunt for ways to understand science and technology and to hope that they can impose some kind of conscious social control over the directions in which they move. Science and technology seem to be taking us, willy-nilly, with them, and they augur even greater changes in the future. While in an earlier era, most people welcomed scientific discoveries and the technological uses to which they were put, today many of us are wary, even frightened, that we, the human race, may no longer be able to direct and guide science and technology, we fear that, as Ralph Waldo Emerson lamented more than a century ago, "Things are in the saddle, and ride men."

We will examine three categories of problems that are caused or exacerbated by modern science and technology: environmental, social, and economic problems, technological inflexibility problems, and political problems. In a vicious circle of technology-based challenges, we will find that each of these clusters of difficulties tends to make the other two harder to manage. Establishing control over these problems requires serious and careful analysis, lest our actions be blind and ultimately more harmful than the problems they are intended to correct. However serious the challenges science and technology present to us, it is clear that they also proffer an array of opportunities and promises we do not wish to forgo needlessly.

We begin by focusing on specific individuals making distinct decisions about real technologies, what they hope to achieve through those decisions, and what steps they take to ensure that the decisions they make are indeed implemented. Our fundamental belief is that whatever larger social, economic, and political consequences or culture-shaping powers science and technology may have, all technologies necessarily involve real people making real decisions; this is the point at which we begin our analysis.

After we identify all of the major participants in the decision making process, we will examine what decision making is like for those individuals. What sorts of different decision-making environments are there? What pressures, constraints, goals, limits, values, definitions, and cultural norms exist in these various decision-making environments, and how do they shape the decisions that individuals make? By doing this, we take a step toward more theoretical explanations of decision making about science and technology, while remaining in contact with the lives and careers of real people.

Our next step is to discover the kinds of interactions that occur between decision makers in one environment and decision makers in other environments. We assume that decision makers in a particular environment pursue specific technological projects but still need certain decisions from decision makers who operate in a different environment. How do they obtain those desired decisions? What steps do they take to encourage, induce, manipulate, or coerce decision makers in other environments to make the specific decisions needed to allow their project to go forward? This is the heart of the politics of science and technology, because while the decision makers who support the technological project are working to obtain facilitating decisions from crucial decision makers, other people may be working to stop or change that technological project and may be trying to get those very same crucial decision makers to make different decisions. Knowing who "wins" and who "loses" in these contests, and why they won or lost, is critical to understanding technological politics. It virtually *is* technological politics.

We then take one more step toward theory by discussing certain kinds of regularized and predictable accommodations that emerge among decision makers. These accommodations frequently involve "understandings" and "agreements" among decision makers who interact often, and they permit certain kinds of decisions to be made with minimal outside interference or opposition. It is at this level of theory, we argue, that we can discuss the larger social, economic, and political consequences of science and technology without getting lost in speculative and conjectural assertions that so often seem to have nothing to do with what happens in the real world.

Following the description of this decision-making framework, we examine technological decision making in several case studies: international economic competition, the military, risk assessment, biotechnology, and the environment. This multilayered model allows us to understand how individual decisions contribute to the three levels of technology-induced problems and sets the stage for suggestions about how to change decision making about science and technology for the better.

No project of this size can be completed without the help, support, and assistance of others. I want to express my special appreciation and thanks to Edward Woodhouse, of Rensselaer Polytechnic Institute, Norman Vig, of Carleton College, and Mark Rushefsky, of Southwest Missouri State University, for their careful readings of virtually the entire manuscript, and to Michael Kraft, of the University of Wisconsin—Green Bay, for his comments and suggestions for the chapters on regulation and the environment. This book is substantially improved for their efforts, while, of course, its errors are mine.

I also thank Sheila Jasanoff and the faculty and staff of Cornell University's Program on Science, Technology and Society for their help and hospitality during a year's very stimulating residence, as this manuscript was completed. Karen Horton and her staff at Prentice Hall also merit sincere thanks for their patient support and assistance in moving this project smoothly through the publishing process. Finally, I commend the good people at Dragonfly Software for the creation of a truly superb, flexible, and powerful word processor, Nota Bene. Managing a manuscript of this length and complexity would have been so much more difficult without this splendid program. It provides an author with everything needed for writing, except the ideas themselves!

Patrick W. Hamlett
North Carolina State University

Chapter 1

Studying the Politics of Science and Technology

When we think of science and technology, we usually imagine men and women in white laboratory coats attending to complex equipment in crowded laboratories or we see highly trained engineers designing and testing complex machines and devices. Everywhere creative activity is visible. We expect cool-headed rationality, precision, objectivity, and experimentation as the order of the day. In this setting, it may indeed seem strange to talk of the politics of science and technology; nothing could seem further from the pulling and hauling of politics than this clean, orderly laboratory.

Yet this pristine view of things is deceptive. Look around you. Most of the major problems and issues facing us at home and around the world are caused or exacerbated by modern science and technology—from pesticide and hazardous waste problems, to ozone depletion and the greenhouse effect, to the nuclear arms race. Most scientific and technical fields are continuously embroiled in political controversy. The combined effects of science and technology have altered our vision of reality, accelerated the pace of social change, and changed forever how we do business, how we work, and where we live. We once believed that these culture-shaping changes constituted "progress," but today we are far less sure about the beneficial effects of some of these changes. Indeed, we have begun to worry about whether we can actually live with some of those changes.

Not only has "progress" changed the way we live, but it has also challenged the capabilities of our political institutions and practices in ways that none could have anticipated more than 200 years ago when the Constitution was written. The speed of technological change creates new problems even as it solves old ones. What is more, the increasing dependence of government policy on highly specialized knowledge and expertise changes the contours of political decision making. Everywhere, it seems, public policy decisions are made by, or strongly influenced by, persons with advanced scientific or technical training. William Lowrance cites just a few examples of the important decision-making roles of technical experts:

Teams of automotive engineers design cars and sell the designs through corporate management to the public. Pharmaceutical experts develop, test, and push drugs toward the market. Nuclear power plant designers weight the ratio of instant to delayed (cancer) death risks they design into reactors. Nuclear managers decide, in cleaning up after an accident, between exposing a few workers to radiation for relatively long times and exposing more workers for shorter times. Much research by social scientists—on the effect of school busing on educational achievement, on the effect of incarceration on criminal recidivism, on the influence of wage incentives in acceptance of occupational hazard—is so integral to policymaking that analysis can hardly be distinguished from advocacy. And of course some scientists and physicians themselves become high official decisionmakers in industry, labor, and government.[1]

Policies concerning the need for new safety features in consumer products, the effectiveness and safety of a new drug, the riskiness of new industrial chemicals, the value of new weapons systems, the possibility of manned space flight, the feasibility and desirability of new forms of genetically altered organisms, the need for greater international economic competitiveness—will be designed by policymakers who pay careful attention to the conclusions reached by technical specialists. When, for instance, a nuclear engineer makes a decision about the safety of a specific reactor design, she is making an important public decision, even though a private utility or reactor manufacturer may be paying her salary.

Science and technology often present government policymakers with their most difficult problems. Given the complexity of many issues, and the potential for grave harm if they make a mistake, should policymakers pay more attention to technical advisers or to their constituents, who often lack technical expertise? How are policymakers who do not have extensive technical training supposed to assess the quality of the "expert" advice they receive? Are the traditional representative practices and procedures of American government capable of addressing issues of such urgency and complexity?

PATHOLOGIES OF TECHNOLOGICAL DECISION MAKING

It is inevitable that phenomena so widespread as modern science and technology would shape—and, in some ways, distort—the larger society in which they operate. It is also inevitable that political authorities would need to manage, if not control, so potent a social force. A vital question, is then, How well does the American political system handle the deep and pervasive transformations introduced by modern science and technology? Unfortunately, there is reason for considerable concern on this score.

Technological decision making in the United States exhibits a number of troubling and undesirable features. Some of these are political in nature, but others, although from outside the political process, still impede effective political decision making. We can identify at least three interlocking levels of problems that affect how technological decisions are made in the United States: social, economic, and ecological problems, flexibility problems, and political problems.

Social, Economic, and Ecological Problems

Mountains of hazardous wastes, air, water, and land pollution, the exposure of workers to dangerous industrial chemicals, the greenhouse effect, dangerous consumer products—these, along with a host of other social and environmental insults, continue to plague us on a most direct and tangible level, despite more than two decades of effort to alleviate them. What is more, we are on the verge of introducing technologies—genetic engineering, more destructive weapons systems, and industrial robotics, among others—that will raise even more troubling issues.

Although these problems continue to fester, worries about international competitiveness seem to require less concern for environmental, health, and safety problems, pitting the economy against ecology. American corporations, eager to take advantage of production savings in low-cost labor markets, shift more and more of their factories overseas, leaving American workers and their communities devastated. New technologies menace jobs of millions, all the while de-skilling those jobs that remain. One of the ironies of technological politics is that often the same sets of decisions that lead to useful innovations in one area also create pressing issues in other areas.

Flexibility Problems

A second level of problems, derived from structural features of current technology, frustrates our efforts to control and correct social, economic, and ecological problems. Simply put, flexibility problems emerge because once technologies are actually in place, their structural features often drastically reduce the range of options available to decision makers. Should unexpected problems arise with an inflexible technology, the ability to respond is highly constricted by the technology itself.

The following discussion is based on David Collingridge's conclusions about several of these features.[2]

Entrenchment   As they are put in place, technologies become economically and socially entrenched and thus harder and harder to alter or modify. As technologies develop and disperse throughout the economy, other technologies and technical systems adjust to the new technology's existence. Over time, enough adjustment will occur that any attempt to alter the first technology will require readjusting many, or perhaps all, of the technologies surrounding it, often at prohibitive expense. This feature of technology reflects the many ways in which different technical systems become interdependently implicated in each other's operations.

Indeed, Collingridge adds, as a technology becomes more and more entrenched, alternatives to that technology gradually disappear. The automobile is an excellent illustration. When the motorcar was new, at least three different power systems were under active consideration: internal combustion engines, steam, and battery power. When the industry settled on the internal combustion engine, experimentation and research on the other two systems stopped. Design standardization is a normal, and critical, step in the evolution of a new technological product (discussed further in Chapter 3). However, decades later, when we needed alternatives to the gas-guzzling, air-polluting internal combustion engine, there were none to be found. A technology, just to the extent that it becomes embedded in an array of ancillary and auxiliary technologies, loses much of the flexibility it had when it was new.

Competition Competition is capitalism's great engine of economic change. Ironically, it can also undermine our ability to manage or control the technologies that the free market engenders. The same competitive pressures that impel a corporate decision maker to pursue promising new technological opportunities also make it very difficult for that decision maker to resist a technological option, once discovered. If one corporation fails to exploit a new technological breakthrough, another will. Each feels the need to preempt rivals by developing the new technical opportunity, lest one lose out for delaying.

Competition means that corporate decision makers necessarily have to limit the scope of relevant issues affecting their decisions. Concerns about environmental, ecological, and health and safety issues, while not wholly absent, necessarily play only secondary roles in the corporate boardroom. This may be good for business, but it is not clear that it is good for everyone else.

Hedging and Lead Time Another structural feature of modern technology that reduces flexibility for decision makers is the propensity of technical planners to hedge against failure to meet projected demand for a technical product by developing or purchasing additional capacity or units. Energy-generating technologies operate this way. Planners, for example, attempting to anticipate public demand for electricity and not wanting to fall short, purchase additional generating capacity before the expected demand occurs. They do not want to face an angry electricity-consuming public without the ability to meet their demands. Because the purchase and installation of new generating capacity take time, decisions to expand capacity have to be made well in advance of when the expected demand actually materializes. Facing only partially predictable public demand in a context of long lead times, planners make advanced commitments to specific technologies. These decisions, once made, are very difficult and very costly to reverse should circumstances and conditions change, thus significantly reducing the decision makers' flexibility.

Scale Another factor, also evident in energy technologies but in others as well, is the desire to obtain economies of scale in the use of such technologies. Deploying very large technological units, such as huge electricity-generating facilities, allows for lower electricity costs to the consumer, just as economies of scale in manufacturing allow for lower shelf prices the products in the marketplace. However, once in place, large technological units are harder to modify should new information make modification advisable.

Technological systems based on large unit size are harder to alter than systems based on small unit size for the technologies in question. When long lead times and hedging against unknowable future demand are joined to large unit size, the result is a technological system that may be very rigid and inflexible and thus very difficult and very expensive to change.

Unfortunately, many, if not all, of the social, economic, and ecological problems derive from well-entrenched, inflexible technologies. Correcting these problems requires facing up to the difficulties of making changes in technical systems that are structurally opposed to such changes. Moreover, important economic interests have important stakes in the technologies just as they exist, and they resist the extensive alterations that may be needed to reduce air and water pollution, maintain employment, and . . . the list is endless.

Political Problems

By themselves, social, economic, ecological, and flexibility problems certainly are challenging enough, but they become even more difficult because the political processes through which we might try to deal with them too often impede our ability to respond effectively. Thus, a third level of difficulty focuses on the political decision making through which we try to resolve these other challenges.

We all know that the American political system was not designed to be the most efficient in the world; the authors of the Constitution feared unlimited power more than they desired efficiency, and they placed institutional obstacles in the way of anyone who would try to wrest control of the government. Thus, we see the familiar separation of powers, checks and balances, and federal structure of the American system of government. Freedom, not efficiency, was their first goal.

The intersection of modern science and technology and our late eighteenth-century form of government is complex. We have ample evidence that technological issues in America are often highly partisan and polarized, with decision makers from one interest group regularly obstructing and frustrating the technological projects pursued by decision makers from other interests. The built-in propensity for conflict between the president and the Congress and our open and freewheeling legislative system seem to invite such obstruction and blocking efforts. When coupled with the American penchant for seemingly endless administrative procedures and alacrity in resorting to the courts to resolve conflicts, controversial technological projects can easily take years, even decades, to complete. Decision makers have nearly unlimited opportunities to fight and refight and re-re-fight each political decision affecting a technological project.

One result of these struggles to dominate the flow and direction of decisions is the loss of technical objectivity. Science and technology policymaking is much more dependent than other policy areas on the availability and flow of technical information. Thus, having a monopoly on technical expertise can be a very real political asset. Having the best available scientific and technical information is crucial to designing and completing realistic technological projects and to defending a project against others who seek to obstruct or block it. Both sides in technological disputes thus try to discredit the scientific expertise marshalled by the other side, thereby reducing the influence of expertise in general and casting doubt on the ability to find unbiased, reliable scientific or technical advice. At the same time, and because of the heated charges and countercharges, policymakers try even harder to find exhaustively complete technical analyses of the issue to guide their decisions.

Thus, too often we find technological issues mired in continuing procedural challenges and delays. Public discussion of technical issues in this environment becomes ever more intransigent, politically polarized, and sensationalized, adding to the policymaking paralysis. Adversaries resort to these kinds of techniques because they expect—and accurately, it seems—opposing decision makers to employ similar tactics. It becomes ever more difficult to assess the technical claims and counterclaims, for policymakers and for the public.

The Vicious Circle

These three levels of problems reinforce each other in a kind of vicious circle. Efforts to relieve air and water pollution run headlong into entrenched, large-scale technologies (which often create the pollution). Those with a stake in such technologies, even though they may endorse environmental protection in general, fight to preserve and protect what represents for them very significant investments of time, money, and talent. To protect those investments, along with the jobs and general prosperity that flow from them, decision makers will make use of the many procedural tactics the political process provides to ward off efforts to curtail or eliminate those technologies. Thus, flexibility problems with the physical technologies we use in our society impede efforts to ameliorate ecological problems created by those technologies.

At the same time, the perception that the social, economic, and ecological problems are worsening exerts increased pressures for political action. But legislative, administrative, and judicial gridlock obstructs the efficient resolution of the problems. The democratic, participatory political processes of American government get used to prevent, delay, and block public decision making on the merits of the issues involved. Political wrangling undermines the policy-relevant cognitive authority of scientific and technical expertise, opening the door to political pressure tactics as the issues work their way through the political system. Frustrated by endless delays and by the use of questionable political tactics, policy adversaries resort to even more agitation, exaggeration, and sensationalism to force decisions from reluctant decision makers. This results in highly polarized political struggles in which opposing positions are rigidly asserted, contributing to yet more political gridlock.

In the face of these kinds of difficulties, even if solutions to the social, economic, and ecological problems of technology finally do emerge, they may appear too late to be effective, or may become watered down or incoherent because of the political compromises needed to elicit sufficient support from contending interests. Surely, we can do better than this.

THE REST OF THE BOOK

How did we get into this fix—and can we extricate ourselves? Answering these questions is part of what this book is about.

We will examine a number of specific cases of technological controversy, exploring the decision-making process in each instance. We will also introduce a general theoretical framework useful for dissecting these and other technological disputes. This framework will help us to tease out of the whirling complexities of technological controversies the most important features and most salient processes. We will finish with a series of recommended changes in how we, as a society, make decisions about technology, recommendations to help us untangle the complexities and confusions found in technological politics and set us on a course to deal with all three levels of problems in technological decision making.

ENDNOTES

1. W. W. LOWRANCE, *Modern Science and Human Values* (New York: Oxford University Press, 1985), p. 6.

2. DAVID COLLINGRIDGE, *The Social Control of Technology* (New York: St. Martin's Press, 1980).

Chapter 2

The Decision-Making Framework

Naturally enough, social forces as powerful as science and technology attract the interest of a large number of scholars and commentators. Even a brief collection of books and articles on modern science and technology would fill a number of library shelves.

Much of the writing on science and technology falls into one of two camps: those who propose "grand theories" to explain the full range of impacts of science and technology and those who produce narrow case studies of specific technical change, but with little or no effort to draw larger theoretical conclusions. Each of these camps suffers from defects that correspond precisely with the strength of the other. Grand theory writings are often too vague and lack much empirical grounding, whereas case studies are, if anything, too narrowly empirical, failing to reach for broader, theoretically interesting conjectures.

What we need for an understanding of technological politics is a middle approach, one that is grounded in the real world of day-to-day technological decision making but can also reach for theoretical significance. We also need an approach that can make specific recommendations about how to resolve the three categories of problems we discussed in Chapter 1.

TECHNOLOGICAL PROJECTS

In simple terms, our approach to understanding technological politics involves focusing attention on the kinds of decisions about technology that get made in our society. Every year thousands of important decisions about science and technology are made: whether to conduct a specific kind of scientific or engineering research, to commercialize a new innovation, to publish the results of a particular experiment, to fund a laboratory or a scientific project, to impose new environmental, health and safety, or other kind of regulation upon a new or an old technology, to protest the use of an existing technology, and on and on. Indeed, a good case can be made that technological politics are, at heart, the sum total of all of the decisions involved with science and technology.

Such a situation, however, leaves us in a theoretical bind. We cannot hope to examine, willy-nilly, each of the thousands of decisions about science and technology made every year. Thus, we use the concept of a **technological project** to encompass discrete, identifiable clusters of decisions associated with specific technological products, processes, or materials. The idea of a technological project will help us to focus attention on a limited number of closely related technological decisions and underscore our interest in the personal and organizational goals of the people who make those decisions.

Technological projects would include, for instance, a chemical company's decision to bring a new agricultural pesticide to market, or an environmental group's attempts to have a specific substance declared a health hazard, or the Pentagon's efforts to develop a new fighter aircraft. The notion of a technological project is specific and concrete. Thus, "biotechnology" is too broad a concept to be a technological project, but bovine growth hormone (a specific application of bio-technology) is a technological project for a number of individuals and groups. "Military technology" is also too broad to be a technological project, although the B-2 bomber is a project for many decision makers. "Nuclear energy," likewise, is too general, but the Diablo Canyon reactor in California is the focus of several competing technological projects.

It is important to note that there may be more than one, sometimes several, technological projects associated with a specific technology. Thus, the chemical firm pursues the technological project of bringing its new pesticide successfully from the laboratory to the marketplace, while the environmental group pursues an opposite course: the technological project of banning or severely limiting, the use of that same pesticide. The two projects are diametrically opposed, and the stage is set for a major political battle between the contending sides. In other cases, different interests and different groups may pursue complementary technological projects, as when both defense contractors and certain labor unions support congressional funding of specific weapons programs. A specific technology, then, may be the focus of several technological projects pursued by various individuals and groups whose interests are affected by the technology.

INDIVIDUAL TECHNOLOGICAL DECISION-MAKER

The next concept we will employ in understanding the politics of science and technology is the **individual technological decision-maker**. Even though we will use abstract concepts during our discussions, at all times we need to keep the individual technological decision-maker in mind.

There are many individuals who make decisions concerning science and technology: corporate executives, plant managers, bureaucrats, the president of the

United States, members of Congress, congressional staff members and aides, judges, grass-roots political organizers, labor union representatives, engineers and scientists, production workers, machinists, and a whole host of others. It is also certain that some of these individuals have more power and more influence in the decision-making process than do others. For some, power emanates from the positions they hold within powerful organizations, such as corporations or government bureaucracies. For others, such as scientists and engineers, power derives from the possession of specialized knowledge. For still others, what power they do have derives from their ability to disrupt or obstruct the decisions made by other, more powerful individuals. Consumer and environmental groups, or even production-line sabotage perpetrated by disgruntled workers, are examples.

As we shall discuss in more detail, individuals involved in making decisions about science and technology have all of the personal foibles, strengths, personal ambitions, faults, emotions, and rivalries of people everywhere. These personality traits affect the kinds of decisions they make in specific technological projects, in allocating resources for science and technology, in deciding to pursue a potentially revolutionary innovation, or in choosing to forgo one promising avenue of research for another. Such traits have a great influence on the direction and speed of technical change, and are yet another reason for never losing sight of the importance of the individual technological decision-maker as we move through our analysis.

TECHNOLOGICAL DECISION-MAKING ARENAS

Having said all this, we must find concepts that will allow us to rise above the realm of the individual, to draw larger generalizations about scientific and technological decision makers. These larger concepts, however, must be rooted in the actions of individuals as they pursue their technological projects, so that we do not lose touch with the empirical foundation of our analysis.

Our third concept, **technological decision-making arenas**, permits this. A **technological decision-making arena** is the decision-making environment in which the individual technological decision-maker operates. Each technological decision-making arena has its own characteristic set of pressures, limitations, attitudes, constraints, norms, and goals that shape and form that specific environment. The thinking, planning, and deciding that individual technological decision makers do as they proceed with their projects will be affected by the specific characteristics of the environments in which they must operate.

We should not conclude, however, that all of the decision makers in the same arena agree with each other on all matters; in fact, many times they will be opponents or competitors. The point is that they are all subject to similar pressures and limitations, pursue similar goals, see their situation in similar ways, and view participants from other arenas in about the same manner.

Not only may there be competition and conflict between units within the same technological decision-making arena, but similar conflicts may exist inside any specific unit. For example, an individual technological decision maker, say, a scientist working in an industrial laboratory or a marketing vice president working for the same company, may come upon a new technological product that he or she wants to see commercialized. The decision maker will have to form alliances with sympathetic decision makers within the firm to push the specific project forward. There will have to be conferences with other people in research and development, in marketing, production, advertising, and so on, in order to organize and orchestrate a coalition to get, and keep, the company's support for the project.

However, there will be many other decision makers within the same firm who will want to see the company's resources directed toward other technological projects. Just because someone has a good idea is no guarantee that the company will even recognize it, much less devote considerable resources to developing and marketing it. It takes effort and skill to bring a technological project forward successfully.

This same sort of internal coalition building is needed in other technological decision-making arenas. Thus, specific decision makers in environmental or consumer groups must work to convince others within those groups to adopt specific technological projects, often in competition with other people who want the organization to move in other directions. Within the Pentagon, to cite another example, individual technological decision makers work long hours to ensure that the specific weapons they are working on continue to receive adequate funding, while others naturally want those same funds for different weapons systems.

The concept of technological decision-making arenas allows us to see the world in the same way that a specific decision maker sees it, and thus gain a better understanding of the pressures and forces that help to shape the specific decisions that he or she makes. We rise above the concrete, empirical realm of the individual technological decision maker without losing touch with the significance of that individual for the larger process of technological decision making.

A careful look at who is involved in technological politics reveals at least eight separate decision-making environments in America today; each arena is a special focus of personal, institutional, social, and political pressures affecting how technological decisions are made in U.S. society. The eight environments are the corporate-managerial arena, the executive arena, the legislative arena, the regulatory arena, the judicial arena, the popular mobilization arena, the academic-professional arena, and the labor arena.

Corporate-Managerial Arena

This technological decision-making arena encompasses business enterprises, corporations, firms, factories, plants, corporate research and development facilities, and major industries that operate most often within a market pattern and for which technological products, materials, and processes form a significant portion of their output. Companies in this arena vary greatly in size, resources, diversity of product lines, extent of marketing and distribution networks, and levels of R&D investments. All, though, operate under broadly similar market conditions.

New technologies often present important financial and career risks for decision makers in the corporate-managerial arena. A new product innovation may simply fail—indeed, most do—because it lacks performance characteristics significantly different from products already on the market, or has flaws or defects that emerge only over time, or may face other, unforeseen problems. Great investments may, and sometimes are, lost in such risky enterprises. Yet not to compete through innovation may mean losing one's customers and one's market to more aggressive, creative, and risk-tolerant competitors.

Technological innovation presents more than financial risks for the corporation. Personal careers also ride on the outcome of new ventures. Many people entertain an overly rational concept of the processes of corporate technological decision making; in fact, corporate technological decision making is cross-cut with personal ambitions, jealousies, rivalries, hesitations, and occasional desperate gambles. Donald Schon has done a good job of describing some of the ways in which the real process of technical growth differs from the overly rational decision-making model. He shows how corporate decisions to invest or not in new technologies often hinge on the personality, perspicacity, and tolerance for risk of key personnel.[1]

Today, decision makers in the corporate-Managerial arena face formidable economic and technological challenges from overseas. No longer secure within the overwhelmingly dominant economy in the world, U.S. corporations find themselves in very intense and unexpected competition with Japanese, European, South Korean, and some Third World manufacturers. A successful response to these challenges requires not only that manufacturing technologies change, but that the social and political culture of the corporation itself must adapt to a new environment. The existing, traditional distribution of decision-making power within the corporate-managerial arena may be the greatest obstacle to the re-invigoration of American enterprise. Whether decision makers within the arena can make the adjustments needed remains to be seen.

Executive Arena

All of the next four arenas are located within the federal (and state or local) government, although each is different enough from the other three to warrant separate treatment.

The executive arena encompasses all of the executive branch departments, bureaus, and agencies that purchase technology or support basic and applied research. Decision makers within the executive arena work under a different set of constraints, limitations, and goals than those found in the corporate-managerial arena, although decision makers in both environments frequently operate in tandem to achieve common goals.

By far the largest executive arena involvement in technological politics is in national security. The federal government expends hundreds of billions of dollars annually to develop and purchase the most sophisticated weaponry and intelligence technologies, knowing that in a very short time the technologies will be obsolete and require even more expensive replacements. In addition, executive agencies purchase and support a wide array of civilian technologies, from energy production and conservation, to agriculture, to space and aeronautics, to medical and biomedical research.

While many of the executive arena decision makers directly involved in affecting technology are bureaucrats, and thus largely insulated from changing political trends, their agencies are often caught up in presidential politics and the alterations in party control of the administration. They must implement each new chief executive's policies according to changing sets of priorities and in response to the pressures of different electoral coalitions. Alterations in the upper-level leadership positions may also affect the continuity of established programs, restructure offices and staffs, and change budgetary or spending priorities.

Although the executive branch focuses on the president, the executive arena itself is very large and diverse. It often happens that various parts of the executive branch end up working against each other, either because of the inherent difficulties of coordinating activities among agencies with different tasks and agendas or because of intentional obstruction resulting from the unavoidable jockeying for power and influence within the arena. While we think of the president as "in charge" of the executive arena, he may find the toughest job is to keep the government from governing without him.

Legislative Arena

The legislative arena differs from the executive in three ways: its multiple centers of power, its decentralized organization, and its highly constituent-centered operating style.

Congress lacks the centralized coordination found in the executive branch of government; the committee and subcommittee system largely precludes a unified institutional approach to technological issues. However, congressional control of the federal budget makes it a truly formidable, if often unpredictable, partner in government technological decision making. Eventually, every technological initiative in the executive arena must run the gamut of congressional budget-making.

Congress is generally more susceptible to sectional or local interest group pressures than is the executive, which can balance such interests against each other in its national constituency. Not so for most members of Congress, who as a rule depend on special interest groups in their home district. All changes in the federal budget or even small alterations in federal agency plans and policies concern Congress; minor cuts in federal spending may spell massive dislocations for the home district and adverse economic consequences for important constituents. The closing or moving of a federal facility, such as a defense plant, research institute, or military post, can mean electoral disaster for the member thought to be lax in protecting the economic well-being of voters back home.

Congressional decision makers exhibit as much of the idiosyncratic, personal, nontechnical (and sometimes nonrational) traits visible in both the corporate-managerial and the executive arenas. Although "cozy" relationships often exist among congressional subcommittees, federal bureaucracies, and the relevant interest groups, the relationship is never wholly predictable, and can change dramatically with changes in personnel, party control, or movements among the other lobbying interests.

Regulatory Arena

The regulatory arena is similar to both the executive and legislative arenas, but distinguishable in its perspectives and by the constraints under which it operates. Federal regulatory agencies are commissioned to protect the public through the promulgation and enforcement of a host of rules, regulations, and standards that affect virtually every aspect of technological production, marketing, distribution, finance, performance, and safety. Of all the arenas, only the regulatory possesses what might be termed a general distrust of technological products and processes, coupled with a willingness to intervene in the private production and provision of goods and services.

There is much controversy about the effectiveness of regulatory agencies. Members of the corporate-managerial arena complain loudly about unnecessary interruption and interference from government bureaucrats and about the imposition of overly stringent regulations and standards that strangle the corporation's ability to compete effectively in national and international markets. On the other hand, decision makers in the popular mobilization arena accuse the regulators of callously neglecting their mandated duties, of being "captured" by the industries they are supposed to regulate, and of willingly abandoning the public interest in favor of the economic interests of major corporations.

The regulatory arena's combination of executive, legislative, and judicial powers in the formulation and enforcement of regulations, and the sometimes wide discretionary powers it possesses make the regulators inviting targets for interest group pressures. Their budgetary dependence upon Congress also makes them liable to pressures from that quarter. Both the crusading member of Congress making a name in the media and the member dependent on corporate favor for reelection will bring pressures to bear on the regulators.

Judicial Arena

Members of the judicial arena are among the more reluctant participants in technological decision making. However, as the social consequences of modern technology proliferate, older definitions of legal rights and responsibilities change, requiring the courts to pass judgments in new, and to them, foreign, terrains. Privacy issues in the computer age, the legal ownership and patentability of artificial life forms, damage claims from toxic waste disposal, and a dozen other scientific and technological problems crowd the court dockets. Judges versed in law and precedent are required to pass judgment in areas of great technical complexity.

Moreover, the frequent difficulty in reaching political decisions about science and technology (discussed in Chapter 1) lead many decision makers to seek resolution in the courts. There, at least, decision makers will not ordinarily duck or evade questions, and some kind of decision will finally be made. Whether judges and jurists are qualified to pass judgment in areas of high scientific and technological complexity is an issue that concerns many. Certainly, courts are expert in applying legal reasoning, but this may not be the best guide to specific decisions involving science and technology.

Popular Mobilization Arena

The most disparate and atomized, the popular mobilization arena is composed of hundreds of different groups, movements, and organizations. Each seeks to affect the decisions taken in all of the other arenas, but most especially within the corporate-managerial arena. Triumphs in the protection of consumers and the environment, in shaping the national security debate, in influencing classroom instruction, and in the treatment of laboratory animals bespeak the collective, if not always coordinated, power of these participants. No member of the corporate-managerial arena (and the executive arena, for that matter) can afford to make decisions without carefully calculating the probable reactions of decision makers in the popular mobilization arena. Corporations and government agencies often wage expensive campaigns to appear at the forefront of such movements, while at the same time attempting to blunt or divert the power of the groups involved.

Not only must the nationally organized and professional members of this arena be considered by other arenas when contemplating action, but there is always the prospect that ad hoc groups of all shades of ideology will form around local issues. Frequently motivated by romantic ideals, these groups employ sophisticated publicity tactics, which makes them formidable opponents. It is difficult to generalize about their aims and methods, and thus they are all the more feared by corporations investing in long-range technology projects. Because of their grass-roots base and their often "motherhood and apple pie" image, such groups are also effective in influencing Congress, thereby adding yet another uncertainty to investment calculations.

Academic-Professional Arena

At first glance, the academic-professional arena appears to be the least independent of all the arenas. Because scientists, engineers, and technicians often depend on decision makers in other arenas for research support, their position vis-à-vis those arenas would appear hopelessly compromised. While there is some degree of truth to this, we must also consider the different ethos or work ethic that attaches to the academic and professional worlds.

Scientists (especially those affiliated with universities), engineers, and technicians owe considerable allegiance to their respective professions and to the codes of ethics and conduct that help establish their credentials among other professionals. This dedication can lead to conflict with those who sponsor their research. In the private sector one often hears critics of R&D establishments accuse researchers of being more dedicated to furthering their professional careers and raising their professional status than to furthering the aims of the firm that employs them. When scientists or engineers blow the whistle on corporate or government decision makers by going public with problems or malfeasance, their professional standing greatly increases their credibility as witnesses.

Professional career concerns can interfere in many ways in the technological roles that researchers and other technical specialists play. The career path for academic scientists requires that they produce experimental results of high enough quality to be accepted by professional journals for publication. Such articles are subjected to peer review by other experts in the field, and thus the choice of research programs and projects can affect radically one's standing in one's field. Consequently, the better trained and more talented scientists can make powerful demands for autonomy and freedom of action from their corporate or government sponsors. To devote a significant portion of one's career to a research project that may be cancelled because of bureaucratic or budgetary changes is a sizable risk, a concern both employers and researchers need to weigh.

While scientists maintain a professional tradition of political neutrality toward social causes (a tradition that still places constraints on their actions), in recent years many scientists have taken public positions on technological developments proposed by government and industry. The environmental release of bioengineered materials, the depletion of the ozone layer, nuclear power plants, and the debate over the strategic defense initiative are examples of issues in which scientists have lent their prestige to one side or another in public controversies.

Labor Arena

Working conditions in America would be vastly different today were it not for unions and union activities. But, in recent decades, the role of labor unions has changed substantially. Collective bargaining now receives legal protection, labor regulations have improved, and some major national unions can claim an unquestioned position among the most established of Establishment political institutions.

At the same time, labor union membership has swelled and receded in recent years, so that today fewer than 20 percent of U.S. workers are union members. Workers' reactions to changing technologies have varied, depending upon how directly they perceive themselves to be affected. In recent years, they have, first, fought the loss of jobs due to technological change and then worried about insufficient technological change and the need to "reindustrialize" American industry. Foreign competition and the need for import protection accompany worries that traditional smokestack manufacturing industries may never recover to earlier employment levels. Workers in the newer industries also complain that their working conditions are stressful and that they have too little control over their daily activities.

ARENA INTERACTIONS

Yet another concept, **interarena relations,** is needed for our framework. It is not enough to describe the various participants in scientific and technological decision making and the different environments in which they operate. We must also catalog the various ways in which decision makers in each technological decision-making arena interact with decision makers in the other arenas.

Central to our analysis is the understanding that decision makers within one arena cannot bring their technological projects to successful completion without obtaining needed facilitating decisions from people in other arenas. A chemical firm wishing to market a new industrial chemical finds that it cannot do so unless it receives a regulatory clearance from the Environmental Protection Agency. Or a manufacturing firm wants to dispose of its wastes in a specific location, but finds that local (and maybe national) environmental groups have formed in opposition to that decision. Perhaps a high-tech electronics firm wants to obtain a Defense Department contract, but needs the go-ahead from both the relevant congressional committee and the Pentagon. In each case, the arena decision maker needs to obtain favorable decisions from one or several decision makers in other arenas; he or she is not able to complete the technological project simply on his or her own. Indeed, a decision maker responsible for a technological project may need to obtain a whole series of decisions from other decision makers as the project moves from one phase to another.

One strategy for obtaining the desired decision from those in the other relevant arenas is to *manipulate* the internal pressures, goals, constraints, and limitations facing decision makers in those other arenas so that the specific technological decision maker, responding to those changes in his or her own environment, makes the needed decision. Another strategy, *co-optation,* involves designing technological projects in such a way that each of the involved arenas obtains some benefit from the project. By finding ways to let the arena decision makers who cannot be ignored profit from the project, one can have greater confidence that they will make the kinds of determinations needed to bring the project to fruition, or at least will not needlessly block or obstruct the project.

Effective decision makers may use both manipulation and co-optation at different times; indeed, a decision maker may use both techniques at the same time, depending on circumstances and what looks like it might work. The key is to get the decision makers in the other arenas to make the kind of decision you want them to make so that you can go ahead with your technological project. All the while, decision makers from other arenas may be trying to get those same targeted decision makers to make very different decisions that might make your project impossible to complete. The story of technological politics is how one goes about obtaining the needed decisions in this kind of environment.

DOMINANT CONFIGURATIONS

One final concept completes our framework: **dominant configurations.** This concept refers to certain kinds of interarena relations in which interactions among decision makers in different arenas become so *routine*, so *regularized*, and so *predictable* that we can speak of those relationships as "dominating," or structuring, the relationship of the decision makers in the various arenas.

Because uncertainty and unpredictability undermine long-range planning, and because manipulative relations with decision makers in other arenas can drain valuable resources, decision makers in various arenas sometimes form relatively stable accommodations with each other. When such relationships persist over time, both the collaborators in the accommodation and decision makers in other, nonparticipating arenas come to understand that the terms of the accommodation are, in effect, binding, if unwritten, "ground rules" for all arena interactions involving this technology. Even Arena decision makers not directly participating in the accommodation may find the order and predictability such relationships provide useful.

Most dominant configurations rest on a basis of cooperation among the participating arena decision makers, although there can also be a good deal of competition and manipulation *within* the configuration. But whenever there is a threat to the dominant configuration from outside, the members nearly always set aside their differences and act to protect and preserve the accommodation. Because all who participate in it benefit from it, there is every incentive to protect and maintain the configuration, even in the face of intermittent reversals that may occur within it.

Dominant configurations succeed by maintaining tight control over decision making concerning a specific technology. A common strategy for maintaining control within a dominant configuration is to find ways to exclude decision makers on the outside from the decisions made inside the accommodation. Too many participants would undermine the accommodation. This is sometimes done by asserting that only decision makers who possess certain credentials can address the issues involved. For instance, during the early days of the civilian nuclear industry, there was a general assumption that only scientists and engineers trained in the arcane technologies should participate directly in decision making. Today, some argue that average citizens should not be involved in making decisions about genetic engineering because they lack the requisite expertise to address the issues. Likewise, technological projects in national security are protected by a "need to know" limitation on information.

Other techniques used to exclude outsiders from dominant configuration decision making include the invocation of accepted cultural norms, such as "free market" and "competitiveness" claims. If a specific technological project is "required" by "market forces," or because of international "competition," opponents of the project may have trouble being heard at all. If this fails, an alternative is to permit an array of "symbolic" participatory mechanisms, such as public discussions, hearings, or expert studies. The goal is to allow just enough penetration of the dominant configuration to assuage public concern without allowing significant disruption of the configuration itself.

Persistent demands for decision-making participation in a dominant configuration by excluded groups may be met by efforts to co-opt gradually the most malleable representatives into the accommodation, where it is hoped they would eventually begin to support and protect the accommodation against other outsiders.

If techniques of this sort fail to rebuff or deflect demands for wider participation, the dominant configuration may simply fall apart. Although powerful, dominant configurations are not immortal.

CONCLUSIONS

Using our five concepts—technological projects, the individual technological decision maker, technological decision-making arenas, arena interactions, and dominant configurations—we are prepared to analyze the variety of scientific and technological decisions made in our society. Thus, as an individual technological decision maker, operating within a particular technological decision-making arena, you make decisions about which specific technological projects to pursue. However, in order to bring those projects to successful completion, you must obtain needed decisions from decision makers who operate in different arenas, subject to different pressures, constraints, limitations, and goals. You must find ways to induce those decision makers to make the right decisions that will permit your project to move forward.

Often, however, decision makers in other arenas may decide to pursue their own technological projects, focused on the same core technology you are concerned with, which may directly oppose your project. Your opponents will also try to obtain decisions from many of the same decision makers you are trying to influence. If they succeed, your project may well fail, and therefore you must find ways to blunt their projects, just as they are trying to obstruct your project. Thus the stage is set for intense political struggle.

The argument put forward here is that before we can do anything about the three levels of technological decision-making problems examined in Chapter 1— social, economic, and ecological problems, flexibility problems, and political problems—we must trace those problems back to the specific decisions made by specific decision makers from which they arise. When we understand how those decisions are made, who benefits from them, who loses, and the reasons why, we may be in a position to deal more effectively with the array of political problems those decisions give rise to.

You may have noticed that in describing the individual and organizational decision makers who influence technological politics, we have included many who are not in the government. The inclusion of nongovernment decision makers in technological politics is unavoidable, in large part, because of the market-oriented economy and representative political process that has dominated the United States from its very beginning.[2, 3]

The inclusion of nongovernment decision makers in technological politics is not, in itself, unique or even remarkable. All political systems throughout the world involve both government and nongovernment decision makers. What is important in the United States, however, is the degree of decision-making influence accorded to the corporate-managerial arena. In political and economic systems such as ours (which include, incidentally, most of Western Europe, North America, Japan, and several other economies in Asia), many important public policy decisions are, in effect, delegated by the government to decision makers in the corporate-managerial arena. Private decision makers greatly shape the development and the use of modern technologies, as Charles Lindblom notes:

> Corporate executives...decide a nation's industrial technology, the pattern of work organization, location of industry, market structure, resource allocation, and, of course executive compensation and status...In short, in any private enterprise system, a large category of major decisions is turned over to businessmen, both small and larger. They are taken off the agenda of government. Businessmen thus become a kind of public official and exercise what, on a broad view of their role, are public functions.[4]

Of course, as we shall discuss, public decision makers can influence corporate executives in a number of ways. Still, in the end, fundamental control of many important economic decisions rests with individuals not subject to election or other forms of public political accountability.

Scientists and engineers also make important political decisions about technology, although, for the most part, they do not have formal government office. In addition to advising government officials on technical matters, these decision makers shape both science and technology through the decisions they make about research projects and priorities, the publication of experimental results, communication with colleagues, and other professional activities. Decision makers in the other two nongovernment arenas, the popular mobilization and the labor arenas, also shape technological politics without holding government positions. Both kinds of decision makers depend on their ability to mobilize nonexpert, public concerns about technology.

The collective influence of these nongovernment decision makers produces what Edward Woodhouse calls "a rival system of governance."[5] The traditional, properly elected or appointed institutions of government share power with decision makers whose power has not been ratified in democratic ways and are not subject to democratic accountability. This arrangement is acceptable because we believe that we have effective, although nondemocratic, mechanisms for assuring that corporate-managerial arena decision makers will protect the common good, instead of simply enriching themselves at everyone else's expense. Specifically, corporate-managerial decision makers are restrained by the discipline of the marketplace. The "invisible hand" of capitalism, we are told, guarantees that, although they may pursue their own private good, they also contribute to the general welfare. Other societies, not so trusting of the marketplace, do not delegate such important decisions to corporate executives, but maintain government control.

There is another important characteristic worthy of some mention. There are many different ways to view how society operates and, more specifically, how science and technology influence social, economic, and political institutions. Technological optimists, for instance, argue that technology has been overwhelmingly beneficial for people, making their ordinary lives easier, more healthful, and more prosperous. Technological pessimists assert that, on balance, technology has been bad for people, increasing the risks and dangers in their lives, depersonalizing human relationships, and forcing people to behave in ways they otherwise would not. Technological apathetics do not think much about technology at all, although they tend to make use of it all of the time.

Other observers, such as Marxists, argue that economic class struggle dominates social decision making, including decisions about science and technology. The capitalists, the currently dominant class, use their power to direct science and technology decisions in ways that strengthen their control of the means of production. Others assert that in advanced technological societies, the technical classes (what we call the academic-professional arena) form a hidden "technocracy," making the real decisions for all of us, regardless of what formally elected officials do. Yet others argue that technological decision making is dominated by the "military-industrial complex," a powerful cabal of the military and weapons industry.

The approach we use here does not depend on or assume any of these theoretical positions. Instead, we employ our five concepts as an analytical framework that will focus our attention on who participates in making political decisions about technology, what they seek to achieve, what techniques and resources they bring to bear on the decision process, and whether or not they are successful. Our argument is that understanding how decisions get made will tell us a great deal about the source of many contemporary political problems involving science and technology and may also point the way toward possible solutions.

This does not mean that we are uninterested in philosophical explanations of technology's power. It does mean, however, that before we can explore such theories, we must have a clear grasp of what actually happens when political decisions about technology are made. Philosophical, ethical, and social theories about technology can have meaning only if they are grounded in the actions and decisions of real people who spend their lives shaping, and being shaped by, technology. What we do here is try to describe what those people do.

ENDNOTES

1. D. K. Schon, *Technology and Change: The New Heraclitus* (New York: Delacorte Press).

2. Charles E. Lindblom, *Politics and Markets: The World's Political-Economic Systems* (New York: Basic Books, 1977).

3. Robert A. Dahl, *A Preface to Democratic Theory* (Chicago: University of Chicago Press, 1956).

4. Lindblom, *Politics and Markets*, pp. 171–172.

5. Edward J. Woodhouse, "Decision Theory and the Governance of Technology," *Teaching Political Science: Politics in Perspective*, 14, no. 4 (1987), 171–177.

Chapter 3

The Corporate-Managerial Arena

In order to use our decision-making framework, we need first to explore in greater detail each technological decision-making arena. We need to discover each arena's special and unique values, goals, pressures, influences, limitations, and constraints—its "culture," so to speak. These make up the environment that shapes and influences the kinds of decisions individual technological decision-makers will reach and the kinds of tactics and approaches participants in other arenas will use when trying to influence those decisions. It is by focusing on the kinds of decisions reached within each arena and on the pressures that shape those decisions that we will be able to illustrate each of the three levels of problems discussed in Chapter 1 and then, perhaps, to suggest potential solutions to those problems. Discussion in succeeding chapters will examine each of the other arenas and their members before we begin to look at how the various arenas interact in specific scientific and technological decisions.

Because, in many ways, decision makers in the corporate-managerial arena are the most influential in American technological politics, we will describe this arena in substantial detail. It may seem odd to begin a book dealing with technological politics by describing a nongovernment decision-making arena, but, as we will see several times, nongovernment decision makers play very important roles in technological politics.

THE ROLE OF TECHNOLOGY IN THE ECONOMY

Corporations, and the individual decision-makers who work for them, must decide when and how to use their resources most effectively to fight competitors and maximize the company's potential for profit in the marketplace. Among those decisions will be many technological projects: the introduction of new product lines or extensive modifications of existing products, capital improvements in production processes, new manufacturing machinery and equipment to replace old or outdated equipment, investments in research and development, purchases from competing pollution abatement equipment suppliers, and many, many more. All of these decisions, made thousands of times by thousands of different firms and companies, collectively influence the direction of scientific and technological change in very important ways.

In recent years, observers have tried to deal with technological innovation directly, as an important variable in its own right. Such studies have provided some fascinating insights into the role of technical innovation and development in the larger processes of market economies. Their findings show us how complex the corporate-managerial arena really is. Many people, often decision makers in some of the other arenas, simplistically approach corporate-managerial decision makers as though they all represented identical companies, pursuing identical goals, and sharing identical values.

IMPACT OF TECHNOLOGICAL INNOVATION

A decision to invest in the research, development, testing, and marketing of a new technical product, process, or material may promise substantial profit for a company; certainly, failure to pursue a technological option when one's competitors are known or suspected to be investigating the same option is to put a company's competitive edge, market share, and perhaps even its ability to survive at risk. On the other hand, most new ventures fail, and a foolhardy chase after a technological innovation that bombs can be just as damaging. Thus, technology poses both a potential risk and a benefit, depending on a company's size, product line or lines, internal resources, level and style of competition, market reputation, established market contacts, and, of course, the state of technical skill and knowledge at the company's command.

William Abernathy and Kim Clark offer a very useful framework for understanding the risks and promises of technological innovation for corporate leaders.[1] They point out that technological innovation has the potential of either weakening or strengthening two sets of critically important corporate resources: *production competences*—(the skills, experience, knowledge base, technological design, capital equipment, production facilities, materials, supplier relationships, production systems and organizations, and so on, needed to *produce* a commercially viable product)—and *market competences*—(linkages to markets and customers, marketing networks, distribution channels, service networks, customer communication, and so on, needed to *sell* the product). Companies spend a great deal of effort, money, and time in acquiring both sets of competences, and are naturally unhappy to see technical changes that threaten to make those competences obsolete. In the marketplace, however, there is a constant risk that one or both of these sets of resources may be lost because of technical innovation.

While Abernathy and Clark agree with Joseph Schumpeter that, in the big picture, technological innovation is "creative destruction," in which certain sets of knowledge, skills, technical design, customer linkages, marketing networks, and the like, are necessarily made obsolete, and replaced by new skills, knowledge, markets, and so on, associated with new technologies, they argue that not all technical changes are disruptive for every company every time:

> Clearly, all technological innovation imposes change of some kind, but change need not be destructive. Innovation in product technology may solve problems or eliminate flaws in a design that makes existing channels of distribution more attractive and effective...Such changes conserve the established competence of the firm, and if the enhancement or refinement is considerable, may actually entrench those skills, making it more difficult for alternative resources or skills to achieve an advantage. Such innovation may have an effect on competition by raising barriers to entry, reducing the threat of substitute products, and making competing technologies (and perhaps firms) less attractive.[2]

Their point is that some technical changes can strengthen and enhance a particular company's production and/or marketing skills, just as some technical changes can undermine and weaken those skills: "[T]he competitive significance of an innovation depends on what it does to the value and applicability of established competence."[3] Clearly, a corporate-managerial decision maker who anticipates that adopting a particular technological innovation may make production and marketing skills obsolete for her company faces a tougher choice than a decision maker who believes that a particular technical change will enhance or strengthen those skills and competences for her company.

For some kinds of companies, the specific production and marketing skills they possess may represent very substantial investments in distribution networks, research and development, inflexible and expensive production machinery, specially trained and skilled personnel (with commensurate salaries), and established customer linkages. For such a company, a successful technological breakthrough may mean that it must scrap its existing production processes and/or marketing systems in order to keep up with the new technology. In some dramatic cases, this may be so disruptive that the company is totally unable to adjust. An example is the devastating impact of hand-held calculators on companies that produced slide rules, the new technology literally revolutionized the market, making all of the slide rule companies production competences completely obsolete. In such cases, the company frequently goes out of business altogether, or at least gets entirely out of the product line that has gone through such a complete revolution. Yet, corporate-managerial decision makers cannot hope to preserve existing technologies forever just because a change may be disruptive to the company.

Using technological innovation's impact on a company's marketing and production competences, Abernathy and Clark have devised a conceptual map of four different phases of technological innovation, each of which is associated with a different competitive environment: regular phase, revolutionary phase, architectural phase, and niche creation phase, and have explored what each kind of innovation may mean to the companies involved.

Regular Phase Innovation

Regular phase innovation usually involves improvements in production and manufacturing processes in well-established markets for standardized products (light bulbs, shoes, industrial chemicals), allowing the manufacturer to make the same product more efficiently. It thus serves to conserve existing production competences (production machinery, personnel skills, management hierarchies). Such incremental changes, though not nearly so dramatic as other kinds of innovation, often significantly improve established manufacturing processes, thereby reducing production costs. While "the changes involved may be minor when examined individually, their cumulative effect often exceeds the effect of the original invention."[4]

Management decisions in this phase emphasize systematic planning needed to support engineering improvements and market refinements. Manufacturing process innovations, stability of product design, and predictable sources of materials all contribute to high volume production and the scale economies that allow lower costs to customers. "Every opportunity must be taken to advance quality, improve product features, break bottlenecks in production, and foster process innovations that reduce scrap and increase yields. This is the world of the administrator, and the functionally oriented engineer.[5]

Revolutionary Phase Innovation

Revolutionary phase innovation "disrupts and renders established technical and production competence obsolete, yet is applied to existing markets and customers,..."[6] often by delivering a wholly new product to existing customers that does what the old product did, but better, cheaper, and more accurately. Abernathy and Clark cite the transitions from the reciprocating engine to jet propulsion in aircraft, from vacuum tubes to integrated circuits in electronics, and from mechanical to electronic calculators as examples of industries that have experienced revolutionary phase innovation. In each case, existing linkages to markets and customers were preserved, although the older production competences in each industry became obsolete. Both the regular and revolutionary phases of innovation tend to conserve and entrench existing linkages to markets and customers (marketing networks, customer communication channels, service networks).

In the revolutionary phase, corporate decision makers must be able to sustain intra-company agreement about long-term goals, including investments in technology and investment. "Here the task is to focus possible unruly technical talent toward specific markets and to marshal the financial resources for this purpose. Good technical insight is needed to break established conventions and foster close collaboration between product designers, process engineers, and market planners. The climate must be one that encourages a sense of competitive assault."[7]

Niche Creation Phase Innovation

On the other hand, niche creation and architectural innovation often disrupt existing linkages to markets. Niche creation opens "new market opportunities through the use of existing technology...in which an otherwise stable and well specified technology is refined, improved, or changed in a way that supports a new marketing thrust."[8] Niche creation thus conserves existing production competences because it involves an innovative combination of existing products that together perform a new function. Timex's introduction of cheap, efficient, and stylish mass-produced watches did not involve fundamental innovations in watch technology, but in production processes and marketing. Sony's introduction of its Walkman cassette player was the combination of lightweight earphones and a portable radio, neither constituting technical breakthroughs—until they were combined.

In the **niche creation phase**, decision makers must be attuned to new market opportunities and be prepared quickly to develop a product package to exploit them. Decision makers must lead their companies into market niches rapidly before competitors enter the same niche. As Abernathy and Clark tell us, "Timing is the essence of management in the niche creation phase....Under these conditions, manufacturing must be quick and responsive, insuring timely delivery, responsive service and adequate capacity for quick buildup."[9] Because niche creation innovation is based on existing technologies, it tends to conserve production competences. However, finding a market niche is often a short-lived advantage, because imitators quickly crowd in. Thus, niche innovators must be constantly alert to yet newer applications and markets.

Architectural Phase Innovation

Architectural phase innovation makes obsolete both market and production competences and is thus the most disruptive of the four types of innovation. This type of innovation

> departs from established systems of production, and in turn opens up new linkages to markets and users, is characteristic of the creation of new industries as well as the reformation of old ones.... In effect, it lays down the architecture of the industry, the broad framework within which competition will occur and develop.[10]

Abernathy and Clark describe this innovation style, using the Model T as an illustration:

> The Model T experience...suggests that architectural innovations stand out as creative acts of adapting and applying latent technologies to previously unarticulated user needs. It is the insight and conception about fresh roles for existing inventions and technologies that mark this kind of innovation. Scientific work plays a part in freeing thought, and relaxing old rules of thumb. The challenge lies in linking understanding of technical possibilities to insights about unarticulated needs.[11]

Xerography, the radio, and phototypesetting are other examples of this kind of technical change. In the architectural phase, management decision makers must encourage creativity and new insights into both technical opportunities and customer needs. A tolerance for risk is needed in this phase. Decision makers must constantly scan for technological developments and market needs and integrate creative first-time combinations of resources.

CORPORATE AND TECHNICAL EVOLUTION

These different phases of technical innovation correspond to different stages in the maturation of an industry and to different styles of management. Observers find a typical tendency in corporate and technological evolution: The corporate/technology relationship tends to move from technologies that are disruptive of production and marketing competences and toward technologies that reinforce those competences, from architectural phase innovation toward regular phase innovation.

The key development that triggers this evolution in the firm's organization and structure is the standardization of its product. Standardization, in turn, depends on the emergence of a *dominant design* for the product, out of all the various competing designs. For example, the dominant design of the automobile eventually rejected both steam and electricity as energy sources, in favor of gasoline and the internal combustion engine. When this occurred, continued development in the losing designs all but ceased, as producers rushed to improve the manufacturing processes relevant to the winning concept.

The organization, structure, and management style of companies differ in the prestandardization period from how companies operate after a dominant design for the product emerges—for one thing, in the terms of competition shift. Standardization of product design, as Abernathy tells us

> changes the basis of competition. Battles in the marketplace no longer are fought over the kind of thing a product is or even the kinds of things it should be able to do. The locus of competition shifts to what the product costs. Once the market decides that it knows what a word processor is—or a video recorder or a PBX exchange or an instant camera or, of course, a widget—the task of manufacturers gradually changes from defining appropriate design concepts to achieving efficiencies and economies in production.[12]

Standardization and the appearance of a dominant product design are among the "forces at work in manufacturing industries that tend to drive productive units toward high-volume operations."[13] Before a product achieves standardization, there may be many different versions competing in the market. The manufacturers will tend to be small, informal, and flexible organizations that use flexible, general-purpose machinery and rely heavily on highly skilled design and manufacturing engineers. Once one of the competing designs gains widespread customer acceptance, the others are driven from the market. The manufacturers now emphasize mass production of the product, rather than one-of-a-kind production, become more structured and hierarchical, and shift toward relatively inflexible, specialized machinery and relatively low-skilled workers. Expensive manufacturing equipment may be able to produce only one kind of product and be nonadaptable for anything else, or adaptable only at a significant cost. The emphasis is now on price competition, and manufacturers will invest in very costly production machinery, including much automation, as a way of keeping production costs to a minimum.

As the firm evolves from architectural innovation toward regular innovation, it comes to fear radical technical changes that may make its investment in expensive and inflexible machinery worthless. Significant technical changes may require that whole plants be closed down, with all of the financial losses, economic disruption, unemployment, and other adverse effects, that accompany such closings. We see here some of the root causes of the technological rigidity and inflexibility that we spoke of early on in this book. It can be very difficult and very expensive for a manufacturer of a highly standardized product to change its fixed production processes to accommodate, for instance, new environmental regulations intended to alleviate pollution problems caused by those very same inflexible production processes. Redesigning a standardized product to meet new product safety requirements may also present the manufacturer with very costly changes in machinery, personnel, training, suppliers, and the like. Customers may need to have the old product, with its old characteristics, and be unwilling or unable to redesign their products to account for the changes in the standardized supplies.

We will have reason to question whether this straightforward vision of corporate-managerial "maturation" accurately describes this technological decision-making arena in a later chapter.

DECISION MAKERS

Thus far we have looked at the larger shape and evolution of corporations and their relationships to the technologies they produce and use. Now we need to consider how decision makers operate within this larger decision-making environment.

One of the first things to note about the corporate-managerial arena, a fact pointed out by many commentators, is that the most important decision makers are not, in fact, the owners of the corporations. Rather, they are professional managers, hired because of their supposed expertise and skill. The owners, the stockholders, have relatively little say over the general directions of corporate decisions and no say at all about day-to-day operations. This condition has existed for several decades now, regardless of what we are told about management's subservience to the stockholders and despite the occasionally fractious annual stockholders' meeting. As long as management succeeds in making a profit, stockholders leave them quite alone to run the firm.

The corporation's board of directors has more influence with management, and can fire corporate officers and set corporate policy, among other things. Still, for all practical purposes, even the board does not control management's decisions most of the time. Most board members are not involved in the regular operations of the company. Moreover, management often is able to nominate members of the board, thereby increasing their independence.

The number of management personnel who can influence corporate decisions about technology can be large, depending on the corporation's organization. In large firms, the CEO, vice presidents, directors of the various divisions, plant managers, and line supervisors play important roles. For smaller companies, there will be fewer managerial decision makers involved in selecting technological projects, committing corporate resources, planning tactics and strategy, dealing with outside decision makers, and so on.

In many ways, the specific decisions reached by such decision makers will be shaped by their positions, roles, and responsibilities within the management system: Directors of research and development will pursue technological projects relevant to that division, just as production managers and marketing managers will make decisions required by their corporate stations and duties.

Although the management structure of the company is intended to allow myriad individual decision makers to cooperate in collective projects, it is a mistake to assume that corporate decision making is, in fact, always, or even often, cooperative and amicable. There is ample opportunity for disagreement and conflict within the company, between decision makers who may be pursuing quite different agendas and technological projects.

For one thing, the corporation has limited resources, and there may be considerable competition within the firm about how to use those resources and which projects to pursue. Any individual technological decision maker may face numerous hurdles within his or her own company to the specific technological projects he or she believes the company should select. Carrying a technological project forward may require skillful coalition building with other powerful decision makers inside the company, effective blocking of other decision makers' favorite projects, overcoming obstacles imposed by rivals, thrust and parry, move and countermove. Having survived these struggles within your own company, you are by no means assured of success. You must still account for the actions of other companies with which you compete in the marketplace.

It gets more complicated still. After getting the corporation to back the project and favorably countering actions by your corporate-managerial competitors, you will also have to negotiate a path through the array of noncorporate decision makers who may influence your project. You may have to get permissions, clearances, or exemptions from the regulatory arena, negotiate deals with the labor arena, attract and hold important members of the academic-professional arena, obtain funding from decision makers within the legislative arena, compete for contracts from the executive arena, and fight off attacks from the popular mobilization arena, even to the point of defending your company in the judicial arena!

Of course, not every technological project will face such an array of opposition; still, any sensible decision maker will carefully calculate all possible and probable resistances before launching a technological project. The technology at the heart of the project, as we have seen, may also be at the heart of technological projects pursued by your competitors in other arenas, whose goals concerning the technology in question may be quite inimical to your goals. Bringing your technological project to a successful completion may mean causing other decision makers' technological projects to fail.

Knowing which technological projects to pursue and which to forgo, or, harder still, which to terminate after getting started, is a critical survival skill within the corporate-managerial arena. One's career may well hinge on which projects one associates with, supports, and encourages (as well as which projects one opposes). "Backing the wrong horse," technologically speaking, may mean an abrupt end to a promising management career.

Project selection depends on technical intelligence: knowing the leading edge of innovation in your company's product line, seeing the potential in what might seem to be a minor technical breakthrough, and understanding what your customers are looking for, among other things. Because they understand the need for such intelligence, large corporations expend considerable energy acquiring as much information as they can, from reading professional journals, attending conferences, and conducting market research to maintaining large in-house research and development laboratories. Still, no individual corporate-managerial decision maker will consider every conceivable technological project. Instead, that person will look for technological projects that fit the company's level of resources, degree of industrial maturity, position in the marketplace, intensity of competition, and so on.

Not all technological projects pursued by corporate-managerial decision makers derive from their perceptions of technological opportunities, market advantages, or competitive edge. Decision makers in other technological decision-making arenas, pursuing their own technological projects, can create situations that intrude upon corporate decision makers. Members of the popular mobilization arena, for instance, may try to get decision makers in the regulatory arena to impose tougher environmental and health and safety regulations that may require manufacturers to alter their production processes, change chemical feedstocks, introduce expensive air or water pollution equipment, or even withdraw otherwise profitable, but unsafe, technological products or materials from the market altogether. Similarly, decisions made within the judicial arena may also impose new and costly requirements. Corporate-managerial decision makers have to respond to these technological projects. They may try to get regulatory or judicial decisions reversed, lobby the executive and legislative arenas for changes in existing laws, negotiate with labor unions for modifications of existing contracts, or increase spending on research and development in order to find technological "fixes" for the problems that decision makers in other arenas impose on them.

CONCLUSIONS

We began by asserting that, of all the technological decision-making arenas involved in technological politics in the United States, decision makers within the corporate-managerial arena are clearly preeminent. Because of their central role in managing the national economy, these decision makers exercise important leverage over decision makers in other arenas (although that leverage does not mean that corporate interests always get everything they want from other decision makers). We saw that the corporate-managerial arena is complex, made up of a wide variety of corporations, firms, and companies. We also saw that technological innovation, while vital to corporate success, can also be dangerous terrain for corporate-managerial decision makers.

There are at least four kinds of technological innovation in the corporate-managerial arena, each of which presents decision makers with different problems and opportunities. Following Abernathy and Clark, we focused on two critical corporate resources, production competences and market competences, and considered how the different types of innovation affect those resources. We suggested that corporations typically evolve from the architectural phase of innovation, in which both production and market competences are undermined, toward regular phase innovation, in which both competences are enhanced. We saw that as this evolution occurs, it brings with it predictable changes in corporate organization, from small, informal, and flexible toward large, hierarchically formal, and generally inflexible decision-making structures.

Looked at from the standpoint of decision makers, pursuing technological projects within the corporate-managerial arena can be a very complicated campaign. A corporate decision maker must, in addition to selecting a specific project, garner sufficient support from other decision makers within the company to obtain continuing access to necessarily limited corporate resources. Coalitions must be formed to carry a project forward, and perhaps to block and obstruct others' technological projects that would siphon off needed resources.

Even if you are successful in gathering support for the project within your company, you must also counter the actions of competing firms, reassure skeptical financial centers and stockbrokers, and deal with customers who may be upset by the proposed changes.

Even now you are not yet done, because decision makers from other arenas may take steps to frustrate your project, and you must respond to their decisions, as well. Carrying your particular technological project to successful completion, then, may require multiple strategies for dealing with potential obstacles thrown up by suspicious regulators· antagonistic legislators, indifferent administrators, tough labor leaders, disgruntled scientists and engineers, assertive judges, and mobilized environment and consumer groups.

ENDNOTES

1. WILLIAM J. ABERNATHY and KIM B. CLARK, "Innovation: Mapping the Winds of Creative Destruction," *Research Policy*, 14, no. 1 (1985), 3.
2. Ibid., p. 6.
3. Ibid., p. 7.
4. Ibid., p. 12.
5. Ibid., pp. 20–21.
6. Ibid., p. 12.
7. Ibid., p. 21.
8. Ibid., p. 10.
9. Ibid., pp. 20–21.
10. Ibid., p. 7.
11. Ibid., p. 9.
12. WILLIAM ABERNATHY, KIM B. CLARK, ALLAN M. KANTROW, *Industrial Renaissance: Producing a Competitive Future for America* (NY: Basic Books, 1983).

Chapter 4

The Government Arenas

In this chapter we examine four technological decision-making arenas that have a common characteristic: They are all part of the federal government. Our goal is to delineate the many roles of government decision makers in technological politics by exploring how they make decisions concerning science and technology. Following our decision-making framework, we seek to discover *who* participates in making government decisions about science and technology, *what* they hope to gain, what *resources* and *techniques* they use to push the decisions in one direction or another, and whether or not they are *effective*. We shall discover that the kinds of decisions made in these four arenas are among the most important and influential made in our society about science and technology, and for that reason these arenas are often the site of some very bitter struggles.

The four government arenas are the executive, the legislative, the judicial, and the regulatory. Each arena involves the actions of hundreds and sometimes thousands of individual technological decision makers responding to the pressures, limitations, and constraints that characterize the specific environments in which each operates, as well as to the influence of other decision makers from other arenas.

In some cases, individuals will be acting in common, under direction of specific decision makers authorized to set goals and assign tasks. In other cases, decision makers will be acting virtually on their own, with little or no overarching direction or control. Often, they will disagree with each other, or with decision makers from other arenas, and in the course of their interactions will have to resolve conflicts over long-term goals, short-term priorities, and resources. And, quite often, the precise nature of the decisions they make will be affected by the duration and fervor of their disagreements and conflicts.

While it is possible to separate and distinguish the government arenas from each other, all four share a common framework of constitutional and legal responsibilities and limitations. Certainly, their relationships would be different if the

United States had, for instance, a parliamentary style of government instead of the separation of powers form as mandated by the Constitution. It is equally clear that our federal system, with one national government, 50 independent state governments, and 80,000 local governments, imposes a common structure on all, regardless of the governmental arena within which they operate. Yet, for all the unifying influence of the Constitution, considerable flexibility and room for maneuver remain for the various branches and agencies that make up government.

THE EXECUTIVE ARENA

When we think of the executive branch of the U.S. government, we naturally think of the president of the United States. The decision-making environment we call the **executive arena**, however, comprises many more people than just the occupant of the White House. Indeed, we must think more in terms of the presidency rather than just the president if we are to comprehend technological policymaking.

The modern, twentieth-century presidency has become quite a substantial bureaucracy, made up of several agencies and individuals whose task is to assist the president in fulfilling his duties. The executive arena, while obviously centered on the person of the president, also involves the Executive Office of the President (EOP), 14 executive departments, and several additional agencies. Indeed, as more than one observer has noted, the president's chief task can be simply getting all these people to work together to accomplish his goals rather than those of the departments and agencies.

Today, executive branch activities in the area of science and technology are extensive, accounting for several hundreds of millions of dollars of federal expenditures each year. Within cabinet departments, virtually every federal body creates, uses, and dispenses scientific information; some departments, such as Defense, sponsor major programs of scientific and technological research and development and application. Scientific and technological programs for civilian use emerge from the Departments of Agriculture, Commerce, Energy, Interior, Housing and Urban Development, and Transportation, as well as the Nuclear Regulatory Commission (NRC), the Federal Energy Research Commission (FERC) within the Energy Department, and the National Aeronautics and Space Administration (NASA). Federally supported medical research is sponsored by the National Science Foundation, the National Cancer Institute, and the National Institutes of Health.

The Evolution of Presidential Involvement

Presidential concern with and support for science and technology dates back to the earliest days of U.S. history, with the first several presidents offering continuous, if relatively low-level, support for government activities related to science and technology. George Washington was a civil engineer and surveyor, and Thomas Jefferson was a noted naturalist and inventor. The Lewis and Clark expedition, which Jefferson commissioned, was intended in part to accumulate useful geographic and botanical information about the newly purchased Mississippi-Missouri River valley. Federal support for land-grant colleges and for agricultural and mechanical experimentation also signaled presidential, and congressional, interest in improving the quality of life for farmers in America. In 1863, President Lincoln signed the charter of the National Academy of Sciences, to provide up-to-date scientific advice to the government.

In the period just after the Civil War, and continuing until World War I, executive branch interest in science and technology declined substantially. The onset of the Great Depression of 1929 rekindled a limited interest in what science and technology might offer as solutions to the economic calamity. However, with the more urgent problems attendant with 25 percent unemployment, President Franklin Roosevelt gave scant attention to the longer-term promises of a technologically led recovery.

Science Comes of Age in Washington

It was not until World War II that science and technology came of age in the nation's capital. The successful prosecution of the most destructive war in human history, fought on four continents and all seven seas, required the concentrated efforts of our entire society, including the efforts of our scientists and engineers. President Roosevelt created the Office of Scientific Research and Development (OSRD) to mobilize this effort. Some of the most sophisticated weapons that came out of World War II—radar and sonar, proximity fuses, guided missiles, and, of course, the atomic bomb—owe their existence to the concerted work of scientists and technicians from a dozen or more countries.

The National Science Foundation

The dramatic successes of the scientific and technical community during the war led several executive agencies and departments, especially the Department of Defense, to seek ways of creating or expanding their "in-house" scientific capabilities. However, with Roosevelt's death in 1945 and the inauguration of his vice president, Harry Truman, the cozy wartime arrangement seemed threatened by the changeover from wartime to peacetime economic policies.

Early in the Truman administration, a concerted effort to organize a federal role in the support of science produced the National Science Foundation, an agency commissioned to administer federal funding for scientific research. The initial NSF proposal, put forward by presidential science adviser Vannevar Bush, was very controversial because of its call for large-scale federal financial support for science with little public accountability, and actually produced a presidential veto when first passed by Congress.

Science Advisers in the White House

On October 4, 1957, the Soviet Union launched the first man-made artificial satellite, Sputnik I. The Soviet achievement shattered the postwar complacency about U.S. scientific superiority and produced a major crash program for basic science throughout U.S. education.

Because of the public concern over Sputnik, President Eisenhower was compelled to "do something" to demonstrate that he was in control of the situation. One of Eisenhower's responses was to constitute the President's Science Advisory Committee (PSAC). Located in the White House, its chair officially serving as the president's science adviser, the organization represented for the first time direct access for the science community to the inner circle of presidential aides. The creation of PSAC was more than mere window dressing, however. Having a personal friend, George Kistiakowsky, as science adviser, Eisenhower at last had an in-house ability to defend himself against bureaucratic agencies pressing their parochial interests. Prior to the creation of PSAC, the White House did not have much expertise in scientific and technical issues, and was thus largely dependent on the information—and biases—of the various executive bureaucracies.

The Kennedy Administration The expansion of the scientific community's influence within the executive branch continued under the Kennedy administration. The Harvard-educated Kennedy had close, personal relationships with the academic community generally and with important members of the scientific leadership. One of his first steps was to upgrade science advice in the White House through the creation of the Office of Science and Technology (OST) as an official body within the EOP.

OST under Kennedy proved to be a good platform for giving the science adviser both the status and the bureaucratic leverage needed to oversee the panoply of executive branch science policies. Jerome Wiesner, of MIT, was selected by Kennedy to be his science adviser. Wiesner maintained his personal contacts with Kennedy, and used his position to strengthen the science advisory apparatus throughout the executive branch. Under his guidance, and with the active support of the president, assistant secretaries for science were appointed in all relevant departments and agencies, while White House control and coordination were substantially consolidated. So effective at organization and coordination had OST become that Wiesner was even accused of making himself a "science czar" by other top-ranking scientists.[1]

Kennedy made ample use of this enlarged science advisory structure, according to James Everett Katz:

> Scientists gave Kennedy advice which went beyond the bounds of policy making within their formal purview. Some advice touched the very underpinnings of foreign policy. For example, Wiesner made Kennedy "the best informed layman on the subject" of nuclear disarmament and nuclear blast detection during the

test-ban treaty negotiations.... The Council of Economic Advisers (CEA) was also an active source of advice; social scientists were also active in setting up programs for civil defense, counterinsurgency, and the Peace Corps—all areas which had considerable personal importance for President Kennedy.[2]

The upgrading and restructuring of the science advisory system under Kennedy had significant consequences for both the quality of presidential leadership in science and technology policies and for the relationship of the science community to government in general.

The Johnson Administration   The close relationship between science advisers and the president that was characteristic of the Kennedy years did not survive Kennedy's assassination. Where Kennedy was pleased to support basic scientific research generously, for Lyndon B. Johnson, the "[e]mphasis in science was on results, the application of science to problems, not on broad basic research which might lead to new applications in the future."[3] Johnson, pursuing his dream of a Great Society, insisted that research funding in science be targeted on concrete solutions to existing social problems.

Ironically, the very successes achieved by OST under Wiesner in developing a cadre of science advisers throughout the federal bureaucracy worked to undermine the influence of the White House advisory structure. With greater scientific expertise available throughout the various departments and agencies of the federal government, the role of OST as principal guardian of science policy was diminished. More and more of the functions of OST were turned over to the scientific staffs of the various agencies. With their need for OST's policy advice diminished, Johnson's White House staff made little use of its services.

Something new to science policy did appear, however. Tests of political loyalty were applied to anyone responsible for science policy in the Johnson administration. The demand for distinctly political loyalty to the president from science advisers was a dramatic change in the traditionally nonpartisan character of the science adviser's post under previous administrations. That Johnson's science Adviser, Donald Hornig, proved unable to hold that support together, especially as the Vietnam War progressed, also undermined the White House's perception of his utility to their goals.

The Removal of the Science Adviser   The estrangement between the president and his staff and the science advisory staff grew even more intense during the Nixon administration. Intense pressures for political loyalty to President Nixon's policy goals, and to Nixon himself, were applied to the science advisory staff: "In the Nixon administration, the prime appointment criterion was loyalty to the president and his policies."[4] And this included support from the academic-professional arena for Nixon's Vietnam policies, for the antiballistic missile, and for the supersonic transport aircraft. Some scientists who served on the science advisory staff or as consultants, came out in very public opposition to the administration's position on these questions. Many scientists publicly opposed some of the Nixon administration's domestic policies as well.

Indeed, as Katz recounts, the Nixon White House treated the existing science advisory staff in the White House like a nest of untrustworthy and disloyal critics:

> This hostility was manifest in a number of attacks launched by the OMB staff members, both on a personal level through invective and vilification, and on an institutional level by weakening and disrupting of OST's channels of communication and influence. The science advisers were unable to bring their position to the attention of the president or his top staff. Nixon had no inclination toward science, and at any rate, he was quite remote from nearly everyone. This guaranteed that his science adviser would have little contact with him. Ideological congruence between administration insiders and science advisers was practically nil.[5]

The conflict came to a head in January 1973, when the Nixon administration formally abolished the post of presidential science adviser, shifting that job out of the White House and into the National Science Foundation. The OST was abolished, and while the president's Science Advisory Committee continued to exist in name, it lost all significant function. Thus, the tradition of science advice immediately available to the president, begun under Eisenhower, ended, with the academic-professional arena effectively banished from any direct role within the executive arena. However, as 1973 became 1974, it was the Nixon administration itself that was ending, mired in the Watergate scandal and followed by Nixon's resignation from office just ahead of what most believe was a nearly certain impeachment.

The Restoration of Science Advice in the White House   The administration of Gerald Ford was more sympathetic toward science in general and less inclined to see scientists as foes. Ford cooperated with an effort in Congress to restore a more amicable—and closer—relationship between the scientific community and the White House. The end result, known as the National Science and Technology Policy, Organization and Priorities Act of 1976, was signed into law on May 11, 1976. The law created a series of organizations aimed at providing science advice to the executive branch, including a legislatively mandated Office of Science and Technology Policy (OSTP), whose chair would serve as the president's science adviser, the Federal Coordinating Council for Science, Engineering, and Technology Advisory Council (FCCSET), an Intergovernmental Science, Engineering, and Technology Advisory Council (ISETAC), and a President's Committee on Science and Technology (PCST).

Thus, after the Nixon hiatus, a formal science advisory apparatus was re-established. This time, the science advisory apparatus was created by action of Congress rather than by presidential decision, allowing greater legislative arena involvement in how science information was to enter into the decision-making processes of the executive arena. For one thing, the science adviser is now subject to congressional subpoena, and OSTP is supposed to provide science advice to Congress as well.

Science, Technology, and the Institutional Presidency

There are some useful lessons to be drawn from this history. We can see, not surprisingly, that science and technology policies are not, by themselves, critical policy issues for the president, although science and technology may be very important for other policy goals. Science and technology policies are important because they contribute to these other policy ends. Science and technology, as a policy domain, can be important within the executive arena whenever there are concerns about the health and vigor of the U.S. scientific establishment or if some specific heavily science and technology-oriented goal is established, such as NASA's space programs or the war on cancer.

Another lesson, also not surprising, is that presidents do not come into office with much expertise in science and technology. Thus, in this policy domain, perhaps more than most others, presidents must rely on the special competence of scientists and engineers for advice and information. This means that staff support is especially necessary for decision making by the presidency in science and technology areas. It is to this staff support structure for science and technology decision making in the executive arena that we now turn.

Subpresidencies   Given the array of tasks that befall the modern president, no individual could hope to stay abreast of all the policy domains requiring presidential leadership and decision making; reliance on staff support is inevitable. Following Henry Lambright, we can speak about the staff support structures of the modern, bureaucratic presidency as comprising various "subpresidencies."[6] A subpresidency refers to a particular group of individuals and agencies, including the president, devoted to a distinctive policy area. Thus, the national security subpresidency, for instance, includes the president, of course, but also several personal advisers and professional staff agencies within the executive arena who provide the president with information, data, and policy advice.

Lambright says that there are five kinds of decision makers in any subpresidency: principals, budgeteers, professionals, administrators, and the vice president.

Principals are persons upon whom the president relies most often when making particular policy decisions. Often, principals are personal friends of the president, and have influence over a wide range of issues. Their advice will often include both policy analysis and political considerations. Thus, principals often are policy generalists, rather than specialists, and have impact across a range of policy problems.

Budgeteers, who work in the Office of Management and Budget (OMB), are professional staff members who (with the exception of the director of OMB) usually continue working at OMB regardless of who is president. These decision makers must make countless choices about national spending priorities. Lambright tells us that budgeteers "adapt to different presidential perspectives, but develop their own points of view and give continuity to presidential management.... They

[are] an extension of presidential power by virtue of their centrality to the president's use of the budget as a primary management tool."[7]

Professionals participate in the subpresidency less because they are personally or politically close to the president, but because they provide a specialized expertise needed for certain kinds of decisions. Professionals will try to reflect the policy goals of the particular president for whom they work or what they think the president wants. As professionals, however, such advisers also owe an allegiance to their professions and to their career ambitions, and thus their activities on behalf of an individual president may be impeded by professional codes of ethics or other outside demands. Thus, professionals must appear to principals—and perhaps to the president as well—as having divided loyalties. At any rate, their policy advice cannot be seen as dictated solely by their concern for president's goals.

Administrators include the heads of departments and independent agencies. Administrators, according to Lambright, face important problems of identification within a subpresidency: "They are appointed by the president and expected to represent presidential perspectives to their agencies, as well as to advise him on policy. Administrators are supposed not only to support the president, but also to administer their agencies. The latter task frequently results in a conflict of interest. What is good for the agency may not be good for the president."[8] From an administrator's viewpoint, the current president is only a temporary occupant of the White House, for whose sake the administrator may not be willing to make very many important sacrifices. After all, when this president is gone, both the agency and the administrator will still be on the job. Administrators see themselves as part of the "permanent government," a status the president cannot claim.

Under recent presidents, the *vice president* has played a more central role in policy development and administration. This is particularly the case in science and technology policies. Lyndon Johnson, as vice president to John Kennedy, took a major role in developing space policy, as did Hubert Humphrey when he was Johnson's vice president. Walter Mondale and George Bush, vice presidents for Presidents Jimmy Carter and Ronald Reagan, respectively, played enlarged roles in policymaking as well.

Subpresidencies in Action   How well the participants in a subpresidency work together in making policy decisions hinges on who is president; it is each president's unique management style and policy priorities that set the general tone and direction of policy, even if the subpresidency develops the specific policy options. This is true of all policy domains, whether it be national security, education, industrial policy, or science and technology.

When a particular president exerts leadership in a policy domain, subpresidency participants line up behind the president's goals. If, on the other hand, the president exerts only nominal leadership in a policy domain, or is simply uninterested in it, policy leadership—such as it is—will emerge from the pulling and hauling of the subpresidency decision makers. The political skills and clout of the various sci/tech subpresidency participants will determine what programs and projects work their way up to the president for ultimate decision. The special political acumen and bureaucratic effectiveness of those decision makers will largely determine which projects go forward and which are delayed, set aside, or even terminated.

OSTP and OMB   Within the science and technology subpresidency, the two most important agencies are the Office of Science and Technology Policy (OSTP) and the Office of Management and Budget (OMB). Often these agencies have opposed each other, with OSTP working for expanded federal support for science and OMB struggled to restrain spending.

OSTP has several functions: (1) providing advice to the president on issues involving science and technology, (2) analyzing policy proposals from federal agencies, (3) interagency coordination and even sometimes management of certain policy areas, (4) recruitment of science advisory personnel throughout the executive arena, and (5) serving as a communications vehicle between the executive branch and the academic-professional arena, among other tasks.

OSTP's Political Enfeeblement   However, OSTP's position within the executive arena is politically precarious, as Ted Greenwood, a former OSTP staff member, tells us: "First, there really is nothing that happens in the Executive Office of the President that could not happen without OSTP. Second, OSTP does not own a presidential process. Third, although OSTP is a very small unit, its mandate is truly enormous; this puts the office under great pressure."[9]

Greenwood's assertion that OSTP is not essential to the operations of the executive arena does not reflect his opinion about the importance of scientific advice for the president, but rather recognizes the political reality that such advice is readily available from many other sources within the executive branch, and that if OSTP did not exist, the government surely would not grind to a halt. However, Greenwood asserts, OSTP, as a centralized agency, can serve to make science advice more efficient and perhaps more effective than advice coming from disparate sources.

The second point, that OSTP owns no formal presidential process, illustrates the significantly weaker political position of this executive arena agency when compared to other, more powerful organizations. OMB, for instance, controls the president's budget, while the Council of Environmental Quality manages environmental issues and the National Security Council runs national security affairs. OSTP does not have a special preserve of its own; it controls no specific, formal policy agenda. What this means is that the political influence of OSTP and of its head, the president's science adviser, rests on how each individual president chooses to use OSTP. OSTP has, in Greenwood's words, "no automatic source of influence."[10]

It also means that the president's science adviser and his staff depend heavily on the more powerful agencies within the executive office for the information needed to do their jobs and for access to the policy decision-making process. Greenwood summarizes: "If one wants to close the science adviser out of a particular issue or render him generally ineffective...all one needs to do is to cut off the paper flow and not invite him and his staff to meetings."[11] We can see that OSTP's bureaucratic independence is compromised by its lack of an institutional base of policy involvement and influence. The science advisory staff must establish and maintain good relations with other agencies, lest they lose their ability to shape policy altogether.

Finally, Greenwood notes that OSTP's staff is necessarily small when compared to the huge dimension of its tasks, creating considerable pressure for time and other resources. In many policy areas, OSTP has had to compete with other agencies, such as the budgeteers at OMB, or other applied agencies, such as the Department of Defense or NASA. Such agencies have their own scientists and experts and often feel more capable of making policy suggestions than the scientists working at OSTP, with the result that the formal science advisory structure within the executive arena has often been cut out of the decision-making process by better established and more politically powerful competitors. Lambright tells us that OSTP has consistently dominated science policymaking only in the area of support for basic research.

OMB's Political Power   The Office of Management and Budget is the chief institutional competitor to OSTP and often plays the role of science policy coordinator and manager. James Katz explains: "Executive-branch positions on science-policy questions are usually handled by the OMB.... The OMB is generally the executive spokesman whenever the Congress challenges the administration position on politically charged science-policy issues."[12]

Federal resources simply cannot be stretched to support all useful projects or programs, and OMB is the agency that sets spending priorities, including science policy priorities. Since all federal agencies must submit budget requests to OMB as part of pulling together the president's overall budget, the agency's decisions have real impact. For instance, as Richard Barke notes, it was decisions made in OMB that stopped federal contribution to the Mohole project in the early 1960s, compelled NASA's decision about a nuclear-powered rocket, and cut out "social research" funding in various federal agencies.[13] On the other hand, OMB can be pushed toward certain science policy decisions, by the president, by Congress, and sometimes by interest groups.

While made up largely of policy generalists, OMB has developed considerable technical expertise. OMB, however, is unable to monitor all of the diverse projects, facilities, programs, and research funded by the federal government. Instead, OMB singles out those science and technology policies it considers important to the president's larger policy goals. Katz explains:

> Prior to giving congressional testimony all executive-branch employees, including officials with science-policy responsibilities, must submit their statements to the OMB for review and approval. Bitter conflicts often ensue over what can be and is said during congressional testimony. The testimony itself is often "massaged" after its presentation until the "proper" viewpoints are expressed.[14]

Katz is making a very important point here: Presidential leadership in science and technology issues—whether for industrial competitiveness, environmental protection, risk management, national security, or whatever—is always at least partially a political process. Whatever other politically neutral goals the executive has, we must never be so naive as to assume that the political costs and benefits of these decisions play no role in decision-making within the executive arena. Presidential power, influence, and prestige are permanent elements of the decision-making environment of every decision maker in the executive arena.

THE LEGISLATIVE ARENA

Members of Congress must deal with a very wide array of often complicated issues. However, the **legislative arena** lacks the central leadership and control exercised by the president. Congress's decentralized and fragmented operating style makes it very difficult for the congressional leadership to impose discipline upon members of either house. This means that the decision-making environment of the legislative arena differs markedly from that of the executive arena.

To deal with its large and growing workload, Congress subdivides its work among more than 100 committees and subcommittees, each of which has a powerful chair who jealously guards the policy areas within the committee's jurisdiction. What is more, those jurisdictions can sometimes overlap, with more than one committee claiming influence over a policy domain. Thus, when dealing with science and technology policy issues, or with issues containing important scientific or technological components, the two major science committees (the Committee on Commerce, Science, and Transportation in the Senate and the Committee on Science, Space, and Technology in the House of Representatives) and their assorted subcommittees may find themselves challenged by others with similar or related jurisdictions.

Scientific and Technical Competence in Congress

While Congress must regularly deal with very complex, technical issues, neither house of Congress can claim substantial scientific or technological expertise among its elected members. Senator Pete Domenici, (R–New Mexico) tells us about his chamber:

> ...today, sixty-five of our 100 Senators were trained as lawyers. A dozen Senators have a business background. There are four farmers, two bankers, plus a variety of other occupations, from a former social worker to a former pro basketball star. With all this talent, one broad discipline is missing. Not a single member of today's United States Senate is a scientist. The closest we come is our civil engineer (Senator Evans of Washington) and our astronaut (Senator Glenn of Ohio).[15]

Scientific and technical expertise is no greater among members of the House of Representatives.

Legislative Staff Competence

This, however, does not mean that the legislative arena has no scientific or technical competence. Legislative arena expertise resides primarily in the congressional staff, now numbering approximately 40,000 persons. Congressional staff members are crucial to the operations of the legislative arena. Many congressional staffers serve for many years on the Hill and thus form a significant pool of expertise about both the general legislative process and specific policy areas. The best staffers are pursued by various Congressional and committee offices, and, as they gain experience, they often move from lesser to more important members and committees. It is quite clear to all that the work of Congress simply could not be done without them.

Legislative Staff Agencies   Each member of Congress has personal staff members, as do both the majority and the minority leadership of all committees and subcommittees. In addition, there are four full-time staff agencies working exclusively for Congress: the Office of Technology Assessment (OTA), the Congressional Research Service of the Library of Congress (CRS-LOC), the General Accounting Office (GAO), and the Congressional Budget Office (CBO). All four agencies possess important scientific and technical capabilities. Other sources of scientific and technical expertise available to Congress include the National Research Council of the National Academy of Sciences, the National Institutes of Health, and the Nuclear Regulatory Commission, among others.

The Office of Technology Assessment   Congress created the Office of Technology Assessment in 1972, specifically because many members of the legislative arena recognized that science and technology play a growing role in the issues the legislature faces and that Congress needs an in-house capacity for independent, professional, and nonpartisan investigations of the impact of technology on society. OTA, it was hoped, would allow Congress to anticipate the positive and negative consequences of technological change before they occur, rather than, as usual, dealing with them after they appear, by which time they might well be irreversible.

On the more political side, OTA provided Congress with a way of challenging the technical basis of policy decisions coming from the White House. During the early 1970s, members of the legislative arena were angered by outright distortions of scientific analyses coming from the executive arena, in particular concerning the antiballistic missile and supersonic aircraft programs of the Nixon administration. As David Dickson tells us:

> Many had been made acutely aware of their lack of access to scientific information when new data about the impact of supersonic transport on the ozone layer were released only hours before a major vote in the Senate on the administration's plans for the SST; their unease was only heightened when evidence emerged that the executive summary of a technical report on the environmental impact of SSTs had been slanted to give a more favorable conclusion than the body of the report

itself—for example, by describing the climatic effects of thirty Concordes as "smaller than minimally detectable."[16]

In the years since its founding, OTA has been criticized by a number of observers, usually for not meeting the high expectations of its founders. While designed to provide high-quality, broad-based, and nonpartisan assessments of new technologies—a kind of "over the horizon" view of the technological future—OTA has been pressured politically to engage in what one observer calls "technology monitoring,"[17] that is, short-term reviews of current technologies that are politically important to members of Congress.

Others argue that many shortcomings in OTA's technological analyses reflect the array of demands, limitations, and pressures imposed on the agency by the committees of Congress. In other words, because Congress as an institution operates on a short time frame and responds most effectively to popular concerns and demands, OTA—a creature of Congress—must shorten its time horizon, too, and must focus on scientific and technical issues of the moment, rather than taking the longer-range perspective of its founders.

OTA's analyses often serve as political ammunition in the legislative battles of Congress; as such, all sides of an issue are very interested in pushing and shaping OTA's assessments to their advantage, or at least to limiting the potential damage such assessments might present. OTA Director John Gibbons describes the political complexities of even defining the scope of an OTA study:

> There usually has to be a lot of horse trading about the scope of the study. For example, if the Senate Armed Services Committee asks for something on arms control, the first thing we do is find out not only the committee chair's interest, but also the ranking minority member's interest. Then we go to the other committees that have jurisdiction—the Senate military appropriations subcommittee and similar groups on the House side—to find out how they would like us to treat the subject. By the time we have put a proposal together, we will have identified the stakeholders in Congress and combined their interests into a single piece they can abide by.[18]

This should remind us that for the legislative arena the political dimension of decision making is never far from view. Congress is, whatever else we may say about it, a preeminently political institution, peopled by decision makers who must, perforce, pay careful heed to the political consequences of their actions, or inactions. It's the political needs of reelection that set the short-term horizon seen in so much of Congress's policymaking, just as reelection worries contribute to the highly constituent-oriented operating style of most members of Congress.

As we will have the opportunity to note in subsequent chapters, much of the political gridlock that characterizes technological decision making in the United States has its embodiment, if not its origins, in the working of the legislative arena. It is here that decision makers from various contending arenas, each pursuing separate and often contradictory technological projects, know that they can often find sympathetic decision makers who are willing to take their side, as long as they can make a connection between their technological project and the legislator's desire for reelection. To forget this is to miss the point of much that happens on Capitol Hill.

Technologically Responsible vs. Democratically Responsive Policies

In the larger sense, Congress faces the problem of fashioning science and technology policies that are at one and the same time technologically responsible and democratically responsive. Technologically responsible policies need to take the longer view, to anticipate what the future will look like and what steps the nation needs to take in order to be prepared for that future. Responsible technological management requires an extended view of social change, as well as the willingness to take risks and to accept the inevitable dislocations that accompany technical change. Sometimes, unfortunately, such policies create considerable disruption in the lives of individuals who are committed to outdated technologies.

Democratically responsive policies, on the other hand, are likely to be more sensitive to the pains that technological change imposes on people, and thus are likely more often to try to protect people committed to obsolete technologies, even if doing so is disruptive to long-term technical growth. Protectionist trade policies, for instance, may give some people relief from foreign technologies, at least for a short time. Given a great clamor from endangered constituents, it is difficult for members of Congress to think any further than the next election.

What we are saying about the legislative arena as an environment for making science and technology decisions is that so much depends on the largely nonscientific and nontechnical influences that shape all congressional decisions. Thus, even if the relevant committees, staffers, and members should come up with a well-informed, well-designed, far-sighted scientific or technical policy, the institution as a whole might well reject it because it fails to address the distinctly political needs of its members.

Examples abound. In the area of federal funding for scientific research, for instance, Congress's decisions have been made largely independent of local interests. Today, however, there is growing demand from many states and localities that federal support monies be more "fairly" distributed, that in the past certain preeminent universities have received the lion's share of funding. So clamorous have these complaints become that Congress now regularly specifies which kinds of projects at specific research universities will receive funding, a process called "pork barrel science." It seems clear to many observers that the best science can be done only at the best equipped and staffed research facilities, and that dispersing federal support geographically can only weaken the overall quality of the research. Yet Congress, mindful of local constituent demands, persists in allocating research dollars according to nonscientific standards.

THE JUDICIAL ARENA

The decision-making environment of the **judicial arena** is closely limited by both law and tradition. Legally, the judicial arena is constrained by the U.S. Constitution and the Supreme Court's interpretations of it, statutory enactments, common law, and administrative law. Decision makers within the judicial arena are also limited by the traditional norms of judicial passivity and impartiality expected of members of the bench. We in the United States have sadly grown accustomed to elected officials in both the executive and legislative arenas who often duck or evade the hard choices presented by modern science and technology; however, we still expect the courts to make decisions fearlessly, basing their judgment on the objective circumstances of each case and an impartial reading of the law.

The judicial arena can claim at least as long an involvement in resolving scientific and technological issues as the other three government arenas. Norman Vig reminds us that courts have a centuries-long tradition of handling personal injury cases, injuries very often the result of industrial and technological developments.[19] With the development of newer and often more dangerous technologies, the courts have indeed encouraged an expansion of traditional nineteenth-century legal doctrines of trespass, negligence, and liability, and have allowed easier access to the courts for individuals and groups seeking redress.

Such steps serve to encourage lawsuits by aggrieved parties: "In 1980, an estimated 10,000 suits were pending over damages due to exposure to asbestos alone, and residents of Love Canal in New York had begun approximately 1,200 actions seeking $15 billion in compensatory and punitive damages for exposure to hazardous chemical wastes."[20] In some cases, huge awards have been made, as in the Karen Ann Silkwood case, in which the Silkwood estate was awarded $10,500,000 because of her exposure to plutonium.

In recent years, the judicial arena has frequently taken on the task of resolving conflicts concerning a host of new developing technologies. The spectrum of cases addressed by the courts has included computers and personal privacy, the patentability of genetically altered life forms, the exposure of industrial workers to hazardous substances, environmental pollution, and the scientific foundations of regulations governing toxic and carcinogenic chemicals such as DDT, polychlorinated biphenyls (PCBs), vinyl chloride, benzene, diethylstilbestrol (DES), asbestos, and radioactive wastes.[21]

Traditional Judicial Remedies

Traditional legal remedies seem unable to resolve many of these thorny issues. The tremendous degrees of uncertainty in many cases of health or environmental litigation make establishing clear lines of responsibility and liability very tricky, as we will see in more detail in Chapter 8. Moreover, while the adversarial techniques of the courtroom may be useful at ferreting out the truth in a criminal case, they are not very useful in handling cases involving scientific uncertainty, as Vig tells us:

> Lawyers on each side will present the strongest possible case regardless of its scientific merit. They will selectively cite expert opinion and evidence which supports their argument, while seeking to discredit that of the adversary by whatever means are available. Judges are then left to pick and choose among conflicting scientific evidence, much of it distorted in the process.[22]

David O'Brien agrees, and adds to the list of defects in traditional judicial doctrines and practices when confronted by the complexities of modern science and technology:

> Scientific uncertainty over the risk of toxins and carcinogens is impossible to resolve within adversarial proceedings. Rules of evidence limit the introduction of some forms of scientific data and testimony. Statutes of limitations frequently foreclose even the possibility of claiming injuries involving diseases with long latency periods, such as cancer.... Private-law adjudication of science-policy disputes is costly, cumbersome, and time-consuming. Adjudication in turn discourages lawsuits and promotes out-of-court settlements since litigation becomes economically unreasonable for individuals suffering and in need of compensation.[23]

Partially in response to the perceived weaknesses of traditional legal remedies in dealing with the kinds of challenges presented by modern technology, during the 1970s Congress enacted some 31 major statutes curbing toxic and carcinogenic substances, creating new labor health and safety standards, and establishing clear air and water programs, along with the regulatory agencies to administer these programs. In many cases, the new laws made explicit provision for judicial review of the decisions made by the regulatory agencies and allowed broader opportunities for the public to bring suit for failure to perform mandated duties. In a break with its traditional deference to regulatory agency decisions, the courts today display a willingness to review intensively and extensively both the decision-making procedures employed by federal agencies and the substantive decisions themselves.

Part of this development stems from the courts' willingness to expand an individual's right to sue a government agency on the grounds of procedural or substantive impropriety. Courts in the past imposed stiffer conditions before a person could bring suit in court to reverse an agency decision. Now, because of increased judicial leniency, it is possible to bring class action suits in which a whole group of individuals is represented even though proof of direct, personal loss cannot be established.

In adding explicit court review provisions to the regulatory programs, Congress clearly desired to use the judicial arena as a brake on the extensive discretionary powers it was granting to decision makers in the regulatory arena.

Many of these programs were created in an era of growing demands for more public participation in government decision making at all levels.

Judicial Decision-Making Strategies

The decision-making environment of the judicial arena is complex, not the least because the judges are individual technological decision makers in our framework and often have strong opinions about their roles and responsibilities. We must remember, as Vig tells us, that

> Judges do not...simply respond to the particular statute and controversy at hand; they are also motivated by their own norms and doctrines. Among other things, they make "strategic" choices on how to approach their reviewing task, what decision-rules to follow, and how far to intervene in administrative affairs.[24]

Following Vig, we can isolate at least four different strategies used by judicial arena decision makers concerning science and technology.

Type I: Constitutional Process   Type I is the most traditional and least controversial decision strategy adopted by many judges. Using this approach, the court focuses on whether or not the agency being challenged properly exercised its legitimate authority in making its decisions; whether the agency's actions conform to the language and intent of the law. At a broader level, the court may need to determine whether Congress originally acted properly in delegating the agency's authority, or whether it failed to clarify the statutory purposes.

Type II: Administrative Procedures   In Type II review, the judge's objective is to examine the administrative procedures used by the agency. While concerned about procedures for a long time, in recent years the courts have intensified their procedural reviews, forcing regulatory decision makers to document the full reasoning behind their decisions. Existing administrative law, such as the Administrative Procedure Act, creates general requirements of proper notification, public participation, and adequate record keeping for all federal agencies. The courts often look quite closely at such procedures when agency decisions turn upon the latest scientific and technological issues.

Type III: Substantive Rationality   The courts go beyond examining administrative procedures in Type III reviews. Judges who apply this decision strategy will examine in close detail the substance of agency decisions, including scientific and technical evidence, methodologies, and conclusions. The court seeks to determine if the agency decision, in addition to following correct administrative procedures, is adequately supported by the best available scientific and technical evidence.

For this sort of determination, the judge must become familiar with the fundamental sciences and technologies involved and try to reach conclusions about the uncertainties necessarily involved in the specific case under question. In some cases, the court calls upon outside experts, while in others judges rely upon the abilities of their clerks to search adequately the relevant scientific literature. This is the most controversial decision strategy, since it is open to the challenge that scientifically untutored judges should not try to resolve complex technical issues and questions that experts in the relevant fields cannot resolve.

Type IV: Interest Balancing   In Type IV reviews, the court's objective is to find a balance between contending interests and conflicting values. This is a traditional part of judicial arena resolution in civil law, but is sometimes applied to scientific and technological issues as well. Often the language of the statute under question may be unclear or ambiguous, and some judges have been willing to read a kind of cost-benefit logic into their decisions.

Court Shopping   These four judicial strategies are so well understood by decision makers in other arenas that parties to prospective litigation will "shop around" for a sympathetic judge who will employ a desired strategy: "parties to administrative appeals will often spend tens of thousands of dollars in elaborate (and even bizarre) "races-to-the-courthouse" to ensure that a particular appellate court will hear an appeal from a scientific rulemaking."[25]

Certain judges and certain courts develop reputations for using one or another decision strategy, and it can be crucial to the success or failure of a particular technological project that a case be filed in a specific court. Barke describes how far some participants will go to get a case before a particular judge: "When the EPA was about to issue a final rule banning the chemical Compound 1080, used in the control of predators, one law firm continuously occupied the only public telephone near the issuing office so that a colleague in the Tenth Circuit Court in Denver could be notified immediately. Other would-be litigants have used walkie-talkies and human signaling chains."[26]

Also, the multilayered court structure adds a degree of complexity to these issues, as Vig reminds us: "There are more than a hundred federal district and circuit courts which often make inconsistent decisions. Although the Courts of Appeal and ultimately the Supreme Court resolve some of the most important differences, judicial outputs can be as diverse in the aggregate as those of the other branches of government."[27]

THE REGULATORY ARENA

The **regulatory arena** presents a diverse decision-making environment because regulatory decision makers face different kinds of legislative mandates and disparate responsibilities. Whether it is the Environmental Protection Agency, responsible for monitoring toxic waste disposal and air and water pollution, or the Occupational Safety and Health Administration, responsible for protecting worker health and safety in plants and factories, or the Food and Drug Administration, answerable for regulating food additives, new pharmaceuticals, and various genetically altered organisms, each agency must deal with its own agenda and its own specific array of technological problems. The legislative arena has not been consistent in establishing either the jurisdictions or the enforcement standards to be used by these agencies. Added to these complexities must be the powers of the judicial arena.

Types of Regulatory Decision Makers

One way to get a handle on how this arena operates is to draw distinctions among the different kinds of decision makers found here. Following James Wilson, we can find at least three different kinds of decision makers operating within the regulatory arena: careerists, politicians, and professionals.[28]

Careerists, the first type, are agency employees who identify with the agency in which they work and who entertain no larger ambitions. Thus, they appeal to no other constituency outside the agency itself. Careerists tend to be political realists, recognizing that they sit at the center of a maelstrom of political pressures. This realization makes careerists, and the agencies they work for, rather conservative. Wilson tells us that "government agencies are more risk averse than imperialistic. They prefer security to rapid growth, autonomy to competition, stability to change."[29]

As Wilson points out, what can threaten an agency like EPA, OSHA, or FDA is a major scandal or crisis in an area within the agency's responsibilities. For agencies charged with protecting the public from the worst consequences of modern science and technology, a dramatic loss of life or other catastrophe traceable to agency action—or inaction, could quickly undermine the agency's political support, even its future.

To avoid such a crisis, careerists in the regulatory agencies take steps to avert potential disaster:

> That agencies are risk averse does not mean they are timid. Quite the contrary: their desire for autonomy, for a stable environment, and for freedom for blame gives these agencies a strong incentive to make rules and to exercise authority in all aspects of their mission. No agency wishes to be accused of "doing nothing" with respect to a real or imagined problem; hence every agency proliferates rules to cover all possible contingencies. The process is known familiarly in the bureaucracy as "covering your flanks." The more diverse the organized constituencies with which an agency must deal, the more flanks there are to be covered.[30]

Thus, many of the actions taken by careerists in the regulatory arena are bureaucratically defensive, risk-averse, scandal-avoiding steps intended to deflect outside criticism. Decision makers from other interested arenas certainly need to be aware of these motivations in order to plan successful interactions with this group of regulatory decision makers.

Wilson's second type, the *politicians*, are agency employees who quite often are appointees, having been selected perhaps as a repayment for other political services, campaign help, or for some assistance they provided to the president. They often entertain future elective or appointive office outside the agency as well. Such politicians are often assigned to the higher management levels within the agency, where they are expected to pursue the president's policy agenda for their agency. Often, politicians have little technical background in the workings of the regulatory agency they head, and are thus heavily dependent on the careerists they supervise, at least until they come to understand the agency's operations. The political and policy views of these appointed decision makers can be very influential in diverting agency decisions.

Professionals, Wilson's third type of agency employee, are also members of the academic-professional arena. They are scientists and technical staff members who owe an allegiance to the agency in which they work, but also owe an allegiance to the profession in which they have standing. Physicists, chemists, engineers, physicians, public health specialists, lawyers, and other professionals—these regulatory decision makers seek the approval of professional peers outside the agency and the self-respect derived from behaving according to external professional norms. Such professional standing can be as important as the approval from one's superiors within the agency.

There is plenty of room for conflict among these three kinds of decision makers within the regulatory arena. For example, in some cases, political appointees to regulatory agencies have had explicit political agendas in mind for the agencies they head. Thus, President Reagan's appointment of James Watt as secretary of the Interior and of Anne Burford Gorsuch as head of EPA were seen by both those in support of and opposed to the administration's policy goals as highly ideological appointments.

Because both Watt and Gorsuch pursued new policies that departed radically from the existing policy directions of the agencies they headed, their decisions were controversial and engendered substantial opposition from members of the popular mobilization and the legislative arenas, as well as from within the very agencies they led. In many cases, the inside information used by critics of the Watt/Gorsuch policy agenda was provided to members of Congress and others by careerists and professionals working in those agencies. Knowing that there is potential for such conflict can be of great value to technological decision makers from other arenas, who hope to use such tensions to advance their own technological projects.

Regulatory Responsibilities

Another aspect of the regulatory arena's decision-making environment is the tremendous array of responsibilities and duties regulators shoulder. For example, EPA alone is responsible for administering the Clean Air Act, the Clean Water Act, the Noise Control Act, the Safe Drinking Water Act, the Resource Conservation and Recovery Act, the Toxic Substances Control Act, the Marine Protection,

Research and Sanctuaries Act, and the Federal Insecticide, Fungicide, and Rodenticide Act, among other enactments. Each of these acts encompasses a large range of activities that EPA is required to carry out.

This staggering burden of administrative, regulatory, investigative, and standard-setting responsibilities lies at the outer edge of contemporary science. The reality is that we have reliable tests on the health risks of only a smattering of the 50,000 industrial chemicals in use today. Likewise, scientific determinations of how best to dispose of hazardous wastes safely, of the environmental impacts from waste disposal dump leaks, and of the long-term health consequences of different levels of exposure to toxic and hazardous wastes are simply not yet available. Walter Rosenbaum summarizes the perplexing problems facing an agency like EPA under these mandated programs:

> These regulatory programs, each a thicket of administrative and technical complexity, all were passed within a period of less than four years. The EPA and other responsible governmental agencies thus were confronted with an avalanche of new regulatory mandates, bristling with insistent compliance deadlines, for which they were expected to be rapidly prepared. It is doubtful that the agencies could have satisfactorily discharged these responsibilities under the most benign circumstances.... By the mid-1980s most TSCA and RCRA programs, mired in administrative and technical complications, were running years behind statutory schedules.[31]

All of these obligations fell on an agency that suffered a 30 percent cut in its operating budget and a 23 percent reduction in staff between 1980 and 1983. By 1983, the EPA's enforcement budget had been cut by 45 percent as well.[32] One result of such reductions is that it will be decades before EPA can hope to review carefully all of the thousands of industrial chemicals, pesticides, effluent discharges, and hazardous waste sites that are part of its statutory responsibility. Other regulatory agencies face different, but quite demanding, tasks as well.

CONCLUSIONS

Clearly, this is a diverse selection of technological decision-making arenas. While all four are components of the federal government, each is a unique decision-making environment, with many different decision makers who are responding to a complex and changing array of limitations, incentives, constraints, and pressures.

Decision-Making Challenges

Decisions made in any one of the four government arenas can have tremendous implications for technological projects pursued in the other arenas. In fact, the history of any specific technological project may require decisions from two, three, or all four government arenas, and there is no reason to expect those decisions to be consistent with each other. A technological decision maker in one of the other arenas will need to plan very carefully how to shepherd a technological project through the maze of potential obstacles presented by the four government arenas. To do this, such a decision maker will need to obtain specific, desired decisions from one or more government arena decision makers; and to do this, an understanding of the incentives, constraints, and pressures operating in each Arena is essential. A difficult part of the planning for decision makers is the unpredictability of which government arenas might become involved in one's technological project. A skilled decision maker must know how to push the right buttons, bring the right pressures and influences to bear at the right time, to obtain the desired decisions from decision makers in those arenas.

It can require considerable effort, time, and resources to mount a serious effort to influence science and technology decision making by the executive and the legislative arenas. Neither the White House nor Congress makes such decisions rapidly, and there may be many opportunities for decisions to support a particular scientific or technological project to change, because of budgetary problems or other changes in priorities. Outsiders must maintain steady pressure on the executive and legislative arenas to ensure that undesirable reversals or outright cancellations do not occur. Of course, decision makers in one government arena can be used to block or reverse decisions made in other government arenas.

A decision maker in, for instance, the corporate-managerial arena, who has guided a specific technological project through the maze of his or her own corporation, fending off other corporate decision makers who also want limited company resources for other projects, is not going to sit quietly while someone in, for instance, the regulatory arena undermines many months or years of work by issuing a rule or regulation that makes it impossible to bring the project to a successful completion. Many thousands and hundreds of thousands of dollars and whole careers may hinge on delivering a new technological project profitably to market.

Likewise, members of the popular mobilization arena are also very interested in what kinds of decisions are made by members of the regulatory arena. If they believe that the new chemical substance, which decision makers in the corporate-managerial arena have worked so long to research, develop, and to market, presents critical health or environmental risks, they will want the regulatory arena decision maker to issue rules and regulations imposing limits on the chemical's use or banning it altogether. Clearly, we are on course for a major political battle, and the decision makers of the regulatory arena are right in the middle of it.

Executive and Legislative Involvement

Interestingly, Wilson tells us, neither the executive arena nor the legislative arena ordinarily plays a major role in this battle. Certainly, the White House can try to influence regulatory arena decisions through the naming of political appointees who agree with the specific policy goals of the administration to top agency management positions. Still, in most cases, the White House staff does not take the time to do an in-depth review of a potential appointee's positions on issues coming before the agency, and, like judges, the political appointees often do not follow the president's agenda (at least not as closely as originally hoped).

The executive arena can impose broad guidelines on some regulatory agencies, as when the Reagan administration issued Executive Order 12291 requiring the use of cost-benefit analysis before issuing any new, major regulation. Yet even here, the order does not apply to all regulations and all regulatory agencies, some of which are required by their original legislation to ignore cost considerations when issuing new rules or regulations.

In the legislative arena, Wilson comments, the relevant committees usually ignore policy questions when handling agency budgets. Fundamentally, there are few votes to be gained by intensive congressional review of regulatory decisions. Indeed, as Wilson tells us, there may be political incentives to leave the existing regulatory machinery alone: "There are scarcely any votes to be had from…intervening in specific regulatory issues. If an outraged constituent demands intervention, a politician can always promise to "look into" the matter and make a pro forma inquiry. If nothing happens as a result, it is, of course, because of "arrogant" or "unreasonable" bureaucrats."[33]

Since regulatory decisions do not ordinarily have a high enough priority within the executive arena for careful review, and do not offer sufficient incentives for the legislative arena to get involved, most regulatory disputes end up in the judicial arena for resolution.

Judicial and Regulatory Involvement

Under the Administrative Procedures Act, the federal courts are empowered to review regulatory decisions, specifically to determine if the agency followed mandated procedures about timely notice of public hearings, proper publications of proposed rules or rules changes, adequate opportunity for affected parties to comment on such changes, and so on. In addition, the courts require regulatory agencies to maintain a detailed record of these steps, along with a clearly stated explanation of why the agency chose to take the steps it did.

Because scientific and technological conflicts often exist at the cutting edge of scientific knowledge, regulatory decisions must often be made with "very few 'hard facts,' many assumptions and inferences, large uncertainties, and the unavoidable exercise of policy judgment."[34] The court reviews regulatory decisions to make sure that they rest on solid scientific reasoning, rather than the unsubstantiated, personal preferences of the regulators.

Moreover, the new regulatory enactments contain explicit provisions allowing appeal into the federal court system by individuals and groups affected by those decisions. Indeed, so frequently are regulatory arena decisions challenged in court that some observers speak of a new "partnership" between the federal appellate courts and regulatory agencies, creating a new era in administrative law. O'Brien summarizes:

> The federal judiciary...has an important participatory role in the formulation and implementation of federal regulation. Litigation has become part of the regulatory process. Agencies inescapably must defend all major regulations in judicial forums; federal regulation appears to require the judicial imprimatur.[35]

Members of the popular mobilization arena regularly seek to influence science and technology decisions by using the relaxed access to the courts. They believe, with some justification, that corporate-managerial decision makers have greater influence in both the legislative and executive arenas. Besides, trying to influence objectionable technological decisions made by members of the corporate-managerial arena through legislative action is both time consuming and expensive. Court cases, while also costly, are less expensive than mounting a major lobbying effort in Congress. Also, because courts must resolve specific cases, they are more likely to produce clear, definitive decisions than would the legislature. Naturally, decision makers in the corporate-managerial arena are aware of these tactics, and must take steps to counter them, if they can.

Appealable Questions   These cases present the courts with a dramatically expanded range of issues, when compared to more routine cases. While typical criminal or civil cases may generate three or four issues important enough for appellate courts to resolve, cases arising from scientific rulemaking in the regulatory arena can involve dozens of major appealable questions and hundreds of secondary issues. With many thousands of research and development dollars already invested, and the potential for perhaps millions of dollars in sales at stake, the contending lawyers in such appeals work very hard to undermine the position of their opponent, as Thomas O. McGarity points out:

> The lawyers for the aggrieved parties comb the lengthy and usually disorganized [regulatory rulemaking] record for facts and arguments that undermine the agency's articulated reasons for the rule. With the help of scientific experts, they identify weak spots and potential contradictions in the technical support documents. Finally, inventive lawyers even dream up plausible sounding "seat-of the-pants" generalizations in the hope that the reviewing court will spin out a "homespun scientific aphorism" to justify a remand of the rule to the agency.[36]

Aggressive lawyers, willing to exploit the inevitable ambiguities found in regulatory disputes, can make even carefully crafted regulatory decision rationales appear to be arbitrary, capricious, and scientifically baseless, and thus increase the chances that the court will overturn the decision. Of course, lawyers representing the agency's position will argue that the decision in question was the best possible, given existing scientific knowledge and legislative responsibilities. In the end, the decision must rest with jurists who themselves are untrained in the scientific issues at issue, and who face court dockets crowded with all kinds of other cases requiring their attention.

Scientific Competence of the Courts   Many people, including federal judges themselves, comment on the problem of increasing the levels of scientific and

technical expertise possessed by the courts. Recommendations range from the elimi-
nation of adversarial procedures in cases involving science and technology, to the
hiring of well-trained technical experts as court clerks, to formal panels of scientists
and other specialists who would be on call to judges, to the creation of special "science
courts" to handle adjudication involving complex scientific or technical issues.

The role of the latter would be to bring forward the best scientific analysis
of specific issues in a nonadversarial manner, thereby carefully delineating what
science knows with surety about the issues at question from what science is not sure
of. A science court would deal exclusively with the scientific elements of disputes,
not with the policy elements.

None of these steps, however, is likely to resolve the problems of how
decision makers in the four government arenas reach their decisions. Outside
expertise is useful only up to a point, when policy considerations, not science, take
over. Because so many science and technology issues inevitably involve policy
choices, the specific policy preferences of individual technological decision makers
will continue to play central roles in technical disputes, and members of other
arenas will continue in their efforts to shape and influence the decisions reached.

ENDNOTES

1. JAMES EVERETT KATZ, *Presidential Politics and Science Policy* (New York: Praeger,
    1978), p. 41.
2. Ibid., pp. 41–42.
3. Ibid., p. 46.
4. Ibid., p. 52
5. Ibid., pp. 50–51.
6. W. HENRY LAMBRIGHT, *Presidential Management of Science and Technology: The John-
    son Presidency* (Austin, Tex.: University of Texas Press, 1985).
7. Ibid., p. 13.
8. Ibid., p. 15.
9. TED GREENWOOD, "Science and Technology Advice for the President," in *The Presi-
    dency and Science Advising*, ed. Kenneth W. Thompson (Lanham, Md.: University
    Press of America, 1986), p. 29.
10. Ibid., p. 31.
11. Ibid.
12. KATZ, Presidential Politics, p. 67.
13. RICHARD BARKE, *Science, Technology, and Public Policy.* (Washington, D.C.: Congres-
    sional Quarterly Press, 1986), p. 56.
14. KATZ, Presidential Politics, p. 67.
15. PETE V. DOMENICI, "Science and the US Senate," in *Science and Technology Advice to
    the President, Congress, and Judiciary*, ed. William T. Golden (New York: Per-
    gamon Press, 1988), p. 405.

16. DAVID DICKSON, *The New Politics of Science* (New York: Pantheon Books, 1984), p. 236.

17. W. D. KAY, "OTA and Congress: The Management of complexity and Uncertainty in the Regulation of Technological Change," paper presented at the annual meeting of the American Political Science Association, Washington, D.C., September 1–4, 1988, p. 29.

18. JOHN GIBBONS, "How John Gibbons Runs Through Political Minefields: Life at the OTA," *Technology Review* (October 1988), 48.

19. NORMAN J. VIG, "The Courts: Judicial Review and Risk Assessment," in *Risk Analysis, Institutions, and Public Policy*, ed. Susan G. Hadden (New York: Associated Faculty Press, 1984).

20. DAVID M. O'BRIEN, "The Courts, Technology Assessment, and Science-Policy Disputes," in The *Politics of Technology Assessment: Institutions, Processes, and Policy Disputes*, ed. David M. O'Brien and Donald A. Marchand (Lexington, Mass.: Lexington Books, 1982), p. 90.

21. Ibid., p. 79

22. VIG, "The Courts," p. 65.

23. O'BRIEN, "The Courts," p. 92.

24. VIG, "The Courts," p. 66.

25. THOMAS O. MCGARITY, "Judicial Review of Scientific Rulemaking," *Science, Technology, & Human Values*, 9, (no. 1) (1984):97-107, p. 98.

26. BARKE, *Science, Technology*, p. 109.

27. VIG, "The Courts," p. 64.

28. JAMES Q. WILSON, "The Politics of Regulation," In *The Politics of Regulation* ed. James Q. Wilson (New York: Basic Books).

29. Ibid., p. 376.

30. Ibid, p. 377.

31. WALTER A. ROSENBAUM, *Environmental Politics and Policy* (Washington D.C.: CQ Press, 1985), p. 204.

32. Ibid., pp. 54-55.

33. WILSON, *The Politics of Regulation*, p. 388.

34. MCGARITY, "Judicial Review," p. 98.

35. O'BRIEN, "The Courts," p. 93.

36. MCGARITY, "Judicial Review," p. 100.

Chapter 5

The Expertise, Mobilization, and Labor Arenas

In this chapter, we examine the last three technological decision-making arenas deeply involved in technological politics. The three are the academic-professional arena, the labor arena, and the popular mobilization arena. Each of these arenas has significantly less overall influence on the directions of American technological politics than the other technological decision-making arenas that we have already examined. This, however, does not mean that these arenas are insignificant participants in technological politics; indeed, as we shall see, each can affect technological politics in very important ways, even if they do not possess the resources and power of the other arenas. No one in the corporate-managerial or in any of the government arenas can afford to ignore decision makers in these three arenas.

ACADEMIC-PROFESSIONAL ARENA

At first glance, we might expect academic-professional decision makers to be among the most powerful and influential in technological politics. As scientists, engineers, technicians, and other expert personnel, they are the originators and possessors of the most significant resource in an advanced, technological society: knowledge. Members of Congress, the executive branch, the courts, consumer and environmental organizations, labor leaders, and corporate-managerial decision makers all regularly consult with members of the academic-professional arena, relying on them for information, data, technical analysis, and technology assessments, and they pay careful attention to what they hear. Nevertheless, as we will see, scientists and engineers are far less powerful participants in technological politics than are decision makers from other arenas.

The academic-professional arena comprises a very large number of decision makers. For instance, there are nearly 5.5 million scientists and engineers in the United States, divided almost evenly between scientists (2.6 million) and engineers (2.8 million). Computer specialists lead in total numbers (710,200) followed by life scientists, such as biologists, agricultural scientists, and medical scientists (460,400), and physical scientists, encompassing chemists and physicists (311,400). Mechanical engineers are most numerous among engineers generally (649,200), followed by electrical and electronics engineers (639,200), civil engineers (337,900), chemical engineers (149,600), and aeronautical and astronautical engineers (118,600).[1] In addition, we have to include the thousands of technical staff personnel who construct and operate laboratory equipment, calibrate measuring devices, record data, and the like.

Scientists and engineers are scattered throughout society, working in the corporate-managerial arena, in the executive and regulatory arenas, in state governments, for consumer and environmental groups, and in all levels of education. For instance, just about 55 percent of all scientists work for business and industry, while about one quarter are employed by educational institutions. Among engineers, however, an overwhelming 80 percent work for business and industry, and only about 4 percent work in education.

They also differ in the tasks they perform. For instance, among scientists, about 20 percent engage primarily in research and development, while one third of engineers do so. Among scientists, about 25 percent are involved primarily in management and administration, including managing R&D activities, while for engineers, just under 30 percent are primarily in management.[2]

These diverse employment situations constitute very different decision-making environments for academic-professional arena decision makers. For those who work in universities and colleges, a crucial attribute is academic tenure. The tenure system was created explicitly to guarantee scholars protection against losing their positions because of what they say, thus encouraging the freest, most open expression of ideas, concepts, and theories within the university setting. Scientists and engineers working for business and industry, on the other hand, have no such protections, and, as has happened, can lose their jobs should they too freely speak their minds on issues considered sensitive by the company that employs them. Also, scholars in universities are at liberty to pursue research projects of their own choosing (assuming that they can obtain funding), while researchers in the corporate-managerial arena pursue projects constrained by corporate needs.

There are also differences in career requirements between industry and academe. In the university, scientific careers depend on the publication of research results in the highest quality, peer-reviewed scientific journals. Associated with such publications is the competition to be the first to document discoveries, the maintenance of research facilities, access to the brightest graduate students, and external funding, among other things.

A key aspect of academic science research involves the free and rapid access to the laboratory results of other researchers, through an unimpeded worldwide network of scientific communications. This network involves formal publications in science journals, but also the presentation of research results at professional meetings, symposia, conferences, scholar-exchange programs, and so on. With the introduction of new forms of electronic communications, using satellites, computers, fax machines, and so on, these even more rapid communications systems will become part of the scientific network.

Scientists who work for corporations also have a professional need to publish the results of their research, attend professional meetings, and tap into the worldwide science communications network. However, their employers sometimes have a very different view. For corporate-managerial decision makers, scientific knowledge developed in company laboratories is proprietary information, produced by corporate investment and intended for profitable commercialization. The idea that corporate scientists would publish the results of corporate research willy-nilly in the open media, or simply discuss the details of corporate research at professional meetings, is unsettling, to say the least. Thus, for many scientists in the corporate world, career advancement through typical steps found in academe are not available.

Career paths for engineers differ. Unlike scientists, engineers have long had an intimate connection with the corporate-managerial arena (see Noble[3] for an extended history of the engineering profession in the United States). Some engineering specialties, such as aeronautical, chemical, and electrical engineering, had their origins in the scientific breakthroughs of the late 1800s and early decades of this century. Today these fields continue to have a close affinity with the professional norms of science. Other, older engineering areas, such as mining, civil, and mechanical, however, began not in the science lab but on the manufacturing shop floor or in operating mines. Formal academic training in these fields began only in the late 1880s, and for a long time, college-trained engineers were often sneered at by those who learned their craft in the old way. These fields, while heavily involved in science today, still show their affinity with the craftsman norms from which they arose.

Both science-based and shop floor–based engineers, however, see the corporate-managerial arena as a natural employment home, and engineering schools continue to instill norms of loyalty to corporate goals in young engineers. As we saw, the vast majority of engineers work within the corporate-managerial arena, with only about 4 percent employed in colleges and universities. And, among those who do have the protection of academic tenure, a large number also work as consultants for corporations and have their university research funded by business and industry. This means that engineers, as professionals, depend heavily on corporate/managerial decision makers and therefore are, by and large, unlikely to take public positions that oppose corporate interests. Indeed, for many young engineers, the goal of moving into corporate management is high on their list of career priorities.

Even though academic scientists have the advantage of tenure to protect them from retaliation for things they may say, they are also highly dependent on outside funding sources, from both the government and industry. Modern research is a very expensive and very competitive business, with the best equipped research laboratories easily costing hundreds of thousands of dollars to set up and maintain. In recent years, less federal research money has made the task of paying for academic science much harder, and has led to a gradual blurring of the traditional distinctions between basic research, to be done at universities, and applied research, usually done in industrially sponsored laboratories. Corporations, sensitive to the speed at which basic research discoveries can enter the commercial market, have been willing to form partnerships with universities eager to find alternative sources of research funding.

One reason, cited by Henry Etzkowitz,[4] that academic scientists have been more willing to cross the line dividing academic from industrial research is that academic research has come to resemble industrial laboratories:

> This change in the beliefs of scientists has been to some extent a consequence of the development of team research which has, over time, acquired characteristics increasingly like those of a private business firm. In some respects, research groups in universities have become "quasi-firms," continuously operating entities with corresponding administrative arrangements and directors of serious investigations responsible for obtaining the financial resources needed for the survival of the research group. The specialization of labour in scientific research, the increasing use of highly specialized and complicated equipment, the pressure to produce results quickly to ensure recognition and continued financial provision have changed certain aspects of scientific activity. The emergence of the professional scientist working in a group in industry has its parallel in the entrepreneurial scientist in the university, or in an institutionalized collaboration of the university and an industrial firm.[5]

Neither scientists nor engineers are especially well organized for political activism; indeed, virtually every scientific or engineering professional association explicitly rejects political advocacy in its official charter. Organized to advance the professional goals of the members, for such associations to take partisan positions would simply alienate those of their members who politically disagree with the position taken.

While remaining nonpartisan, some professional associations—for example, the American Association for the Advancement of Science (AAAS), the National Academy of Sciences (NAS), and NAS's research arm, the National Research Council (NRC)—have sponsored analyses of various pressing technical problems. At first these reports were prepared at the behest of the White House, but in recent years, Congress has requested studies as well. These reports and commentaries have played sometimes influential roles in the public debate on the issue involved, although, as usual, both sides in most disputes can find some evidence for their respective positions in those reports or can find recognized specialists to criticize them.

For most scientists and engineers, politics means voting in elections and occasionally attending to local community issues; for most members of both professions, political activity is about the same as it is for any other average citizen. In fact, surveys of political attitudes among physical scientists and engineers show them to be by and large more conservative than the rest of the nation's population.

However, both scientists and engineers do sometimes get involved in major political controversies, and when they do, they can have significant impact. Joel Primack and Frank von Hippel[6] illustrate how sometimes just a handful of scientists and engineers have been able to influence important public decisions in national security, pesticides and other environmental issues, and public health concerns. Because they enjoy considerable public prestige and trust, when scientists and engineers decide to go public about a problem, they will be listened to and interviewed on television and will often mobilize public involvement in the issue at hand.

Occasional forays into the public spotlight can garner a lot of short-run notoriety, even celebrity status, for individual scientists (one has only to think of Cornell astronomer Carl Sagan or Harvard anthropologist Steven Jay Gould, as examples). Still, it is difficult to assess the real impact such efforts have in the larger picture of technological decision making in the United States. Public posturing by scientists can affect only a tiny fraction of the thousands of technological decisions made each year. The rest simply are made by other people, subject to other pressures.

Rather than look to those instances where scientists and engineers have made public statements or protests, the real impact of academic-professional decision makers in technological decision making most likely occurs in the relative quiet of corporate and government conference rooms. Access to those conference rooms for scientists and engineers rests on the policy-relevant cognitive authority of science, on the general public perception that science provides reliable and ideologically neutral data that can be turned into useful technologies.

Those members of the academic-professional arena deemed to be "reliable," "sound," and "sensible" by decision makers in the corporate-managerial, executive, regulatory, and legislative arenas quietly help to frame the issues and delineate the range of policy responses considered by other decision makers. By helping to shape the thinking of decision makers in other, more powerful arenas, at least some academic-professional decision makers exert sometimes considerable influence over the direction of technological politics. What power scientists and engineers enjoy comes less from their willingness to appear as witnesses at congressional, regulatory, or judicial hearings or to hold highly visible press conferences than from their access to decision makers and willingness to offer informal advice and analysis.

POPULAR MOBILIZATION ARENA

Of all the decision-making arenas, popular mobilization is the most disparate and fragmented. The central feature common to all members of this arena, that allows us to cluster them together, is their dependence on the mobilization of the general public as a vehicle for influencing the technological projects pursued by decision makers in other arenas. All of the groups and organizations within this arena are small, when compared to other political pressure groups, and they frequently operate on no more than a shoestring budget. What gives them impact in technological politics is their ability to move ordinary citizens (who often are not members of the organization) to demand changes in specific technological decisions and in how technological decisions are made in general.

There are dozens, even hundreds, of groups and organizations within this arena, and the range of issues they are interested in is very wide indeed. For example, many groups are involved in the consumer protection movement, seeking to influence how products are manufactured, advertised, sold, and repaired in the marketplace. Other groups are concerned about technology-induced injury to the natural environment. Still others try to alter how national security decisions are made, especially in the area of nuclear weapons design, development, testing, and deployment. Other groups, of a fundamentalist religious orientation, try to shape science instruction in public schools, seeking to remove scientific theories they find objectional (particularly evolution) from American classrooms. Yet others are agitated about the use of live animals in scientific research.

Thus, while all these efforts focus on science and technology, the specific issues of interest (consumer protection, environmentalism, peace issues, creationism, animal rights) scatter across nearly the entire range of politics. Groups within the popular mobilization arena are mostly political outsiders. They lack most of the features common to more traditional pressure groups: connections with established Washington power brokers, professional lobbying staffs, large war chests for campaign contributions, and general recognition as powerful players.

Lacking these "insider" resources, popular mobilization arena groups must rely on other assets and other tactics. Each group depends on its ability to shape public opinion, to arouse and mobilize supporters, and to engage in unconventional forms of political pressure, including massive letter-writing campaigns, staged media events, angry marches and demonstrations, site occupations, and other forms of passive resistance and even, for the most extreme, a limited use of violence.

And it is clear that such tactics do work in many cases. Both consumer and environmental groups have succeeded in pushing decision makers in the legislative and executive arenas to address their concerns and to enact a long list of statutes aimed at protecting both consumers and the larger environment. At least the larger consumer and environmental groups have taken on the trappings of more traditional interest groups: Washington offices, professional lobbyists, sophisticated media programs, and so on. They are still small when compared to the resources of, say, corporate-managerial trade associations, but they are gradually joining the ranks of the Establishment in government. Most others, however, remain on the outside, looking in.

The Consumer Movement

In traditional economic theory, there should be no need to take special care of consumers, because the marketplace itself offers all the protection needed. Any seller who consistently produces defective or dangerous wares or goods that simply do not meet the demands of buyers will rather quickly be driven out of business by competitors ready and able to meet consumer needs. In the end, the competition of the free market provides the surest protection for consumers. This scenario, of course, exists only in an ideal, perfect market. In the real world, there can be a lot of slippage from the ideal, and the consumer movement in the United States exists to make up for the defects of real market systems.

Beginning with the thalidomide scare of the early 1960s (thalidomide was a drug developed in Europe that produced grotesque birth defects when taken by pregnant women, but was never approved for use in the United States thanks to the effort of one FDA official), public concerns about the safety of consumer products, especially about drugs and other medicines, led to greater demands for government intervention in the marketplace on behalf of consumers. Partly as a result of the efforts of several consumer "policy entrepreneurs" such as Ralph Nader, a flurry of consumerist legislation was enacted: the Child Protection Act, National Traffic and Motor Vehicle Safety Act, Fair Packaging and Labeling (Truth-in-Packaging) Act, Consumer Credit Protection (Truth-in-Lending) Act, Interstate Land Sales Full Disclosure Act, Natural Gas Pipeline Safety Act, Poultry Inspection Act, and Radiation Health and Safety Act, among many others. The history of consumerism illustrates that, even though interest in consumer matters waxes and wanes on the larger political agenda, when mobilized, consumers can have dramatic effect in the political process.

Critics might complain that most of the consumer legislation has been no more than symbolic politics and that manufacturers are able easily to evade legal restrictions. While this charge is certainly true at least some of the time, perhaps the best evidence that decision makers in the corporate-managerial arena take consumers seriously is the creation of consumer departments within their companies, staffed by individuals trained to respond quickly to complaints or safety problems.

These and other attempts by the corporate-managerial decision makers to head off consumer complaints signal just how effective consumer movements are seen by decision makers in corporate boardrooms. The costs of continuously resisting new consumer legislation in the legislative arena, of defending company products in liability lawsuits in the judicial arena, and of bearing the tremendous expenditures of a major product recall ordered from within the regulatory arena have made decision makers within the corporate-managerial arena much more wary about simply ignoring consumer interests.

These achievements are all the more remarkable in light of just how small and concentrated the consumer movement is. Organization theorists and others have known for some time now that consumers, although they number in the tens of millions, are among the hardest groups to organize for effective political action. In many cases of consumer fraud, the actual amount any individual consumer may lose to an unscrupulous manufacturer is quite small, although the "take" for the manufacturer may be very large. Even a few pennies per item, if millions of items are sold, can be a fortune.

For any individual consumer to try to recover from consumer abuse may cost more than the amount lost, not a wise investment of time and effort. Even when serious injury is involved, as in defective products, in the end it might be cheaper for the manufacturer simply to pay off the few consumers who will have the time and resources to seek damages than to redesign a product so as to remove the danger for everyone. Because they are so scattered, because the injury any individual may experience is likely to be marginal and localized, and because effective action requires coordination, time, and effort, consumers as a class continue to be unusually difficult to organize politically.

Robert Mayer makes a distinction between the "core" elements of consumerism, those for whom consumerism is central to their activity, and "secondary" consumerists, those for whom consumer interests are secondary to the real purpose of their political activity.[7] There are a number of groups, for instance, labor unions and some environmental groups, that occasionally participate in consumer struggles but whose energies are most regularly employed in pursuit of alternate goals. Indeed, he argues, sometimes strictly consumer groups depend heavily on support from sympathetic groups outside the core of consumerism.

The core groups in the consumer movement include, for instance, several small organizations founded by Ralph Nader, such as Public Citizen, Congress Watch, the Litigation Group, and the Center for the Study of Responsive Law. Also included are the Consumer Federation of America, the Consumers Union, and the Center for Science in the Public Interest, along with a variety of small groups that focus specifically on such issues as automobile or airline safety. Although organizations like the Consumers Union may list 3 or 4 million consumers as members, the core of active participants remains quite small. Mayer gives us his estimate of the size of consumerism's leadership: "Building on a base of widespread but unchanneled consumer discontent, the consumer movement at any given time is run by perhaps fifty full-time professionals. Their continuing employment depends on their ability to solicit dues-paying members, sell publications, and find patrons."[8]

In addition to these groups that operate at the national level, many have state and local chapters that work on localized consumer problems. None of these organizations is very large, yet they have political clout out of proportion to their size or financial resources.

The Environmental Movement

According to Walter Rosenbaum, the environmental movement, like consumerism, can also be divided into a "core coalition," "close allies," and "fellow travelers."[9] Within the core coalition of environmentalism are a number of national organizations, often with active state and local chapters. Well-known national organizations, such as the Sierra Club and the Wilderness Society, fall into this camp. Another component of the core coalition are the recreationists, such as the National Wildlife Federation and the Izaak Walton League. Yet another segment of the coalition are groups dedicated to the protection and preservation of endangered species and wildlife habitats, such as the National Audubon Society and the Conservation Foundation. Finally, there are a number of environmental organizations that specialize in litigation and regulatory interventions, such as the Environmental Defense Fund and the Natural Resources Defense Council.

In addition to the core coalition, environmental groups often receive help from sympathetic interests that are not focused exclusively on environmental concerns. The League of Women Voters, Common Cause, Public Citizen, the Union of Concerned Scientists, and the Center for Science in the Public Interest, among others, are examples of groups that frequently align themselves with environmentalists but pursue wider agendas themselves. And, finally, there are the fellow travelers: organizations that will support environmental issues when such support also serves the group's central purposes. Labor unions have often worked with consumer and environmental groups, especially when issues of toxic chemicals and wastes in the workplace are involved.

Peace Groups

Traditionally, national security has been one of the most restricted policy domains. Because of the requirements of secrecy and, even more importantly, of technical competence, participation in decisions about national defense, weapons design and deployment, arms control negotiations, and similar issues has been limited to a small array of technical and policy specialists.

Ever since the atomic bombs were used in World War II, several organizations and groups have led various efforts to restrict, restrain, and eliminate the nuclear arms race. Ironically, a number of the scientists who participated in the Manhattan Project to develop the atomic bomb have joined or led such actions. All such efforts, however, have failed to have much impact on the evolution of the arms race. Members of "Ban the Bomb" are seen as cranks, oddballs, or appeasers. As such, their efforts and arguments can be safely ignored by those charged with making national security policy.

In the early 1980s, however, a movement emerged that seriously challenged the dominance of national security by "technical experts," and eventually prompted one of the most pro-defense presidents in recent memory, Ronald Reagan, to alter his policies. The Nuclear Freeze Movement, begun by Randall Fosberg, was able to cut through the maze of complexities surrounding weapons development and capture the public's imagination with a simple and direct technological message: The way to stop the arms race was for both superpowers mutually to stop testing new weapons. For Fosberg, weapons testing was the crucial choke point through which she hoped to strangle the arms race.

No nation, she argued, would willingly rest its national survival on strategic weapons it had not tested, not just once but several dozen times. If no new weapons were tested, no new weapons would enter the nuclear arsenals, and the arms race would come to a halt. What is more, testing of major weapons systems is nearly perfectly verifiable. Except for the testing of components, major nuclear weapons must be tested outside the laboratory, where everyone can see it. This is especially true for strategic missiles. Both sides could easily observe each other, since it is impossible to mask a missile test.

The Nuclear Freeze Movement's goal—end the testing of new nuclear weapons—was technically sophisticated, yet the essence of political simplicity. Ordinary people could grasp it immediately, even if they did not understand throw weights, fractionizing, MIRVs, reentry vehicles, SLCMs, GLCMs, inertial guidance systems, or any of the other technical arcania common to traditional national security debates. The movement took the country by storm, with several small communities declaring themselves "nuclear-free zones," a number of states considering nuclear freeze initiatives, and the U.S. Congress seriously debating a freeze resolution of its own, led by such well-known politicians as Democratic Senator Ted Kennedy and Republican Senator Mark Hatfield.

In the end, the Reagan administration succeeded in fighting off the freeze resolution, but only after it altered its bellicose public rhetoric toward the USSR, along with making freezelike proposals of its own. Although the public enthusiasm for the freeze idea has ebbed in recent years, it is clear that popular mobilization around a comprehensible arms control program can have a major impact on the policy process.

Creationists

Creationism is one of the most unusual components of the popular mobilization arena (see Nelkin[10]). The central aim of creationists' efforts is the removal from public classrooms of any references to the theory of evolution, which, they argue, is not scientific and is actually an element of a religious movement known as "secular humanism." Instead, or at least alongside, of evolution, a pseudo-scientific amalgam of assertions collectively known as "creation science" should be taught, they argue.

In recent years, creationists have been successful in getting various state governments to adopt "equal time" legislation requiring that creationism be given equal time in any class that discusses evolution. Creationism, they argue, is just as much a science as evolution and thus deserves equal time in public schools. Although such "equal time" legislation has been overturned by federal courts as violations of the establishment clause of the First Amendment to the U.S. Constitution, creationists remain active. They have been involved deeply in textbook selection decisions made by state textbook boards and by individual school districts. By focusing their efforts in major states, such as Texas and California, they hope to influence textbooks everywhere in the country. Most textbook publishers cannot afford to produce different versions of texts for different states, and since Texas and California are the largest purchasers of textbooks in the country, affecting textbook choices in those two states has impact everywhere.

Some members of the academic-professional arena have organized efforts to oppose creationists, urging textbook boards to intentionally select only those texts that treat evolution fully. Scientists, by and large, ignored the creationist campaigns. The issue of teaching evolution, they thought, had been resolved 50 years ago in the famous Scopes "Monkey Trial," and scientists were too busy with their own research to fend off the efforts of misguided cranks. The successes of the creationists, not only in getting laws passed but, more importantly, in shaping high school textbooks led some scientists to organized resistance. However this struggle ends, it is clear that groups with broadly antiscience goals can also influence decision making through popular mobilization.

The Animal Rights Movement

Animals have been used for scientific research for more than 2,000 years, dating back to Greek physicians about the third century B.C.[11, 12] Beginning in the 1700s and 1800s, various groups, called antivivisectionists, appeared in opposition to the use of animals in laboratory research, on the grounds that the pain and suffering inflicted on them were unjustified.

Throughout the first half of the twentieth century, the antivivisectionist movement faded into obscurity, as the public generally supported the claims of research scientists that animal studies were essential to finding cures for human diseases and ailments. And, indeed, medical research seemed to provide an unending array of new vaccines, medicines, and surgical treatments. It became difficult to argue with the scientific community's case for the necessity of animal research, in the face of cures for polio and a host of other dread diseases, as well as heart, lung, and kidney transplants and an array of other life-saving procedures.

However, beginning in the late 1970s and continuing throughout the 1980s, public attitudes have changed. There is greater concern for the well-being of laboratory animals, especially when animals forced to endure severe pain, not for medical advances, but merely to test whether, for instance, a shampoo formula would irritate human eyes, received media coverage. Many people began to doubt the claims of laboratory researchers that animal experiments were both necessary and productive. Occasionally, a new episode of maltreatment would be disclosed, often with gruesome pictures of apparently maimed or injured animals confined in small cages. The animal rights movement, a late twentieth-century continuation of the antivivisectionism of earlier centuries, has focused on forcing changes in how animals are used in modern science.

To many in the academic-professional arena, the animal rights activists seemed like irrational, antiscience cranks. How, the scientists asked, are cures for cancer, for heart disease, for AIDS to be discovered if researchers are not allowed to use laboratory animals? The animal rights activists argued that there were other options besides live animal tests, but that scientists did not care about animal suffering. At the most extreme, some animal rights activists urged the total end of animal research; indeed, some activists have taken to guerrilla tactics, breaking into labs at night and releasing all of the animals. Others, less extreme, allow that some kinds of animal research may be needed, but want much more rigorous government regulation to ensure that animals are kept in humane conditions, that they are not forced to endure unnecessary pain, and that scientists exhibit a clearer commitment to the decent treatment of all research animals.

The animal rights movement has been able to force reconsideration of animal treatment in both the executive and legislative arenas. The U.S. Congress conducted hearings into the mistreatment of laboratory animals, at which some of the most egregious and horrifying examples were prominently displayed. Clearly, just the threat of direct legislative intervention has led the academic-professional arena to preempt this issue by making internal changes in animal treatment. The

National Science Foundation and the National Institutes of Health have reexamined existing animal treatment standards and have issued more stringent requirements for researchers receiving federal funding.

LABOR ARENA

One of the most controversial and widely debated points of contact between technology and the larger society is in the workplace. Indeed, what industrial technology does or does not do to workers is at the very core of political ideologies that have shaken the world. From syndicalism to socialism to communism, on the one hand, to liberalism and the free market, on the other, theorists and philosophers have charged that industrial technology either liberates or enslaves ordinary workers, that it facilitates the spread of wealth or concentrates it in fewer and fewer hands, that humankind has become the master of technology or its poor, befuddled slave.

Because today unions are among the most established of Establishment institutions, we tend to forget the bloody history of union organization in the United States. In the early decades of this century, labor organizers were regularly hounded, beaten, and threatened by goon squads hired by management. In more than one case, local police, national guardsmen, and even federal troops had been used to put down labor agitation, often with much violence, blood, and death. Surely, the working conditions in American factories, stores, offices, and other institutions would be vastly different but for the sacrifices and efforts of labor unions. Peter Drucker comments:

> There is no parallel in history to the rise of the working man in the developed countries during this century. Eighty years ago American blue-collar workers, toiling 60 hours a week, made $250 a year at most...And they had no "fringes," no seniority, no unemployment insurance, no Social Security, no paid holidays, no overtime, no pension—nothing but a cash wage of less than one dollar a day. Today's employed blue-collar worker in a unionized mass-production industry...working 40 hours a week earns about $50,000—half in cash, half in benefits. Even after taxes, this equals...25 times the worker's 1907 real income...And the rise in social standing, and especially in political power has been greater still.[13]

These improvements are due in largest part to the work of labor unions.

Today, however, organized labor faces some of the most severe challenges in its history. The problems no longer center on managerial resistance to union demands, although this still happens. Instead, the entire economy is changing beneath the unions, and with it, much of the rationale for traditional labor unions, as well. Drucker, again:

> There is also no parallel in history to the abrupt decline of the blue-collar worker during the past 15 years. As a proportion of the working population, blue-collar workers in manufacturing have already decreased to less than a fifth of the American labor force from more than a third. By the year 2010—less than 25 years

away—they will constitute no larger a proportion of the labor force of every developed country than farmers do today—that is, a 20th of the total....The decline of the blue-collar worker is not a matter of "competitiveness," of "government policies," of the "business cycle," or even of "imports." It is structural and irreversible.[14]

The structural, irreversible changes Drucker talks about stem in large part from changing technology. As the national economy shifts away from its traditional base in smokestack manufacturing industries—automobiles, paper, steel, rubber, petroleum—and toward "knowledge-intensive" industries—computers, finance, insurance, science-based R&D—the role of the traditional union-worker has changed dramatically. Automation has eliminated many jobs, admittedly many tedious and dangerous ones. However, the kinds of skills and training most in demand in the "factory of the future" have little to do with traditional labor. Now, a worker is expected to be able to operate complex computers, or to be completely replaced by one. Harley Shaiken comments:

> The flexibility of microelectronics extends computer technology to every corner of manufacturing. On one automobile assembly line, for example, 98 percent of over 3,000 welds on the car body are by performed swiftly moving robots, computer-controlled mechanical arms. In an aerospace machine shop, the complex contours of a jet-engine support are carved out by the whirring cutter of a numerically controlled machine tool, itself directed by a computer that is simultaneously supervising over a hundred other machines. In a diesel engine factory, bearings are removed from one of over 4,000 identical bins by a cart that glides silently down 100 yards of a darkened aisle and lifts its forks three stories into the air. In an engineering office, the structural properties of a part are tested by an engineer sitting at a cathode-ray tube...in Cologne, Germany, and then the finished design is instantaneously transferred to a computer in Dearborn, Michigan.[15]

While such changes clearly increase manufacturing efficiency and contribute to international competitiveness, they also present an array of social and political problems that will be very hard to resolve. Robert Kuttner notes:

> As the economy shifts away from its traditional manufacturing base to high-technology and service industries, the share of jobs providing a middle-class standard of living is shrinking. An industrial economy employs large numbers of relatively well-paid production workers. A service economy, however, employs legions of keypunchers, salesclerks, waiters, secretaries, and cashiers, and the wages for these jobs tend to be comparatively low.[16]

The introduction of computer controls into the workplace means more than the replacement of redundant workers by machines; it also means much greater control of those workers who remain in what Robert Howard has called the "Brave New Workplace."[17] Computers allow management to achieve effective control of the entire work force, completing a process of regimentation that actually began as the factory system emerged nearly three centuries ago. The goal of "scientific management," associated with Frederick Winslow Taylor at the turn of the twentieth century, has been to so reduce the range of options available to workers in the performance of their tasks that there would be virtually no loss of shop floor control by supervisors and managers. Now, microelectronics permits a degree of supervision undreamt of by Taylor and his followers, in the office as well as the factory.

Computers can, and do, keep track of precisely how efficient each of hundreds of workers are, of how long it takes each one to complete a specific task, even of how often a worker leaves his or her station to use the restroom. These data are then used to assess the worker's performance. The computer has become the stern, unfeeling "boss" who looks over one's shoulder every minute of the working day. Indeed, a whole level of management consultants has emerged whose work goal is to facilitate management's desire to reduce the work force and to bring the remaining under tighter control. One such consultant, quoted by Howard, admits that "our job was eliminating people. In fact, that's the way we had to justify our fee. We always had to be thinking, 'How many people can we get rid of? How can we get the paperwork through faster?' the whole thrust of office automation is to reduce the work force in one fell swoop."[18]

As if these problems were not enough to occupy decision makers in the labor arena, there is also the whole problem of international competition. Modern manufacturing technologies also mean that production of high-quality products can take place virtually anywhere in the world. Corporate-managerial decision makers have shown themselves eager to take advantage of the significantly lower labor costs available in Latin America and along the Pacific Rim, and have moved more and more of their factories overseas. It is in this rapidly changing environment that decision makers in the labor arena must try to influence technological politics. What is more, the traditional political clout of organized labor has shrunk, with less than 15 percent of the nation's workers joining unions. Labor's traditional alliance with the Democratic party is actually seen by some commentators as a political liability today. Labor's declining power is best seen, however, in the string of contracts they have had to accept in recent years. Not only did they forgo the usual pay raises and benefit improvements, but they had to endure actual reductions ("rollbacks") in wage and benefit packages.

ROLES IN TECHNOLOGICAL POLITICS

Ideological Diversity

It is important to note that there is no ideological orthodoxy to be found in any of these three technological decision-making arenas. Indeed, in the popular mobilization arena, for instance, considerable differences in priorities and policy goals can be found among the various groups and organizations.

Consider for a moment the array of groups within the environmental movement. At one end of an ideological spectrum are the "hard-line preservationists," who oppose the multiuse development of wilderness areas. Preservationists are the least willing to make accommodations with various development plans or planners. More amenable are the recreationists. These groups also support the preservation of wilderness areas, but not simply for the sake of preserving pristine regions from development. They seek to protect such areas so that they may be used for hunting, fishing, and other recreational activities, and have been more willing than preservationists to tolerate some economic development of natural resources and multiple uses for public lands, as long as game and recreational uses are not affected. Protectionists, a third cluster within environmentalism, are more concerned about the protection of endangered species and their shrinking habitats.

Thus, environmentalism does not speak with one voice on all issues. The different groups involved, while they often cooperate, often pursue quite different agendas, sometimes at odds with each other. Thus, recreationists may assist preservationists in the preservation of specific wilderness areas, but disagree with them on, for instance, the creation of access roads into those wilderness areas. Both groups may cooperate with protectionists, but there may be room for disagreement between those who want to protect certain wildlife species and those who hope to use wilderness areas for hunting and fishing. Preservationists may quarrel with both recreationists and protectionists about how much the movement should compromise with developers, and may find themselves insisting upon more stringent judgments than the others think is wise.

A similar spread of opinion can be found within the consumer movement. Mayer distinguishes between "reformist" and "radical" consumer activists. Reformists, by and large, work within the existing market system, trying to find ways to overcome "market imperfections" that put consumers at a disadvantage, for example, lack of adequate product information or obstacles to redress for harm. He asserts that much of the recent success in consumer legislation derives from the skillful activities of reformers.

Radicals, on the other hand, hold that the plight of consumers results not from isolated problems with a market system that is, on the whole, functioning as it should, but from deep-seated problems with the market system itself. Thus, while reformers applaud the creation of government agencies charged with protecting consumer interests as one very useful way of correcting the failings of an unfettered marketplace, radicals, Mayer argues, assert that government agencies simply serve to cover up the misdeeds of greedy corporate decision makers by lulling the public into believing that government regulations will cure the problems. Radicals argue that in America big corporations have so much power they can abuse consumers with little fear of discovery or punishment. For radicals, tinkering on the margins of the existing market system will not solve the problems. What is needed is a wholesale change in the national economy and in the structure of the corporate-managerial arena.

Reformers have been more willing to use the traditional means of pluralist politics—lobbying in the legislative arena, dealing with Regulatory Arena decision makers, and bringing lawsuits in the judicial arena—than have radicals, who rely more on public boycotts and efforts to place consumer advocates directly on corporate boards of directors. However, Mayer may be overstating the degree of difference in tactics between reformers and radicals, just as he may be overstating how different these two groups are from each other. It may be that reformers have been as successful as they have in part because they can point to the even more extremist threats of so-called radical consumer activists, in a kind of "good cop/bad cop" tactic. The demands of reformers may seem more acceptable to decision makers in the corporate-managerial arena than having to fight off their more zealous cousins.

Both creationists and animal rights activists also display a range of beliefs and views. Some within the creationist movement honestly believe that creation science is every bit as scientific as is evolution, and thus deserves equal time in public classrooms. Others, recognizing that creationism cannot in any sense qualify as a science, really hope to use the claims for equal time to intimidate textbook publishers into eliminating any discussion of evolution from science textbooks.

Among animal rights groups, there are reformers and radicals, too. The reformers, as we saw, are willing to permit some limited amount of animal research, granted that certain stringent standards are met by the researchers. "Animal liberation" groups, on the contrary, oppose all forms of animal research as "speciesism," akin to racism or sexism, and have been willing to break the law to free laboratory animals.

Decision makers from other arenas who anticipate that groups or individuals from the popular mobilization arena may interfere with the completion of a specific technological project will need to know what kind of group is likely to step in, what its specific goals are, how willing it is to compromise, and so on. It would be as serious a tactical error simply to assume that all such groups can be lumped together and treated in the same manner as it would be for popular mobilization arena decision makers to assume that all corporations are the same and that all corporate-managerial arena decision makers can be treated alike.

There is also considerable variation within both the academic-professional and labor arenas as well. Skillful decision makers from other arenas are well aware of the divisions and differences in these arenas and will attempt to exploit those differences in order to blunt opposition to specific technological projects. If, for instance, a corporate-managerial decision maker can show that at least some environmental or consumer groups support, or at least do not actively oppose, a specific technological project, this may go a long way toward undermining the power of those groups who do offer resistance. Divide and conquer can be a very useful strategy.

Outsider Strategies

By and large, decision makers in each of the three arenas see themselves as "political outsiders" in the larger game of technological politics in America. Certainly, decision makers in the popular mobilization arena portray themselves explicitly as challengers of the status quo rather than as part of the problem. Given the power and influence of corporate-managerial decision makers, their access to decision makers in the government arenas, and their financial resources, academic-professional, popular mobilization, and labor arena decision makers certainly are not as central to technological decision making.

We do have to be more cautious in talking about academic-professional and labor decision makers as political outsiders, since there are numerous examples of members of these arenas playing very central roles in certain policy decisions. Still, the vast majority of scientists and engineers are no more politically active than are average citizens—which is to say, not a lot—and only a handful of their professional colleagues ever achieve significant policy influence.

Alliances

For academic-professional participants, decision making clout seems to hinge on their ability and willingness to form alliances with corporate-managerial, executive, legislative, or regulatory arena decision makers. Of course, some scientists and other technically trained people form alliances with popular mobilization arena groups, but in doing so take on the outsider coloration of the organization.

This last point needs some elaboration. Many individual decision makers may be occasional or even permanent members of more than one of these three arenas—a scientist or engineer may help a consumer or an environmental group, or members of labor unions may join and support consumer groups, or private citizens may join both consumer and environmental organizations. Indeed, given the small size and relative financial poverty of many consumer and environmental groups, crossover support from the other two arenas may be vital to the success of the group's technological projects.

Still, decision makers in each of these three arenas do have some political weapons at their disposal.

Public Opinion

The manipulation of public opinion is probably the single most effective technique employed by these decision makers. An outraged public can be the vehicle for breaking up cozy relationships between, for instance, corporate-managerial and legislative or regulatory arena decision makers. However, public opinion is an ephemeral and volatile weapon. Capturing the public's attention can be quite difficult, especially for issues that appear distant and unclear to the average person.

Public attention shifts rapidly and unpredictably, so that even if an issue rises to public notice, it may fade or be replaced by a newer issue before effective action can be taken. Indeed, decision makers in the corporate-managerial and in the government arenas often pin their hopes of success in various technological projects precisely on the public's fickle and limited attention span. Keeping the public focused on a specific issue may, in fact, be the central locus of struggle between contending arenas.

Given the wide array of issues competing for public attention, plus the host of entertainments available, groups within the popular mobilization arena often rely on sensationalized and exaggerated claims to garner media attention. A careful, temperate assessment of possible consequences simply will not attract the needed public attention. This does not require dissembling or deceit; it may involve merely emphasizing the most dire of a range of possible consequences following upon a technological project. By now, of course, decision makers in other arenas are fully aware of this technique, and are prepared to come forward with their own assessments, which, while most often do not include outright lies, emphasize the safest of a range of possible consequences of allowing their technological projects to go forward. Thus, the issue at question suffers from a progressive polarization, as the contending sides try to counter what they consider to be the misleading statements of their opponents.

Technical Information

Technical information, therefore, becomes a critical asset for these three arenas. For one thing, airing such information is quite often how issues are brought to the public's attention. The disclosure of malfeasance by executive, legislative, or regulatory decision makers is always newsworthy and brings the media spotlight to the issues involved. Disclosure of unexpected risks or dangers attendant upon specific technological projects puts the sponsors of those projects on the defensive, especially if there is the suggestion that the newly discovered information had been intentionally covered up. It is for these reasons that the sponsors of technological projects often go to considerable effort to maintain a monopoly on technical data concerning those projects—they know only too well that such a monopoly gives them a major advantage against their opponents.

That is also why obtaining such information is so important, especially for consumer and environmental groups. Their credibility is on the line when they come forward with specific charges, and it is important that they be able to back up their allegations with hard data. This, in turn, is why obtaining scientific and technical help from the academic-professional arena is so useful.

In many struggles, a consumer or environmental organization does not have to prove conclusively that a particular technological project, for instance, a new agricultural pesticide, is actually dangerous. It may be sufficient simply to cast doubt on the project sponsor's claims of safety. Having one's own scientists—better yet, finding one of the sponsor's scientists—who can raise public doubts may be all that is needed to derail someone else's technological project. Once frightened, the public is very unlikely ever to accept fully the product, process, or material under scrutiny.

Everyone involved, of course, knows all of this and plans strategy to deal with threats of this sort. Corporate-managerial sponsors, thus, will have at hand an array of tests and research results "proving" that the technological project is not only safe but positively beneficial. Consumer and environmental groups, having decided to pursue a technological project of their own in opposition, will try to accumulate technical research undermining the corporate-managerial assertions.

This dynamic is the chief source of the polarization and intransigence that so often characterize how technological politics operates. We will have opportunities to see this process repeatedly in later chapters.

Litigation

Another effective tactic used by decision makers in all three of these arenas, but most especially by those in the popular mobilization arena, is litigation. Some consumer and environmental groups specifically specialize in regulatory and judicial procedures. The threat of a lawsuit serves several purposes for popular mobilization arena decision makers. A court decision, for one thing, can be a cheaper and quicker way to obtain a definitive decision, when compared to the time and resources needed to effectively lobby for legislative changes. The courts can be a kind of "equalizer" in political struggles between opponents who command vastly different resources.

Threatening a lawsuit can also allow popular mobilization arena groups, who do not ordinarily have any role at all in corporate-managerial decision making, to shape indirectly technological projects pursued by corporations. A corporation may think twice about certain very expensive technological projects if it fears that the completion of those projects may be indefinitely delayed in the courts. Corporate-managerial decision makers may also attempt to allay consumer or environmental concerns by modifying a specific technological project as a way of avoiding expensive litigation in the future.

Court action can also influence decision makers in the regulatory arena. The steps taken to strengthen the right of affected individuals to participate in regulatory decision making, including specific legislative authority to bring suit in federal courts, mean that regulatory decision makers must pay closer attention to the claims and demands of groups that have proven to be willing and able to use the courts to reverse undesirable regulatory decisions. The openness of the American judicial system, plus the skillful use of legal actions by popular mobilization arena groups, contributes directly to the massive administrative gridlock that bedevils technological decision making in the United States.

ENDNOTES

1. National Science Foundation, *U.S. Scientists and Engineers: 1988—Estimates* (Washington, D.C. 1988), NSF 88–322.
2. Ibid.
3. DAVID F. NOBLE, *America by Design: Science, Technology, and the Rise of Corporate Capitalism* (New York: Knopf, 1977).
4. HENRY ETZKOWITZ, "Entrepreneurial Scientists and Entrepreneurial Universities in American Academic Science," *Minerva*, 21, no. 2–3 (1983), 198–234.
5. Ibid., p. 199.

6. JOEL PRIMACK and FRANK VON HIPPEL, *Advice and Dissent: Scientists in the Political Arena* (New York: Basic Books, 1974).

7. ROBERT N. MAYER, *The Consumer Movement: Guardians of the Marketplace* (Boston: Twayne, 1989).

8. Ibid., p. 55.

9. WALTER A. ROSENBAUM, *Environmental Politics and Policy* (Washington, D.C.: CQ Press, 1985).

10. DOROTHY NELKIN, *The Creation Controversy: Science or Scripture in the Schools* (New York: Beacon Press, 1982).

11. JUDITH C. ZOLA, JARI A. SECHZER, JOAN E. SIEBER, and ANNE GRIFFIN, "Animal Experimentation: Issues for the 1980s," *Science, Technology, & Human Values*, 9, no. 2 (1984), 40–50.

12. HARRIET RITVO, "Plus Ça Change: Anti-Vivisection Then and Now," *Science, Technology, & Human Values*, 9, no. 2 (1984), pp. 57–66.

13. PETER DRUCKER, "The Rise and Fall of the Blue-Collar Worker," *Wall Street Journal*, April 22, 1987, p. 36.

14. Ibid.

15. HARLEY SHAIKEN, *Work Transformed: Automation and Labor in the Computer Age* (New York: Holt, Rinehart & Winston, 1984), p. 1.

16. ROBERT KUTTNER, "The Declining Middle," *The Atlantic Monthly*, July 1983, p. 60.

17. ROBERT HOWARD, *Brave New Workplace* (New York: Viking Press, 1985).

18. Ibid, p. 20.

Chapter 6

Technology and Economic Crisis

Many observers express great anxiety about the health and vitality of the American economy. On so many fronts the U.S. economy no longer exhibits the leadership, vigor, and strength it once had, and many foreign competitors—the Japanese, the South Koreans, the Germans, the Brazilians, and others—either have surpassed American leadership in one industry after another or are threatening to overcome a weakened American lead. In steel production, for example, long a mainstay of the American economy, the Japanese have become the world leader. As economist George Eads laments, "the various studies describing the erosion of competitiveness in the U.S. steel industry show that it took our industry 20 years of hard work to turn an overwhelming competitive advantage...into massive uncompetitiveness."[1]

The Japanese have also gained economic dominance in consumer electronics, such as television sets, video recorders, and radios, while, as we all know, in automobiles they have deeply shaken even the Big Three American manufacturers, General Motors, Ford, and Chrysler. Even in high-tech and service areas, thought by many to be America's ace in the hole in international competition, the Japanese, among others, threaten to overwhelm American companies. The list of "endangered" American industries grows each year: advanced computers, semiconductors, aircraft, industrial chemicals, machine tools, telecommunications, pharmaceuticals, scientific instruments, engines, turbines, plastics, insurance, banking and financial services, engineering services, and on and on.

In the face of this economic deterioration, many analysts have come forward with recommendations through which American economic strength might be restored. In virtually every case, these suggestions involve important interests pursued by one or another of the technological decision-making arenas we have been studying.

For instance, some analysts urge greater reliance on free market forces to restore U.S. competitiveness, steps that involve the relaxation of numerous environmental and health and safety regulations. Such relaxations would be of critical importance to both the regulatory and the popular mobilization arenas. Others favor the introduction of "industrial policies," aimed at increasing the role of government in business decisions, especially in the areas of technical innovation, research and development, and market protection, matters of great concern to the corporate-managerial and labor arenas. Some urge that labor unions reduce their pay demands and agree to various benefit "givebacks" in order to make U.S. manufacturing competitive with low-wage foreign firms. Such steps, of course, would be critical to labor arena decision makers, as are efforts to improve worker productivity through automation, robotics, computers, and word processing software.

The conclusion we draw is that the issues and problems of industrial decline, foreign trade, competition, and productivity involve and affect decision makers in many, perhaps all, of the technological decision-making arenas we are exploring. Despite their differences in specific recommendations, virtually all analysts agree that the American economy, and all of us within it, must undergo some very significant changes during the next several years, many related to changes in technologies. What is more, because these changes will be fundamental, there is ample room for conflict among decision makers from different arenas, as they are affected differently.

COMPETITIVENESS AND THE U.S. ECONOMY

Perhaps the most pervasive and widespread economic problem facing us today is our declining ability to compete in international markets. The effects of our shrinking ability to invent, design, manufacture, and sell high-quality, low-cost goods to people in other lands are felt throughout our economy, in a growing imbalance in international trade, in lost jobs and closed factories, and in a lost technological edge. As one knowledgeable observer put it:

> Our productivity growth rate was significantly lower than that of other countries, and it was declining. Our historically favorable trade balance first diminished, then turned negative. Our trade in technology-intensive products began to reflect a shrinking share of world markets. It was evident that we were not using technology as effectively as we might, or perhaps as well as some other countries were using it. Our innovative capacity was, for the first time, in doubt. A large part of our R&D was for defense and space, and without commercial objectives. Key industries, like steel, autos, and consumer electronics, were in deep trouble. Countries we had been assisting were becoming, to an ever greater extent, successful competitors in world trade.[2]

In many ways, these are new and unfamiliar problems for Americans. We are used to being "number one" in the world economy, leading the way with new technologies, new products, and the highest standard of living in the world. Much of our economic strength, however, rested upon short-lived and transitory circumstances, and now that those circumstances have changed, we find ourselves in a new world of tough international competition.

One reason we led the world for so many years after World War II is that we had the only major economy still intact after that terrible and destructive struggle. Both the victors and the vanquished suffered substantial destruction, and it would take our allies (and our former enemies) many years to recover and rebuild before they would be able to compete with us on an even footing. However, we should have expected and prepared for the day when they would complete their recovery. After all, their recovery was to a large degree financed by the United States, through such programs as the Marshall Plan.

Also, for a long time we relied on the general isolation of our domestic economy, so big and self-contained as to be largely independent of the vagaries of international trade. However, a series of economic shocks, such as the two energy crises of 1973 and 1979, plus the growing presence in American stores of products named Sanyo, Toshiba, Sony, and Minolta—and now including even the Korean Hyundai and the Yugoslav Yugo automobiles—forced us to recognize that our economy is fully penetrated by foreign firms selling products once available only from American companies.

We live in a truly interdependent world with an international economy, and there are several other nations that are as competitive or more competitive than we are. Clearly, we cannot continue to do business as though these developments had not occurred. We must adapt to a very different economic environment.

Many observers look to science and technology to help us adjust to the new international marketplace. Whether they urge a return to free market forces or the introduction of more interventionist, long-range industrial policies, most analysts hope that the long tradition of American technical inventiveness can be rekindled. If we can once again achieve world leadership in commercial technologies, they hope, we might correct our trade imbalances, maintain our standard of living, and beat back the assaults of foreign manufacturers for control of the U.S. economy.

However, restoring American scientific and technological dominance, many argue, will require many alterations in how the American economy is run, and if those in charge—in corporate boardrooms, in labor unions, in regulatory agencies, in Congress and the White House—do not voluntarily make those alterations, many fear that the government may have to force them. Naturally, many participants within the corporate-managerial, labor, regulatory, and other arenas are concerned whenever others begin talking about mandated changes in their traditional decision-making structure, operations, or strategies.

ARENA INTERACTIONS

There are a number of themes and debates going on today concerning the condition of the American economy and the potential role of science and technology in solving economic problems. Let's look at some of the most important debates.

Corporate Management

In the face of such evidence of economic decline, a veritable cottage industry of analysis has appeared, with books and articles decrying the decline and explaining its causes appearing each year.[3-11] And, naturally, there is a lot of finger pointing and blame laying going on, too—and there appears to be plenty of blame to go around.

Many critics maintain that American corporations operate in ways that clearly obstruct their ability—indeed, their very willingness—to invest in, develop, and market the kinds of new technologies that would make them competitive with foreign firms, which clearly do invest, develop, and market commercially successful innovations. A major division of opinion concerns whether the problems lie principally within the corporate-managerial arena or stem from conditions outside the control of corporate-managerial decision makers. The truth appears to be that decision making both inside and outside the corporate-managerial arena contributes to the general decline in U.S. international economic competitiveness.

In a recent, highly regarded study,[12] the MIT Commission on Industrial Productivity, after detailed examinations of the automobile, chemical, commercial aircraft, consumer electronics, machine tool, semiconductor, computer, copier, steel, and textiles industries, isolated six weaknesses of American manufacturing that are at the heart of the economic crisis we face. The following sections discuss these weaknesses.

Outdated Strategies

Many American manufacturers, the commission found, pursue market strategies that have become badly outdated. This takes two forms: a continued reliance on the mass production of standardized products and parochialism.

As we noted in Chapter 3, there is an assumption that the "natural" development for any manufacturer is away from specialized, one-of-a-kind production and toward large-volume mass production. This permits large economies of scale and constitutes what is commonly thought to be "industrial maturity." Mass production, in turn, assumes a market willing to accept essentially the same small line of products everywhere, with little differentiation or specialization of design or function. In the immediate postwar era, this approach worked well for consumer products like toothpaste, cars, television sets, and clothing, as well as for capital products. At the time, this seemed to be the very secret of the uniquely American economic success:

> Indeed, within the United States the triumph of this system was so complete that other patterns of production were virtually wiped out. There was little room left in the economy for the craft tradition, with less-hierarchical work organizations and the direct participation of skilled workers in production decisions, or for other means of serving smaller segments of the market.[13]

Many American industries, the theory suggests, are now fully mature, and, in a world economy where capital and technology cross borders almost unimpeded, simply cannot compete with firms in Japan, South Korea, Brazil, or elsewhere with labor costs one half, one quarter, or even one tenth as high. This is a natural, and basically irreversible, feature of any manufacturing technology once it has become highly standardized and mature. The industrial maturity theory suggests that once a corporation has taken on this kind of organization, it cannot reverse the process, cannot shift back toward the fluidity and flexibility of new product manufacturers. With steel, textiles, shoes, perhaps automobiles, perhaps machine tools, and other industries, the factors that influence competitive advantage have simply shifted away from the United States and toward its trading rivals.

The point is not to deplore what, in any case, cannot be changed, but to shift concern toward those industries and technologies that still require skilled workers and where we still have competitive advantages. Thus, some argue, the United States should gradually concede its losses in the older, smokestack industries of the past century—steel, automobiles, rubber, textiles—upon which the "sun is setting" and turn attention to the "sunrise" industries of the future: computers, biotechnology, electronics, material sciences, and such industrial services as engineering design, finance, communications, and insurance. The older assembly line jobs will inevitably go to Mexico, Singapore, Taiwan, and other low-wage countries. We make a mistake when we vainly try to preserve our investments in these industries.

The industrial maturity thesis has been challenged by scholars who argue that even mature, highly standardized industries can shake off their organizational and technological rigidities and once again become technologically competitive. William Abernathy et al. make a strong case for the possibility of "dematurity" in American industry: "We would argue [that] manufacturing industries can indeed arrest—and in some circumstances even reverse—the maturation process. We would argue for the possibility of industrial "de-maturity."[14] Most significantly, under conditions of dematurity, the terms of competition change. No longer do firms that make essentially the same kind of mass produced product (shoes, automobiles, light bulbs) compete only on the basis of costs, advertising, and styling. Under dematurity, technology becomes the focus of competition once again, as economist Alan Kantrow explains: "...the one dominant force in this dematuring process is technology. Technology has become a kind of lever to unsettle the established terms of competition in a whole range of industries."[15]

Under these new conditions, once sedate industrial organizations, and the decision makers who work therein, find they must change their management practices. This, of course, can be threatening to those whose careers hinge on the continuation of "standard operating procedures," and who are unable or unwilling to change. However, Abernathy et al. urge optimism for corporate managers facing dematurity:

> It is our strong belief that, properly understood, the possibilities of a restored technology-based competition—that is, a mode of competition in which producers once again actively seek out distinctive technical solutions to the product attributes favored by the market—can turn the threat of de-maturity into an attractive program for industry renewal.[16]

What many American manufacturers have missed, the MIT Commission found, is that the market has changed substantially. Customers are much more aware and sophisticated and demand specialized, more tailor-made products, rather than highly standardized commodities. However, "mature" U.S. firms are ill structured to provide such goods. What is more, American corporate decision makers remain too parochial in their outlook, believing that the rest of the world wants what America has and will always accept whatever America produces. Instead of actively finding out what customers in other countries really want, too many U.S. manufacturers continue to think that consumers in Japan, Europe, or Latin America, will continue to purchase what consumers in Topeka and Orlando want. We need, they assert, to reacquaint ourselves with the rest of the world. Our international competitors take special care to meet local needs and wants.

There are significant problems as well, with the idea of shifting economic resources out of older industries and into high-tech industries and services. As a matter of fact, we already face serious foreign competition in many high-skill industries, not only in the older, assembly line industries. Some of these high-tech industries—semiconductors, for instance—have begun appealing to the government for protection against foreign manufacturers. Moreover, foreign firms are also competing in advanced services, with insurance, banking, and engineering design companies displaying Japanese and German names springing up in America. If we plan to abandon the smokestack for high-tech and services, we're likely to be shocked to see our chief competitors already there.

What is more, we cannot successfully base our economy on high-tech and services alone. High-tech firms, it is clear, simply cannot create enough new jobs to take up the employment slack that abandoning steel, glass, automobiles, rubber, and the like would create. Moreover, the vast majority of new service jobs created in our economy have not been at the high-skill, high-wage end of the scale; most have been in the low-skill, low-wage realm, as food service. This is quite a prospect for a laid-off steel worker. More importantly, however, services are intimately linked to old-fashioned manufacturing, and if we abandon our older industries, we'll lose our service industry too:

> If we lose control and mastery of manufacturing production, the problem is not simply that we will be unable to replace the jobs lost with service jobs, or simply that those service jobs will pay less, or that the scale and speed of adjustment will shock the society—and polity—in potentially dangerous ways. It is that the high-paying service jobs that are directly linked to manufacturing will, after a few short rounds of industrial innovation, wither away, only to sprout up offshore.[17]

In short, if our competitors can master the techniques of factory production for traditional manufacturing, they can, and will, master the techniques of high-tech and service industries as well.

Short Time Horizons

A second weakness noted by the commission is the tendency of U.S. corporate-managerial decision makers to take a very short-term perspective about technology. Our competitors, they note, are much better at taking a long view, investing for the more distant future, while American decision makers seem to have trouble planning beyond the next quarterly earnings statement. Effective technological competition requires a willingness to pursue technical opportunities, for years sometimes, before the commercial payoff appears.

Part of the problem is that U.S. corporate-managerial decision makers too often rise to leadership positions with little or no real experience with manufacturing, as noted in a frequently cited article by Robert Hayes and William Abernathy:

> Our experience suggests that, to an unprecedented degree, success in most industries today requires an organizational commitment to compete in the marketplace on technological grounds—that is, to compete over the long run by offering superior products. Yet, guided by what they took to be the newest and best principles of management, American managers have increasingly directed their attention elsewhere. These new principles, despite their sophistication and widespread usefulness, encourage a preference for (1) analytic detachment rather than the insight that comes from "hands on" experience and (2) short-term cost reduction rather than long-term development of technological competitiveness. It is this new managerial gospel, we feel, that has played a major role in undermining the vigor of American industry.[18]

Hayes and Abernathy note that over the past quarter century, the career paths of American corporate decision makers no longer provide future executives with intimate hands-on knowledge of the company's products and production technologies. Instead, managers have risen from the financial and legal offices within American companies. Lacking background experience with actually making the company's products, with little appreciation for complex relationships among producers, consumers, suppliers, and technology, finance-oriented corporate-managerial decision makers too often fall prey to the tyranny of the quarterly earnings report. They make short-term decisions to enhance immediate profitability and avoid making the long-term commitments required for new product or new process technological innovation. This trend is exacerbated by typical executive compensation plans, in which a decision maker's personal income is pegged to the latest corporate earnings statement, thus increasing the executive's willingness to sacrifice long-term growth for short-term profitability.

Technological Weaknesses in Development and Production

Another weakness spotted by the MIT Commission is the tendency in the corporate-managerial arena to downplay the importance of production processes, design engineering, and product quality: "American design engineers too often neglected manufacturability and quality in their product designs."[19] In case after case, U.S. science has produced important technical breakthroughs that have been commercially exploited by the Japanese or others. The commission's indictment is quite explicit:

> American companies evidently find it difficult to design simple, reliable, mass-producible products; they often fail to pay enough attention at the design stage to the likely quality of the manufactured product; their product-development times are excessively long; they pay insufficient attention to manufacturing processes; they take a reactive rather than a preventive approach to problem solving; and they tend to under-exploit the potential of continuous improvements in products and processes.[20]

The MIT Commission noted with irony that, while we remain the world's leader in basic science, we too often fail to bring potentially commercial science-based discoveries to market. There seems to be a breakdown of some sort between discovery and marketing, and others are stepping in to take advantage of our inability. Part of the problem is that a large amount of our scientific research is defense oriented, which has left the "product-realization process a poor cousin." A major contributor to this weakness, the commission noted, is postwar U.S. engineering training, which deemphasizes product realization and process and product engineering and overemphasizes natural science.

Neglect of Human Resources

The MIT Commission also noted that U.S. firms do not make effective use of their workers, treating them as either largely interchangeable commodities or entrenched opponents. In contrast, our major foreign competitors treat their workers as integral to the company's success, investing in extensive training and retraining programs, including them in important decision making, and treating their skills as valuable corporate resources. (We return to a discussion of management-labor relations later in this chapter.)

Failures of Cooperation

We saw in Chapter 3 that corporations evolve along with their products, moving toward highly structured, hierarchical organizations as they shift toward high-volume mass production of standardized products. Divisions, departments, and offices appear where before there had been little hierarchy, few titles, and relatively informal communications among decision makers. Coordination and cooperation become major problems that the MIT Commission believes many American corporations are not effectively meeting.

Too often, the commission says, design engineers do not talk with production personnel as new products are developed, thereby losing the important insights that those who will be responsible for making the product can bring to the design process. Instead, bottlenecks, design problems, and quality control issues are left to crop up later and to be dealt with piecemeal. Our competitors have developed more effective product teams and overcome problems of coordination and cooperation:

> In contrast with their Japanese competitors, American firms have several extra layers of hierarchy arranged as an organizational tree. To communicate with one another, people working in different departments often have to go up the tree to their lowest-level common superior and then back down. In Japanese firms the hierarchy has fewer levels and it is layered rather than strictly treelike: people in one layer generally know and can easily communicate with people in the next-higher and next-lower layers, regardless of departmental boundaries.[21]

It is not argued that U.S. firms should slavishly imitate Japanese firms; indeed, there is evidence that Japanese firms are beginning to behave more like American companies, as their own economy changes.[22] Instead, American companies need to find their own mechanisms for getting around the cumbersome and clumsy decision-making structures that obstruct their ability to coordinate and cooperate.

The commission found that Japanese firms are significantly quicker to bring a new product idea from design, to development, to the store shelf than are American companies, and a good part of the difference is the Japanese firms' capacity to facilitate intrafirm communication and cooperation. In a new market system that emphasizes sophisticated and segmented consumer demand, the ability to respond rapidly to changing consumer desires will be a significant element of competitive strength. American firms, still wedded to mass production of standardized products, remain sluggish and lethargic compared to lean, trim, and very responsive foreign firms.

Government and Industry at Cross-Purposes

The MIT Commission pointed to an array of government policies that affect how decisions are made in the corporate-managerial arena. Tax, regulatory, fiscal, labor, and trade policies all influence corporate-managerial decision makers. Although apologists for corporate-managerial decision makers often cite government decisions as the chief culprit in the declining U.S. competitiveness, the commission disagreed. Government policies do affect corporate-managerial decision making, but many of the problems facing the American manufacturer are self-inflicted, it said.

The MIT Commission offered a series of steps U.S. industry should take to reverse the rapid slippage in American international competitiveness:

1. Focus on the "new fundamentals" of manufacturing. This means that corporate-managerial decision makers must put products and manufacturing processes ahead of finance, establish new measures of productive performance, focus on the effective use of technology in manufacturing, embrace product customizations and production flexibility, and encourage innovation in the production process.

2. Cultivate a new economic citizenship in the work force. This means increasing opportunities for workers to learn for work and at work, increasing employees' breadth, responsibility, and involvement, and providing greater employment stability and new rewards.

3. Blend cooperation and individualism. This means that they must organize for both cooperation and individualism, promote better intra- and interfirm relations, expand partnerships, and strengthen cooperation between labor and management.

4. Learn to live in the world economy. This means they must understand foreign languages, cultures, and practices, shop internationally, enhance distribution and service, and develop internationally conscious policies.

5. Provide for the future. This involves investing in basic education and technical literacy, develop long-term business strategies, establish policies that stimulate productive investment, and invest in infrastructure for productive performance.

The MIT Commission was quick to note that these recommendations require important changes in government decision making, along with new forms of leadership from corporate-managerial decision makers.

THE POLITICAL FIGHT

The political battle affecting corporate management practices is occurring primarily in the legislative arena, with participants from the executive arena and, of course, the corporate-managerial arena active and involved.

Many of the "industrial policy" recommendations put forward by economists and politicians contain provisions to improve and sharpen U.S. management decision-making practices (see, for example, Wildavsky[23]). In some cases, special incentives would be created to encourage more research and development into new products and processes, while in other cases, restrictions on corporate mergers and acquisitions would inhibit what many see as a waste of corporate resources. And in yet other cases, limitations on corporate freedom to close potentially profitable plants or to move production facilities overseas are included.

Other suggestions include the creation of federal agencies charged with channeling public and private investment money into successful, innovative companies, provided they use effective management techniques. Some support short-term federal bailouts for troubled industries, but only if those industries will streamline their operations, reduce expenses, close unneeded and unprofitable facilities, increase their R&D efforts, increase investments in production technologies, and follow other steps to improve their international competitiveness.

Within the legislative arena, such proposals serve many purposes, political as well as economic. For a lawmaker, taking bold steps to correct economic problems pays election dividends, especially if the legislator is from a region suffering economic distress. Most voters are usually not interested in arcane economic theories; however, they do expect office seekers to understand what is happening to the economy and to have concrete plans for dealing with problems, including explicit steps to correct corporate mismanagement. "Industrial policy" proposals are an excellent vehicle for showing one's economic acumen. Having a well-developed formula for economic reform also gives a legislator a posture from which to criticize the incumbent's policies.

For politicians, continued economic drift and the loss of more jobs accompanied by continued large management salary bonuses are very tempting political targets. Whether the proposed solution is industrial policy, importing Japanese or German management techniques, or blatant protectionism, corporate managers are easy targets for attack, invective, and blame. Participants from the corporate-managerial arena are very concerned to block all such efforts to interfere with their management decisions. While they may not be happy with the existing array of federal tax, employment, and investment policies, they do not want to see a spate of new "experiments," whether or not labeled industrial policy, imposed by people they see as more interested in advancing their political ambitions than in actually running a company.

For ammunition, corporate-managerial participants can only point to the familiar principles of marketplace economics. They will zero in on whatever success stories of effective American companies doing business overseas can be found, and they promise firmer, leaner, more effective management practices in their own companies, if only the government resists the urge to interfere with the marketplace. But, as Robert Kuttner notes

> The trouble with this view is that there is no country that prospers via pure capitalism....Our competitors all plan more explicitly than we do, and all use variants of "corporatism"—deliberate business-government collaboration, with or without labor as junior partner. One can identify relatively egalitarian corporatist countries—West Germany, Sweden, Japan—and relatively low-wage, authoritarian ones such as Korea and Taiwan, but no successful cases of pure laissez-faire.[24]

Corporate-managerial decision makers are at a political disadvantage compared to the supporters of industrial policies, especially if their promised management reforms do not produce quick results. Since they are often blamed for the current state of the economy, corporate managers have little room for error and must begin to show significant improvement quickly. Fortunately, there is some evidence of change within the corporate-managerial arena, as corporate decision makers gradually come to understand the precarious position they are in. For instance, in some major American business schools, students are studying with more energy the problems of productivity, international competition, and the virtues of actually knowing something about the products one sells.[25] Whether they learn these lessons soon enough to halt the decline of America's standing in international trade, and before participants in other arenas compel changes in management practices, remains to be seen.

Labor Problems

In general, members of the labor arena seek to maintain their impact on corporate and government decision makers, to find ways of limiting the undesirable impacts of technological change, to maintain jobs in endangered industries, to promote programs of effective assistance for workers who have lost their jobs, and to preserve the positions of labor leadership.

The problem is that most of the recommendations offered to cure the declining U.S. competitiveness appear to involve retreat by organized labor on one or more of these goals. Seeing themselves as most often on the periphery of economic decision making, often allowed only to react to decisions made and imposed from elsewhere, labor arena participants are concerned that the competitiveness problem will eventually be solved only after major sacrifices are imposed on workers, whose living standards and future prospects are at peril. Let's look at some specifics.

Employment

Over recent years many American corporations have responded to increased competition by either closing unprofitable plants or moving production facilities overseas or both. These responses, widespread in many industries, have been called the "deindustrialization of America,"[26] and one result has been the permanent loss of thousands of jobs in affected industries. One estimate asserted that between 1980 and 1982, 2 million manufacturing jobs were eliminated in the U.S. economy[27] through this kind of attrition. While there is a continuous employment turnover in our economy, with many jobs lost and created through this natural process, the problem of deindustrialization focuses on those industrial jobs that are permanently lost.

Decision makers in the labor arena are also concerned that members of the corporate-managerial arena are making decisions about the location of production facilities that are exporting jobs to foreign countries. In response, labor unions and other groups representing workers and the communities in which they live have pressed for legislative restrictions on a corporation's ability to close a plant. Plant-closing restrictions would impose a variety of restraints on corporate decision making: 30, 60, or even 90 days' notice before a plant can be closed, retraining and relocation payments to affected workers, and even compensatory payments to the local community in order to help it weather the economic and social changes that plant closings impose.

The legislative and executive arenas are crucial in this struggle, as labor and corporate-managerial participants pressure Congress and the president concerning proposed plant closing legislation. In this struggle, the labor decision makers probably have the advantage in pressuring members of the legislative arena to make the "correct" decision—that is, support plant closing restrictions—since they can point to the very real impacts such closings have on particular voters, especially in regions of the country already experiencing economic difficulties.

Members of the corporate-managerial arena are not able to use such heartfelt, real-life stories of economic pain and loss. Instead, they must fall back on more abstract arguments about economic efficiency and unneeded interference with market decisions. Such arguments may not work so well with members of Congress besieged by complaints from distressed voters back home.

However, such arguments may work better within the executive arena. To some extent, the executive is less susceptible to the pleas of specific regions or industries and more concerned about national economic policies. Executive agencies, such as the Office of Management and Budget, must often look past the individual impacts of national economic policy, as often must the president. Thus, decision makers in both the labor and the corporate-managerial arenas, each seeking to obtain desired decisions from the legislative and executive arenas, do what they can to manipulate the constraints and pressures in those target arenas.

Job Skills

Labor arena decision makers are also concerned about the changing skills required for jobs. In short, there is great anxiety that changing technologies have "deskilled" many jobs, that technology has reduced the skill levels needed to perform tasks, and thereby reduced the bargaining position of the individuals hired to perform those jobs. What is more, many fear that the deskilling is not a necessary and unavoidable consequence of new technologies but is a conscious choice made by management, intended to reduce the influence and control of workers to an absolute minimum.

The development of the factory manufacturing system over the past three centuries can be seen as a progressive deskilling of workers, as mass production, assembly line work broke skilled crafts down into simpler and simpler tasks. At each point in this development, tasks that previously required skill and training became simpler, allowing management to hire less trained workers to perform the tasks. Unskilled laborers traditionally have far less influence in shaping shop floor conditions, job rules, wage and benefit scales, and the like.

Well-trained, skilled workers, however, can influence their working conditions through the threat of withholding their irreplaceable skills, in a strike, or significantly retarding a manufacturing process in a work slow-down. For management, there is little that can be done except to negotiate with such workers. What bothers participants in the labor arena is that new technologies, especially computers, as applied in the office and on the shop floor will trigger a new onslaught by management against labor's influence on working conditions.

There are numerous examples of how technology is changing the character of work and the specific skills needed to perform it. In two recent studies, historian David Noble[28] and industrial specialist Harley Shaiken[29] have documented the impact of computer technologies on the machining industry. Skilled machinists, who cut metal into the gears, cams, crankshafts, and other precision shapes needed in other machines, have been among the most independent of workers, frequently demanding, and receiving, substantial autonomy from corporate management. Shaiken describes the complex role the professional machinist plays:

> It is the machinist who converts an engineer's conception, whether in the form of a drawing or a verbal description, into a finished part. This involves far more than good coordination and knowledge of which lever to pull on the machine. The skill is one of the brain as well as the hand, and it is learned on the job, transmitted from journeyman to apprentice and mastered only after years of experience....The machinist determines the machine setup, plots the order of operations, and selects the speeds and feeds at which the machine will run....Once the part touches the rapidly rotating cutter, an operator with years of experience is needed to spot potential problems and to react correctly when they do arise. A slight change in the color of the chip may mean the entire part will warp; a small difference in the sound of the machine could mean a poor finish; a mild chatter of the cutting tool might result in a scrapped part.[30]

As manufacturing machinery became more complex, requiring closer, tighter tolerances, the specialized skills of the machinist became more valuable, and machinists had more leverage in their bargaining with management.

One response by management has been the effort to substitute automation for the skills of the human machinist. With much more complex computer programming at hand in recent years, entire workstations have been computerized, with the automated machine capable of making precise metal cuts at a much faster rate and lower error percentage than a human operator and without the need for breaks, rest periods, or demands for increased pay. To a large extent, automated, computer-run machine tools have "captured" the specialized skills of the human machinist in the machine itself. As such, they require only periodic maintenance by workers possessing far less skill than the machinist. The machinist's position has been deskilled, and management's control over the once-independent machinist has been increased.

Other steps taken by management also cause worries among workers. The large-scale introduction of robots into the production process both threatens human jobs and increases management's ability to dictate work conditions. Of course, many of the tasks taken over by robots are dangerous and tedious, such as welding or painting in automobile assembly. Still, these are human jobs lost to machines.

But even more significant than the introduction of robots is the spread of FMS (flexible manufacturing systems) in industry. These computer-based technologies are nothing less than a fully automated manufacturing process, an almost fully automated "factory of the future." In computer-integrated manufacturing systems,

> the computer or computer network manages an integrated system of processes. Here the computer takes on the transcendent role of integrator or coordinator. Not only does the computer control each of the processes in the system, but it also controls the movement of materials to and from each process, changes tools, inspects the product, adjusts machines when deviations occur, and provides its human bosses with information on how well things are going.[31]

Yet a third concern for labor arena participants comes from the introduction of computer technologies, not just in manufacturing plants but in the front office as well. Office automation not only threatens jobs, as computers rapidly replace clerical workers; it also threatens to alter radically the working conditions of the workers who remain.[32, 33]

We know that computers greatly enhance the work productivity of clerical staff, with word processing, financial spreadsheets, online information systems, and computer networking. These new forms of office software also serve to deskill clerical workers, who no longer need to have the in-depth training of precomputer days. As a direct consequence, such workers are in a much weaker position in presenting complaints about working conditions, salaries, promotions, and the like.

More insidiously, those same computers can also manage and monitor workers at their stations in much more detail than was ever possible before, informing management of the speed and efficiency of each worker on a minute-to-minute basis. In some firms, such as telephone operators, sales personnel, insurance claims workers, and airlines reservation clerks, the computer reports to supervisors precisely how much time each employee takes to complete each task, how many errors are made on each task, even how often and how long workers are away from the workstation for breaks, trips to the bathroom, and so on. Similar levels of computer-based monitoring also are available on factory floors.

The new computer-based worker observation systems suggest a distinct lack of trust and respect, as if management expects the workers to shirk their responsibilities unless very closely watched. Workers often feel as though every hour of every workday their managers are looking over their shoulders, looking for mistakes or malingering. In some cases, supervisors actually do have regular daily talks with workers, where their speed, efficiency, errors, absences from station, and the like, as monitored and publicly reported by computer, are discussed; and workers whose performance in these areas falls below "standard" expectations are pressed to improve their performance.

Workers in such offices often report increased fatigue, tension, anxiety, and other health problems caused by such intense scrutiny by management. Glenn Watts, of the Communications Workers of America, comments:

> Research is just beginning to point out that the levels of stress associated with modern technology and the modern workplace are serious, and demand urgent attention from both labor and management. As a result of new technology, computerized measuring sticks for job performance are being rapidly introduced into the workplace. The end result is a work situation where people are under even more pressure....[S]tudies are now beginning to show that office work can, and many times does, involve serious health hazards and alarming levels of job-related stress.[34]

In all four areas—manufacturing workstations that automate specific shop floor tasks, flexible manufacturing systems that automate entire factories, clerical office automation, and computer-based worker monitoring—labor arena decision makers face considerable problems in pressing their concerns. Management can, and does justify the application of these deskilling and surveillance technologies by claiming that they are necessary to restore our international economic competitiveness and that labor opposition is antitechnology obstructionism. Corporate-managerial participants echo General Electric Executive Vice President James Baker's prescription for economic survival in the face of tough foreign competition: "Automate, emigrate, or evaporate."[35]

Labor arena decision makers are hard pressed to rebut this argument, given the obvious decline of U.S. international economic performance and the widespread belief that technological innovation is one sure way to reverse the decline. CAD/CAM (computer-aided design/computer-aided manufacturing) programs, flexible manufacturing systems, computers, and advanced software programs are exciting, cutting edge technologies, the very sort of innovations in which the United States still has a competitive advantage.

Still, labor has achieved some concessions through negotiations. For instance, the United Automobile Workers of America obtained contractual agreements with General Motors providing for advance notification of the introduction of new technologies, corporate-financed retraining programs, and guarantees against technologically induced layoffs of workers with one or more years of seniority and another agreement to develop and launch new business ventures aimed at providing jobs for union-represented employees.

The chief locus of labor and corporate-managerial conflict on the adoption of deskilling technologies remains in the collective bargaining process, with little impact from other arenas. This works to the disadvantage of labor arena decision makers, since they are trying to protect the working conditions of employees whose jobs have already been deskilled and therefore whose bargaining leverage has been reduced by the very technologies at issue. Threatening to take irreplaceable, skilled machinists out on strike is one thing; threatening to take out lower-skilled workers attending automated machining stations is quite another.

What is more threatening, many in the labor arena believe that some technologies being adopted by the corporate-managerial arena are actually intended to serve management's hidden antilabor agenda and are only camouflaged as necessary for economic reinvigoration. As an example of such hidden goals, Noble[36] argues that the selection of the specific automation technology of numerically controlled machine tools, widely used to automate the machinist's work, was *not* dictated by technological or economic necessity. Instead, this form of automation technology was chosen by management over alternative technologies *precisely because it decreases worker influence and, thus, increases management control of the work situation.*

Both Noble and Shaiken assert that other automated machining technologies are available that can both increase productivity and enhance worker importance. However, management adamantly refuses to adopt these alternative technologies. Noble and Shaiken maintain that management seeks to gain and keep complete control over the shop floor and over the entire production process and to eliminate organized labor's influence. The competitiveness controversy, which as we have seen many observers actually blame on unproductive management practices, serves to obscure the true objectives of corporate-managerial decision makers.

ENDNOTES

1. GEORGE C. EADS, "Dangers in U.S. Efforts to Promote International Competitiveness," *The Positive Sum Strategy: Harnessing Technology for Economic Growth*, ed. Ralph Landau and Nathan Rosenberg (Washington, D.C.: National Academy Press, 1986), p 530.

2. N. BRUCE HANNAY, "Technology and Trade: A Study of U.S. Competitiveness in Seven Industries," in *The Positive Sum Strategy: Harnessing Technology for Economic Growth*, ed. Ralph Landau and Nathan Rosenberg (Washington, D.C.: National Academy Press, 1986), pp. 479–480.

3. MICHAEL DERTOUZOS, RICHARD K. LESTER, and ROBERT M. SOLOW, *Made in America: Regaining the Productive Edge* (Cambridge, Mass.: MIT Press, 1989).

4. ROBERT H. HAYES and WILLIAM J. ABERNATHY, "Managing Our Way to Economic Decline," *Harvard Business Review* (July/August 1980), 67–77.

5. JOHN ZYSMAN and LAURA TYSON, eds., *American Industry in International Competition: Government Policies and Corporate Strategies* (Ithaca, N.Y.: Cornell University Press, 1983).

6. ROBERT H. HAYES and STEVEN C. WHEELWRIGHT, *Restoring Our Competitive Edge: Competing Through Manufacturing* (New York: John Wiley, 1984).

7. BRUCE R. SCOTT and GEORGE C. LODGE, eds., *U.S. Competitiveness in the World Economy* (Boston: Harvard Business School Press, 1985).

8. LESTER C. THUROW, *The Zero-Sum Solution: An Economic and Political Agenda for the 80's* (New York: Touchstone Books, 1985).

9. EZRA F. VOGEL, *Comeback: Case by Case: Building the Resurgence of American Business* (New York: Simon & Schuster, 1985).

10. RALPH LANDAU and NATHAN ROSENBERG, eds., *The Positive Sum Strategy: Harnessing Technology for Economic Growth* (Washington, D.C.: National Academy Press, 1986).

11. STEPHEN S. COHEN and JOHN ZYSMAN, *Manufacturing Matters: The Myth of the Post-Industrial Economy* (New York: Basic Books, 1987).

12. DERTOUZOS, et al., *Made in America.*

13. Ibid., p. 47.

14. WILLIAM J. ABERNATHY, KIM B. CLARK, and ALAN M. KANTROW, *Industrial Renaissance: Producing a Competitive Future for America* (New York: Basic Books, 1983), pp. 20–21.

15. ALAN M. KANTROW, "Government Policy and the Competitive Effects of Innovation," in *Competitiveness through Technology: What Business Needs from Government*, ed. Jerry Dermer (Lexington, Mass.: Lexington Books, 1986), p. 6.

16. ABERNATHY, et al., *Industrial Renaissance*, p. 29.

17. COHEN and ZYSMAN, *Manufacturing Matters*, p. 58.

18. HAYES and ABERNATHY, "Managing Our Way to Economic Decline," p. 68.

19. DERTOUZOS, et al., *Made In America*, p. 69.

20. Ibid., p. 68.

21. Ibid., p. 96.

22. DAVID C. MOWERY, and NATHAN ROSENBERG, *Technology and the Pursuit of Economic Growth* (New York: Cambridge University Press, 1989).

23. AARON WILDAVSKY, "Squaring the Political Circle: Industrial Policies and the American Dream," in *The Industrial Policy Debate* ed. Chalmers Johnson (San Francisco: ICS Press, 1984), pp. 27–47.

24. ROBERT KUTTNER, "The Competitiveness Craze," *New Republic*, November 2, 1987, p. 22.

25. "What They Don't Teach You at Business School," *U.S. News & World Report*, July 13, 1987, pp. 44–46.

26. BARRY BLUESTONE and BENNETT HARRISON, *The Deindustrialization of America: Plant Closings, Community Abandonment, and the Dismantling of Basic Industry* (New York: Basic Books, 1982).

27. "High Tech: Blessing or Curse?" *U.S. News & World Report*, January 16, 1984, pp. 38–44.

28. DAVID F. NOBLE, *Forces of Production: A Social History of Industrial Automation* (New York: Knopf, 1984).

29. HARLEY SHAIKEN, *Work Transformed: Automation and Labor in the Computer Age* (New York: Holt, Rinehart, and Winston, 1984).

30. Ibid., p. 18.

31. ROBERT THURD and JOHN A. HANSEN, *Keeping America at Work: Strategies for Employing the New Technologies* (New York: John Wiley & Sons, 1986), p. 26.

32. ROBERT E. KRAUT, ed., *Technology and the Transformation of White-Collar Work* (Hillsdale, N.J.: Lawrence Erlbaum Assoc., Publishers, 1987).

33. BARBARA G. F. COHEN, ed., *Human Aspects of Office Automation* (New York: Elsevier Science Publishers).

34. GLENN E. WATTS, "An Old Problem is a New Technology: Safety and Stress in the Modern Office," in *Ibid.*, p. 304.

35. JAMES BAKER, "Industry Must 'Automate, Emigrate, or Evaporate,'" *U.S. News and World Report*, January 16, 1984, p. 44.

36. DAVID F. NOBLE, *Forces of Production: A Social History of Industrial Automation* (New York: Alfred A. Knopf, 1984).

Chapter 7

Dominant Configurations: Science, Technology, and the Military

In this chapter we explore the most abstract and general of the four concepts of our decision-making model: **dominant configurations.** As we move up the ladder of these five concepts, from technological projects, to individual technological decision makers, to technological decision-making arenas, to interarena relations, and now to dominant configurations, each step takes us from relatively more concrete, specific ideas and experiences to relatively more abstract ones. Each step allows us to grasp a larger array of influences shaping technological politics, influences that cannot be understood properly without using the more abstract concept. However, our goal at each step has been to reach beyond the confines of one concept without losing touch with the real, concrete, specific experiences that are the "stuff" of technological politics.

The concept of a dominant configuration reaches a level of generality that will allow us to examine the validity of some notions about a "technological momentum" or a "technological imperative" that may be driving social, economic, and political change in undesirable and dangerous directions, regardless of human wishes, plans, or desires. Too often ideas of this sort seem to be so divorced from the concrete realities of life in our society that it can be difficult to understand the impact and importance of such assertions. We hope that using the concept of dominant configurations will help to make these ideas more comprehensible.

Up to this point, we have seen how individual technological decision makers operating within different technological decision-making arenas seek to obtain from each other the kinds of decisions each one needs to complete specific technological projects. A variety of techniques are used in different settings to induce an important decision maker to make just the kind of decision needed so that one's own project can move forward. We have seen that technological decision makers and the organizations they work for often expend a lot of time, effort, money, political clout, and other scarce and valuable, if intangible, resources trying to ensure that the desired decisions are made.

Given how costly this can be, it is not surprising that decision makers in various arenas should try to create more stable accommodations with each other. Often, the participants in such accommodations do not share identical goals: Each seeks different benefits, depending on the environmental pressures operating in his or her specific arena, and simply find it useful to work together with members of other arenas in regularized ways. When these stable relationships among technological decision-making arenas persist over time, both the participants in the accommodation and decision makers in other, non-participating arenas come to understand that the accommodation amounts to unwritten ground rules for all arena interactions. Even arenas not directly involved in the accommodation may find the order and predictability such relationships provide useful to themselves. Some, of course, may find such accommodations occasionally to be obstacles to their own goals.

This kind of regularized, predictable relationship among decision makers in different arenas can be seen as "dominating" the interactions of various arena participants, hence, as a dominant configuration of interarena relations. Not every instance of cooperation among technological decision makers constitutes a dominant configuration. We are talking about persistent and well-established accommodations.

Decision making within a dominant configuration is to be more regular, if not necessarily more amicable, than decision making in other areas. In some ways, the operation of a dominant configuration negates policy gridlock as a problem in technological decision making. Since all participants in a specific dominant configuration understand the rules that apply, there is much less chance for endless wrangling, procedural delays, and political polarization so characteristic of technological decision making in areas with no dominant configuration to manage decision making. Often, as we will see, the efficiency of technological decision making within a dominant configuration is purchased by the expedient of narrowing the range of decision makers permitted to participate in the decision-making process. Dominant configurations work because the participants are able to keep outsiders from upsetting the arrangements that the insiders find so comfortable. Here, we are once again presented with the problem of finding a balance between technological responsibility and democratic responsiveness. Dominant configuration may be efficient; they may even be responsible, although this is by no means guaranteed. They are most certainly not democratic, however.

MILITARY-INDUSTRIAL COMPLEX

As usual, things become clearer when we can point to specific examples. The example we will use to illustrate dominant configurations is what is often called the "military-industrial complex": the combination of the military services, Department of Defense bureaucrats, large defense-oriented corporations, scientists and engineers, and others involved in the design, development, and procurement of weaponry and other matériel for the armed forces. There continues to be controversy about the concept of a military-industrial complex (for example, see Slater and Nardin,[1] Pilisuk and Hayden,[2] and Sarkesian[3]), with a number of observers arguing that the concept is too ambiguous to serve as a really useful analytical tool. Nevertheless, the idea of a combination of personal, political, professional, and economic interests focused on military issues will serve our purposes here.

Often the military-industrial complex is blamed for the seemingly unstoppable arms race, with technology contributing directly to that apparently irresistible momentum. The precise mechanism differs from observer to observer. Some blame defense contractors and their allies within the Pentagon for pushing unneeded new weapons for corporate profit, others blame the bureaucratic mentality of Department of Defense officers and civilian leaders for allowing themselves to be controlled by unexamined conclusions about superpower relationships, while still others blame interservice rivalries and competition for the arms race (for example, Baugh[4]).

Technology and the Arms Race

For many observers, however, the powerful but often hidden engine that actually fuels the arms race is the weapons technology itself, creating ever more destructive and ultimately uncontrollable weapons systems. Ralph Lapp bluntly states the case: "It is my contention that missile technology, not man, has dominated the evolution of our defense policy."[5] Herbert York, an experienced defense scientist, has said much the same: "...the root of the problem [of the arms race] has not been maliciousness, but rather a sort of technological exuberance that has overwhelmed the other factors that go into the making of overall national policy."[6] And another important participant in weapons systems development, former Secretary of Defense Robert McNamara, has described the pressures pushing defense decision makers in similar terms: "There is a kind of mad momentum intrinsic to the development of all new nuclear weaponry. If a weapon works—and works well—there is a strong pressure from many directions to procure and deploy the weapon out of all proportion of the level required."[7]

As York, Lapp, McNamara, and many others see it, new weapons technologies develop an irresistible momentum, a "technological exuberance," that policymakers are, in the end, unable to resist: "The possibilities that welled up out of the technological program and the ideas and proposals put forth by the technologists eventually created a set of options that was so narrow in the scope of its alternatives and so strong in its thrust that the political decision makers had no real independent choice in the matter."[8]

Modern, technologically sophisticated weapons can take quite a long time to design, test, and deploy. Therefore, work on them must begin many years before they are needed in the active forces, and years before the elected officials who will make the final deployment decisions take up their duties. It follows from this, as Lauren Holland and Robert Hoover note, that decisions to fund exploratory research and development for such potential weapons must occur even earlier, often before the exact nature of the threat the weapon is expected to counter is known:

> Major decisions about research [on new weapons systems] are made ten to fifteen years before formulation of the strategic doctrine that will be official when the

weapon enters the force posture.... Major decisions about research are undertaken ten to fifteen years before the actual Soviet capabilities against which the weapon will operate is known.... Major decisions about design and development are made five to ten years before formulation of the strategic doctrine that will be official when the weapon will operate is known.... Major decisions about design and development are undertaken five to ten years before the opponent's actual capabilities against which the weapon will operate is known.[9]

Such long-term advance planning cannot be based simply on assessments of current weapons decisions by the Soviet Union, but must rely on projections, often decades into the future, of what they *might* do.[10] Neither side can risk being caught unaware as the other side makes major breakthroughs in weaponry.

Arena Interactions

The chief characteristic of a dominant configuration is the level of cooperative predictability and regularity in interarena relations found there. These characteristics develop over time, as the decision makers within different arenas gradually figure out ways to do business with each other that work to everyone's advantage while avoiding the costly and wasteful pulling and hauling that is too often found outside dominant configurations.

By carefully observing the ways in which participants in each of these defense-related arenas regularly deal with each other, we can explore this specific dominant configuration. The kind of ongoing interarena accommodation we are looking at here is based on a combination of informal understandings among various arena decision makers, formal bureaucratic procedures, and legal enactments (along with, depending on who is speaking, rare or regular illegalities).

Although the dominant configuration surrounding weapons development and procurement dates back to World War I, its major impetus is found in the cooperation experienced between the government and private corporations in manufacturing weaponry and armaments during World War II. After that war, when demobilization began, many thought that the wartime relationship between government and industry would end. However, the onset of the Korean War and the cold war revived the procurement partnership, which has persisted ever since.

During the 1950s, under the cold war regime of intense national security concerns, the arenas involved in defense technology were the corporate-managerial, the executive, the legislative, and the academic-professional. There was virtually no outside interference in weapons design and development, and among these active arenas, very little friction or conflict. The Pentagon recommended goals and systems for weapons development, and Congress willingly accepted and funded these policies, struggling only over which states and congressional districts would benefit from defense contracts. Scientists and engineers saw federal funding for defense-related research and development grow year by year, with universities and private laboratories benefiting from advanced research facilities.

Much changed by the 1980s and early 1990s. Today, corporate-managerial decision makers must take very seriously the job of managing their close contacts with decision makers in other relevant arenas, and have substantially increased the size and complexity of their lobbying offices in Washington in order to manage those relationships better.

Corporate "government relations" offices take the lead in planning and coordinating a company's entire effort to influence decision makers in other arenas, including grass-roots lobbying, PAC (political action committee) campaign contributions, and direct contacts with influential decision makers in both the executive and legislative arenas. The full range of activities handled by a defense contractor's government relations staff is huge, as the following list of activities reported by the Boeing Corporation as part of the responsibilities of its Washington government affairs office illustrates:

- To prepare and implement congressional strategies on Boeing programs.
- Preparing and distributing fact sheets to selected members of Congress to inform them of the effects pending legislation will have on Boeing.
- Preparing and disseminating legislative data to Boeing personnel.
- Following the course of legislation through the Congress and determining when it is appropriate and timely for members of Boeing management to participate directly (testimony) or indirectly (written statements) in hearings on legislation directly affecting the successful management of Boeing.
- Helping to prepare bills or amendments to existing laws, finding sponsors for such legislation, and helping the bill through the legislative process by preparing and presenting material to support such legislation. These duties are only performed when Boeing considers the specific piece of legislation essential to its well-being.
- Attending hearings and sessions of both houses to report directly and timely the actions being taken on legislation of interest to Boeing.
- Overseeing the preparation of data on members of Congress who are seeking support in elections and making recommendations to the Civic Pledge Committee [Boeing's Political Action Committee].
- Encouraging members of Congress, their staffs, and the staffs of committees to visit Boeing plants. Preparing agendas and coordinating the Congressional visits with the various segments and divisions of the company.
- Providing the focal point for coordinating all contacts between the legislative branch of the Government and Boeing. Assuring that all company contacts "on the Hill" in support of Boeing segments and divisions are coordinated with their representatives in the Washington office.[11]

Corporate-Managerial and Executive Arena Relations

For those in the corporate-managerial arena involved in weapons design, development, and production, the decision makers in the executive arena (largely in the Pentagon) are very important indeed. The decisions these individuals make determine what kinds of weapons will be developed, who will develop them, which ones will be moved into large-scale production, who will do the manufacturing, and ultimately how much profit they will earn.

For defense contractors, who may have invested millions or hundreds of millions of dollars in the new system, these decisions can mean life or death for the firm. Thus, corporate-managerial decision makers cannot simply hope that executive arena decision makers make wise choices; they must try to influence those decision makers to make the "right" decisions, that is, the decisions desired by the contractor. This is the mission of the corporate government relations offices. To accomplish this, government relations staff members cultivate contacts with every significant executive arena decision maker, from DOD officials who deal with current or prospective contracts, procurement decision makers in all three military services, to important assistants in the Office of the Secretary of Defense.

Members of the corporate-managerial arena realize that one of the most effective ways to influence decisions made within the executive arena is to hire someone who has worked there, who has an intimate knowledge of the pressures and procedures within that arena, and who has well-established friendships with executive arena decision makers to call upon. Thus, to enhance their positions, contractors frequently try to recruit retiring Pentagon officials to their companies, thus gaining the advantage of those former DOD officials' knowledge of Pentagon decision making and continued association with active Pentagon officers: "Defense contractors regularly hire DoD civilian employees and retiring military officers who bring a wealth of professional experience and useful contacts to the company. From its side the Defense Department hires personnel from the companies, providing the Government with skilled executives."[12]

This "revolving-door" practice continues to be a valued avenue of access to internal DOD decisions. Gordon Adams continues:

> The expertise brought by these individuals is not only technical but political: information on and access to policy-making that helps create a closed network in a community of shared assumptions…. The contractors obtain many benefits from the movement of personnel: information on current and future DoD and NASA plans, especially in research areas; access to key offices in Federal agencies, technical expertise for weapons development and marketing, skilled personnel with an intimate knowledge of both sides of contracting. The "revolving door" enhances the ability of a contractor to develop a successful Government relations strategy and gives the Government useful insights into the contractors' ways of doing business.[13]

Many, perhaps most, of the military officers who work in the weapons procurement system within the Pentagon fully expect to go to work for those contractors when they end their military careers, an expectation that can have subtle but real implications for the kinds of procurement decisions they make while in uniform: "A lot of people who work in the Pentagon expect to go to work for defense contractors later. The prospect may be greater if they make a decision that can mean hundreds of millions of dollars for a company. The temptation is obvious."[14] So strong is the desire to obtain postretirement employment with defense contractors that efforts by active duty military officers to resist the existing accommodation can carry significant penalties, as one defense consultant reported: "Fighting the system gets one blackballed, and future employment are bleak. In this way the industry has come to completely control DOD...even more than its political appointees."[15]

Two additional mechanisms through which members of the corporate-managerial arena attempt to influence decisions made within the executive arena are trade associations and advisory committees. Both of these mechanisms have less to do with manipulating specific technological decision makers in specific decisions than they do with creating and maintaining channels of communications and information between the two arenas. Communication and information can be vital to defense contractors as they seek to stay abreast of weapons program decisions made within the Pentagon.

Trade associations are common throughout the corporate-managerial arena, not simply among those firms that design and build weapons. They serve as communications centers for the various firms involved in an industry and as a spokesman for the interests of the entire industry. They represent an effort by defense contract competitors to pool their resources in order to obtain benefits that help all of the members, as Donald Hall has explained: "Contractors—and their industry associations—are divided by economic self-interest in acquiring the largest possible share of the defense dollar, but the same contractors are unified in common motivation to influence defense procurement and policy."[16]

There are several defense-related trade associations. Among them are Aerospace Industries Association, American Defense Preparedness Association, National Security Industrial Association, Air Force Association, Council of Defense and Space Industry Associations, Association of the U.S. Army, Navy League, Shipbuilders Council of America, and Armed Forces Communications and Electronics Association. According to Gordon Adams, these trade associations meet many needs of individual defense contractors:

> A need for a regular flow of information, especially on forthcoming research and development; general maintenance of the level of defense and space spending; the right to exploit patents developed through contract work; a regular distribution of defense dollars among different types of weapons systems; access to Defense Department and NASA officials in social settings; an influence over defense procurement policy issues in DoD, the White House, (OMB) and Congress.[17]

These trade associations sponsor annual conventions, which are widely attended by military and civilian personnel from the Pentagon. Specialized panels and classified briefings may also take place, along with the distribution of information about forthcoming weapons programs. In Adams's words: "It would be hard to imagine a more efficient setting for gathering information on future R&D trends and becoming acquainted with key procurement and policymaking officials."[18]

Most trade associations also publish newsletters and magazines, providing information on weapons programs, new sources of information on Pentagon planning, discussions of congressional actions, and the like. Trade association representatives regularly testify before Congress, encouraging continued defense spending and supporting specific research and development programs; the associations provide information about the defense industry to DOD and NASA, and information about Pentagon and NASA activities to their members.

Advisory committees also serve as vehicles through which corporate-managerial decision makers maintain regular contacts with Pentagon decision makers and obtain early information about upcoming weapons programs. Defense-related advisory committees are numerous, usually providing scientific and technical advice to the secretary of defense and to the individual military services. The committees are made up of representatives from DOD, scientists familiar with defense science and engineering, and technical personnel from various defense contractors. As such, these committees serve as a very important conduit of information and communication among the corporate-managerial, academic-professional, and executive arenas. Adams lists some of the kinds of advice such committees provide:

- [The] desirable scope, internal balance and, where appropriate, the substance of research, development, engineering, test and evaluation effort that should be pressed by the Dept. of Defense.
- The effectiveness of research and development in providing combat-worthy weapons systems, with attention to prompt and effective utilization of new knowledge; the rapid evaluation of the effectiveness of the projected weapons systems in meeting military requirement.
- [The] preferred management practices and policies for the effective prosecution of these programs.[19]

Since many of the civilian and military decision makers at the Pentagon rely heavily on the advice of technical advisory committees, corporate-managerial decision makers are in a very strong position to influence executive decision making at the earliest stages in the evolution of prospective weapons programs. These activities often serve the interests of the other arenas as well:

[Corporate-managerial] Washington office staffers can become so central to the flow of information that they become the medium for communications between the other [arenas]. According to one Pentagon source, "The best thing about corporate lobbyists is that they pass on to us a lot of stuff that they've learned on Capitol Hill. It's usually the quickest way for us to find out what's happening up there."[20]

Such intense efforts to create and maintain extensive contacts throughout the other arenas pays important dividends for corporate-managerial decision makers. Through corporate participation in advisory committees, attendance at trade association meetings, informal social contacts with Pentagon officials, and so on, defense contractors not only can stay current with ongoing R&D efforts and weapons systems developments, but they also can frequently influence future decisions. The relaxed and relatively free flow of information among technical specialists from all of the relevant arenas allows for considerable cross-fertilization of ideas and concepts, informal discussions of service weapons needs, and other exchanges.

Corporate-Managerial and Legislative Arena Relations

The legislative arena is also critically important to corporate-managerial decision makers. While the executive takes the lead in setting weapons priorities, no funding for defense is possible without congressional appropriations. The committees of Congress can have a huge impact on weapons programs, even those that are rather advanced in their development. Changing perceptions of national priorities, of international tensions, and the like can affect the legislature's willingness to authorize defense spending levels. Thus, corporate-managerial decision makers try to influence the decisions made on Capitol Hill as well. To do this, government relations offices also develop networks of contacts in Congress, especially with members of the major defense-related committees, such as the Armed Services, Appropriations, and Science and Technology. Regular contacts and visits keep the network active, useful as a reserve against those members who question the value of specific weapons systems.

One very important way that corporate-managerial decision makers attempt to influence the decisions made within the legislative arena is through campaign contributions to members of Congress who support defense spending. Defense contractor political action committees (PACs) continue to make significant contributions to the reelection campaigns of politicians known to be sympathetic to defense issues. One study found that eight major defense contractor PACs contributed an average of 59 percent of their funds to the campaigns of congressmen who either have significant defense-related employment in their districts or who serve on House and Senate committees dealing with defense issues. Two PACs, McDonnell Douglas and Lockheed, gave as much as 78 percent, and 67 percent, respectively, of their funds to congressmen from key geographic locales or key congressional committees.[21]

While there is probably no simple, direct connection between specific campaign contributions and specific votes on the floor of Congress, large contributions over several years can make sure that defense lobbyists (often former members of Congress or congressional staffers themselves) receive careful attention when they call upon the members whose reelection has been helped by giving to campaign war chests. The head of McDonnell Douglas's Washington office summarized that defense contractor's views: "We actively support the candidacy of members who would further the interests of the McDonnell Douglas Corporation. We're not going to give to a candidate who consistently recommends that the defense budget be slashed in half. Clearly, if you're on the committee, you can also support the interests, directly, of McDonnell Douglas."[22]

Corporate-managerial decision makers carefully target their campaign contributions to those members of Congress who serve on the crucial Armed Services and Appropriations committees. In a recent congressional election, McDonnell Douglas contributed to the election campaigns of 36 of 39 members of the House Armed Services Committee; Lockheed gave to 36 of 39 as well; Hughes Aircraft gave to 34; General Dynamics to 33; Raytheon to 32; General Electric, 30; Boeing, 29; Rockwell International, 28; and Martin Marietta, 22. That year the ten largest defense contractors contributed a total of $1,544,022 to federal-level campaigns, averaging more than $150,000 for each contractor.[23]

Other financial instruments used by the corporate-managerial arena to influence legislative decisions are speaking honoraria. Paid directly by the corporation or the defense trade association, these honoraria cover the member's costs in attending meetings, delivering speeches, or participating in round-table discussions, symposia, and so on.

A second "revolving door" operates between the corporate-managerial and legislative arenas. Members of Congress who have served on important defense-related committees, upon retirement or loss of an election will often take positions with defense contractors, lobbying before the very committees on which they recently served. Once again, the corporate-managerial decision makers find the former member's legislative knowledge, skill, and contacts very useful in their efforts to induce Congress to make the kinds of technological decisions they desire. In addition, congressional staff members are also valuable acquisitions, since they are also extremely well versed in the legislative process. Bob Adams reports that "[k]nowledgeable sources estimate that at least 30 former congressional staff members—many of whom had key positions with the committees on armed services or appropriations—work for defense firms. Most earn a living buttonholing their ex-colleagues on behalf of the contractors."[24] What is more, those former staffers now can earn incomes sometimes ten times higher than their congressional pay.

One of the most useful ways the corporate-managerial participants manipulate the pressures operating inside the legislative arena is by spreading the subcontracts that come from large weapons contracts among as many congressional districts as possible. With those subcontracts go jobs for voters back home. Nationwide, in fact, some 2.9 million American jobs derive from the manufacture of weapons,[25] and the potential loss of jobs through failure to support weapons manufacturing can be a very effective motivator of congressional support. After all, defense contractors are often the largest employer not only within a congressional district but within the state as a whole.

A classic example is Rockwell International's B-1 bomber. This multi-billion-dollar, technologically sophisticated aircraft has components produced and supplied by 35 major subcontractors and 3,000 suppliers in 48 states. The number of jobs directly related to the B-1 program is huge: 25,200 in California, 16,200 in Ohio, 8,800 in New York, 6,400 in Washington, 5,000 in Oklahoma, 4,800 in Maryland, 4,000 in Tennessee, 3,300 in Texas, 3,300 in Kansas, 3,000 in Georgia,

2,200 in Massachusetts, 1,500 in New Jersey, 1,100 in Florida, 1,100 in Connecticut, 1,000 in Michigan, and lesser numbers in other states.[26]

Not only do corporate-managerial decision makers gain an individual congressional ally by placing subcontracts in his or her district, but they also gain an unofficial, in-house congressional lobbyist, as the affected members press their colleagues to support the specific weapons programs made in their districts. As one defense lobbyist put it: "The more congressmen you have saying to the chairman [of a congressional committee], "I have an interest in this," the more likely you are to win."[27] And the defense contractors make sure that each member knows precisely how much money, and how many jobs, are staked on the future of specific weapons programs.

Additional lobbying pressure is brought to bear on members of Congress when defense contractors orchestrate constituent groups to inundate the member with letters, telegrams, telephone calls, and personal visits. Local business and political leaders are flown to Washington to press for continued legislative support, while local labor unions are encouraged to urge continued funding. These grassroots campaigns are organized and managed, once again, by the corporation's government relations offices in Washington.

Corporate-Managerial
and Academic-Professional Arena Relations

It is estimated that up to 30 percent of the nation's 600,000 scientists and engineers are in some way involved in defense. Of these, the majority work in university laboratories under DOD research grants, although many work in government laboratories as well. By and large, they enjoy not only larger salaries than their brothers and sisters who do not work in the defense area but also a variety of other advantages, such as state-of-the-art research facilities and cutting edge theoretical problems to wrestle with.

However, working for defense contractors or for the government directly carries some professional burdens as well. The necessity for secrecy in defense work imposes itself both when a scientist or engineer enters into the work, through the required security checks and clearances, and while the work is done. Defense scientists are not ordinarily allowed to publish the results of their classified work and often are kept in the dark about the related work of other defense scientists. Also, there is the problem of overspecialization:

> Whereas in nonclassified work both the company and the employee generally benefit from a rich and continuous cross-fertilization of ideas, this is not and cannot be so to the same extent in the blinkered environment of classified work. Rather, one tends to become an expert in a narrowly defined area, while the balance of one's training suffers from disuse. Professionally, this is the kiss of death in fields in which entire technological revolutions take place on the order of every five years.[28]

To spend several years working in a narrowly defined area in defense can make it very difficult to transfer to nondefense work, since the skills honed in defense are often of little value in the civilian market. Given the unsteady and largely unpredictable fluctuations in defense spending from year to year, a scientist or engineer devoted to defense work may also be at greater risk of losing his or her job. The experiences of highly skilled and trained engineers working for NASA show clearly the risks involved, as many such persons were unable to find professional work in their area of specialization after being let go by the government.

We might expect that in the relationship among decision makers from the corporate-managerial, executive, and academic-professional arenas, those in the academic-professional arena are in the weakest position for influencing the decisions made in the other two arenas. And this is surely true, in the general sense that scientists and engineers, unless they have other sources of support, must depend on defense contractors or the federal government for their employment. Some scientists work in university laboratories and have thereby an added degree of independence. Yet even here a scientist may find himself or herself heavily dependent on Defense Department research grants. It is probably only those scientists or engineers who possess paramount expertise in certain critical fields who are in a position to impose their own conditions on participants from the other two arenas.

For scientists of national and international reputation in areas vital to defense work, there can be many opportunities to influence decision making within the executive and corporate-managerial arenas, and in the legislative arena as well, although through somewhat different mechanisms. Often such scientists will be brought in during the early, formative stages in weapons development through service on those advisory councils mentioned earlier. It is here, before a weapons program has taken on much momentum and when ideas are exchanged and challenged, that a scientist can help to shape the program the most. After a program is underway, it is much harder to affect.

Science advice from respected experts is a valuable bureaucratic and political weapon, and for some scientists a common avenue for political influence. Some scientists, serving on the President's Science Advisory Committee or as presidential science adviser, can exercise considerable formal and informal influence on executive arena decision making. Similarly, such respected defense experts can influence legislative decision making through testimony before the relevant authorization and appropriations committees.

However, most scientists and engineers involved in defense work are not so well connected with the centers of political power. Historically, for such outsider scientists and engineers, the most effective way to influence decisions made in the corporate-managerial, executive, or legislative arenas has been through public political action or protest.

Ever since the first atomic bomb was detonated and later used against Japan during World War II, a small but vocal group of defense scientists and engineers have expressed moral ambivalence about their work. Concerned about the terribly destructive forces they have unleashed, these concerned professionals have often led efforts to curb the arms race, to support arms control agreements, and to urge the creation of an international structure of control of atomic and nuclear weapons. While mostly working on the outside of the policy process, that is, not within the central decision-making circles in Washington, these scientists have occasionally had victories (see, for example, Primack and von Hipple[29]). In a broad sense, however, such efforts have had little long-lasting impact on the weapons development process.

President Ronald Reagan's Strategic Defense Initiative (SDI, sometimes called Star Wars) program triggered a ground swell of protest from many members of the academic-professional arena. Citing different motives—from SDI's probable impact on the arms race, to doubts about the program's technical feasibility, to worries about SDI's impact upon other research priorities, to personal moral concerns about participating in the arms race—several thousand scientists and engineers in U.S. and Canadian universities signed petitions protesting the program and pledging neither to seek nor accept SDI funding from the Pentagon.

What is significant about this effort to organize a kind of boycott of SDI among scientists and engineers is the choice of tactic by the scientists and engineers involved. This segment of the academic-professional arena clearly lacks the insider influence possessed by some other scientists and engineers. Being unable to shape the SDI program by participating in the early discussions within the defense community, these members of the academic-professional arena feel that their only point of leverage on the executive arena is through public protest. They also hope that such public displays will influence decisions within the legislative arena, probably less by changing the minds of members of Congress than by giving debating ammunition to those in Congress who already oppose the program. They hope to use their scientific reputations for political goals, just as the executive arena hopes to use the scientific reputations of their scientists and engineers for opposing political purposes.

HOW THE DOMINANT CONFIGURATION OPERATES

How do all of these relationships among participants in different technological decision-making arenas affect weapons development? What kind of military system does this dominant configuration produce?

One feature of corporate-managerial participants in this dominant configuration is predominance of engineers within defense firms. Often between 30 and 50 percent of the total factory work force of the typical defense firm are engineers and scientists,[30] from designer to program manager to corporate officer. One result of this is the considerable emphasis on technology and R&D within defense firms as the preferred solution to military problems, an emphasis that is no doubt communicated to Pentagon officials.

Such firms tend also to be risk minimizers, more interested in technical modifications of existing weapons than on introducing completely new weapons concepts. Jacques Gansler comments:

> An additional effect of this number of engineers in a given plant is that considerable R&D money is spent on engineering work done on systems that are already in

production, rather than on new systems. This practice accounts for the very large number of changes which take place on a typical defense item during its production phase. Frequently the presence of these engineers simply results in changes for the sake of change; for example, where an improvement in capability is only marginal, but the increase in cost is quite significant. In fact, there are many who argue that it is this heavy emphasis on engineering throughout the acquisition process...that results in the so-called technological imperative being the largest single driving force in weapon system development; "because we can do it, we must do it" —regardless of the need or the cost.[31]

Thus, Gansler provides additional evidence that technology, not strategy, too often drives the weapons development process. He continues:

...this technical workforce tends to consume an enormous amount of government R&D expenditure on full-scale developments of weapons systems, where they are doing largely routine work on converting feasibility-demonstrated systems into production drawings and the like—which again uses up government R&D money that could be spent on far more creative activity, more "leading edge of technology" work. Thus these large percentages of engineers in each defense-industry facility tend to result in a very significant share of the work being done on the less creative aspects of R&D.[32]

Here Gansler differs from other critics of the defense industry who argue that it is exciting, exotic new technologies that pull the arms race along. Scientists and engineers, according to this scenario, pursue the latest and most modern technical concepts, and sell these concepts to the Pentagon.[33] Gansler argues, instead, that most defense-related R&D work is often actually focused on modifications of existing weapons lines, not on new, path-breaking concepts. The impetus, according to Gansler, is still technological, but of a more conservative and routine sort.

Indeed, some critics urge that the essentially conservative technological orientation of the major defense contractors has produced a military loaded down with weapons that are too technologically complex. One critic, Mary Kaldor, writes that one "consequence of this elaborate combination of [technological] conservatism and technical dynamism is what economists call 'diminishing returns': more and more effort is expended for smaller improvements in military effectiveness."[34]

It is also clear that those members of the corporate-managerial arena who participate in defense constitute a highly concentrated industry, with relatively few very large weapons manufacturers thoroughly dominating the industry. Such concentration has created in reality a two-tiered defense industry, with a small number of very large prime contractors surrounded by a shrinking array of smaller subcontractors and suppliers.

In recent years there has been a trend toward vertical integration, as the prime contractors either have expanded to be able to do both the R&D work on new weapons concepts and the production of the weapon, once approved, or the prime contractors have bought up previously independent large and small subcontractors. As Gansler notes:

An increasing amount of vertical integration has been taking place in the defense industry for a variety of reasons—for example, to maintain market share, to assure capability for bidding on new programs, to assure the availability of critical parts (in the presence of rapidly diminishing sources), and because of the financial problems at the lower tiers of the defense industry. Thus, subcontractors are being absorbed by prime contractors, and many of the prime contractors are building their own parts sources—for example, their integrated-circuits laboratories and their fabrication facilities for composite materials.[35]

There are a number of reasons for such concentration, many of which evolve from the kinds of decisions that are made in other arenas. For instance, only the larger firms are able to support the high overhead costs of the literally thousands of accounting, auditing, reporting, and security requirements imposed by Congress and the Pentagon. Also, the unpredictability of congressional funding for defense, with budgetary changes occurring from year to year, means that many smaller firms cannot enter or remain in the industry, since they lack the surplus needed to weather the lean years.

Another executive arena decision that affects how the corporate-managerial decision makers operate is the tendency for the Pentagon to award full-scale production contracts, on a single-source basis, to the same firm that submitted the most attractive R&D proposal in the first place. That is, after the R&D phase has been successfully completed and the new weapon has been approved for mass production, DOD tends to give the highly profitable production contract to the same firm that did the original R&D.

What this means is that for a defense firm to win the production contract, it must first win the R&D contract. To do this, it often intentionally accepts financial losses by submitting unrealistically low-cost R&D contract bids—what is called "buying in"—in order to get the profitable production contract. The firm then hopes to recoup its R&D underbid over the several years that it will be producing the weapon. Indeed, the company will likely earn a substantial profit, since the originally approved weapon design will very likely be modified several times during the decade-long production run. What is more, once the production contract is secured, the firm is likely to be the only company making this particular weapon, its "single source."

Gansler estimates that about 60 percent of DOD contracts are awarded on a noncompetitive, single-source basis. Thus, the largest number of executive arena weapons production decisions are competitive only in the early R&D phase. After that, competition disappears, as the winning company gets to handle the entire production of the weapon. Gansler concludes:

The approach of early competition followed by sole-source contracting through the remainder of the program provides no incentives for cost reductions either in the R&D program or later in the production program. In fact, the incentives are in exactly the opposite direction: the contractor is encouraged to increase the development and production costs as much as possible, because this maximizes profits, and because in a sole-source environment there is no risk attached to doing so.[36]

In these and in other ways, we see that substantial advantages for corporate-managerial participants in this dominant configuration derive from the careful cultivation of decision makers in other arenas. One excellent example of such advantages can be seen in the Independent Research and Development and Bid and Proposal Programs (IR&D/B&P) of the Department of Defense. These programs, which "represent a hidden billion-dollar-a-year pipeline for military research and development funds that are doled out free of Congressional control,"[37] reimburse defense contractors for independent R&D projects that they undertake on their own without a DOD contract (IR&D) and for the costs contractors incur while preparing formal bids and proposals for government contracts (B&P). The funds used in these two programs are generally free of congressional oversight and review because

> sums devoted to IR&D/ B&P are hidden in the budget as components of ordinary line items for contract research, development and procurement. Thus, Congress does not know the details of the programs. Moreover, since the projects are lumped into the contractor's overhead for all military R&D projects, and since these costs are not always audited, the Pentagon itself is not exactly sure how much it is spending each year for IR&D/B&P. In 1978 "estimated" IR&D/B&P costs of $1.24 billion amounted to 11 percent of the total budget for "Research, Development, Test and Evaluation," but 31 percent of the budgeted program for "Research, Exploratory Development, and Advanced Development," the earliest states of the R&D process.[38]

Moreover, contractors are allowed to shift their claims for reimbursement back and forth between the two categories, since there are no common standards to separate IR&D claims from B&P claims. While contractors do not necessarily recover 100 percent of their claims, some firms can recover the vast majority of their expenses: "Companies are allowed to recover their IR&D/B&P costs in proportion to the Government's share of their total business. In other words, if 90 percent of a company's business is with the Pentagon and NASA, then the taxpayers pick up 90 percent of its independent research and bidding expenses."[39]

These funds have played important roles in the early development of a number of major weapons programs, including the B-1 bomber, cruise missiles, high-energy lasers, space-based surveillance systems, precision-guided munitions, and others.

Not only do IR&D/B&P funds reimburse defense contractors for their independent R&D efforts, they serve as an entrée for influencing DOD decision making:

> As it works now, the IR&D/B&P programs have come to play a formative role in weapons-acquisitions policy. A 1974 study by the defense industry of the IR&D/B&P programs noted that "on occasion, contractors have recognized Government needs, and have had solutions for a critical deficiency, prior to its recognition by the Government." A less polite description of this practice is that contractors, in their efforts to get an inside track on new military business, routinely peddle the results of their IR&D programs to the military officials in charge of identifying new military "requirements," and *succeed in inducing them to invent a requirement to fit a new weapon* instead of the other way around.[40]

Weapons contractors energetically defend the programs, claiming that they stimulate competition for federal contracts. The evidence suggests, instead, that the programs actually reinforce the industrial concentration characteristic of the defense industry. For example, in 1978, the top ten contractors received 50 percent of the dollar value of IR&D/B&P payments made to more than 90 contractors, while the top 25 contractors received 78 percent of the programs' funding.[41] Nor do the programs' funds go toward breakthroughs in science and technology, as Christopher Paine and Gordon Adams note:

> Air Force and Department of Defense reports [indicate] that 65 percent of all IR&D money is spent not on searching for the "scientific breakthroughs of tomorrow" but rather on relatively short-term projects aimed at winning new defense business. B&P efforts, by their very nature, are even more attuned to bringing home the next contract than pushing back the frontiers of science.... The bulk of the innovations IR&D/B&P–funded projects do produce takes the form of minor incremental improvements in many different military technology areas.[42]

In these and in dozens of other ways the various decision-making arenas involved in weapons development—and the individual technological decision makers who work within them—have worked out predictable accommodations with each other. They have devised a wide variety of ways in which decision makers in each arena help out decision makers in the others. This requires careful attention to the specific pressures, constraints, ambitions, and limitations operating in each arena and a willingness to manipulate those pressures in ways likely to induce individual technological decision makers to make the "right" or desired decisions. Because all of the participants understand the rules of the game, they can conserve resources that often must be employed in shaping multiarena decisions outside a dominant configuration.

CASE STUDIES

Let's review some specific instances of technological decision making about weapons systems to see how the participants involved worked to influence each others' decisions. We will do this for two cases: the development of MIRVs (multiple independently targetable reentry vehicles) and the effort to develop ballistic missile defense systems (the Strategic Defense Initiative, sometimes called Star Wars). Unlike many analyses of these weapons, our concern will not be with their strategic wisdom, or lack thereof, but with the internal mechanisms that affected how the decisions were reached in each case. We will try to decide if the technologies involved controlled or determined the outcome of the decision processes.

The Development of MIRV

One of the most important technological developments in the entire post–World War II era was the deployment of multiple independently targetable reentry vehicles, or MIRVs. A MIRVd missile, unlike conventional ICBMs, carries more than one nuclear warhead; indeed, the larger MIRVd missiles may carry as many as 10 to 15 warheads. What is more, these multiple warheads can be directed toward separate, independent targets. The warheads rise aloft within a "strategic bus" on top of the missile. Once the bus separates from the missile, it continues along its trajectory, periodically "dropping off" one after another of its lethal passengers, each warhead then falling ballistically toward its own target, possibly hundreds of miles away from the targets of other warheads carried on the same missile.

The story of the evolution of the MIRV technology is a classic case of a series of emerging technologies coalescing into a nearly unstoppable technological project. It is a technology that met so many diverse needs of organizations and individuals involved in the military services, in the Pentagon, in the laboratories, and in the boardrooms of defense contractors that, by some accounts, virtually nothing could have stopped its development and deployment:

> MIRV was clearly a technology whose time had come. It was firmly grounded in the technical developments of the 1950s and was primarily an extrapolation of concepts of the same period.... It was rapidly accepted within both the military and civilian sides of the Defense Department, with only a brief and scattered resistance. All concerned increasingly saw MIRV as a solution to their own particular problems.[43]

Thus, while MIRVing American missiles—and Soviet missiles, too—has fundamentally altered the nature of the strategic relationship between the superpowers, and in the opinion of many made that relationship more precarious, it did not constitute a fundamental alteration of ballistic missile technology. Rather, it was an extension and elaboration of existing technologies and applied to new tasks.

The Air Force's Ballistic Systems Division (BSD) had been the agency responsible for the development of the Minuteman ICBM force. BSD and aerospace contractors maintained direct, rapid, and informal communication channels, so that new opportunities and new mission requirements were widely discussed by individuals from both public and private organizations. Indeed, most new projects began within BSD as a result of the interplay between their personnel and their industrial contacts. "Ideas would bounce back and forth for a while until a firm proposal was generated and a contracting team was on board. It would then be presented to the Air Staff for approval and the issuing of formal requirements."[44] Moreover, defense contractors frequently served as advocates for new systems, using their extensive contacts within the civilian level at the Pentagon, as well as in Congress and the White House.

In the Navy, SP (Special Projects Office) headed up the development of the Polaris and Poseidon submarine-launched ballistic missile systems, the Navy's MIRV projects. Unlike BSD, SP did not maintain extensive contacts with the outside scientific community, instead working with naval research scientists and engineers.

It is largely in the interactions among three executive arena agencies—the Air Force's BSD, the Navy's SP, and the Director of Defense Research & Engineering (DDR&E)—along with the defense contractors from the corporate-managerial arena and scientists and engineers from the academic-professional arena, that we find the technical origins of MIRV. These groups and contractors make up a "technological community" with common interests in the development of newer, state-of-the-art missile technologies.

For this technological community, MIRV offered a number of advantages. For BSD, MIRV promised additional work on new and interesting projects, something the agency needed in order to maintain the morale and job satisfaction of its highly skilled technicians and engineers. BSD's desire for new, state-of-the-art missile systems was aided and encouraged by members of the aerospace industry, with whom BSD maintained close contacts. The Special Projects Office of the Navy also benefited from the MIRV program. Graham Allison summarizes much of the technical community's interest in MIRV this way: "The technical community seems to have been driven by the "sweetness" of the technology and the researchers' competitive instinct, which was aroused primarily by U.S. ABM research, since little was known about actual Soviet ABM activity."[45]

The "sweetness" Allison refers to is the technical challenge of developing a way of delivering separately targetable warheads accurately to their targets. The concept itself emerged from a program initially intended for developing penetration aids to overcome a potential Soviet ABM system. The "penaids" project was looking into ways of placing decoys and other elements into the warhead of existing missiles which would be dispersed as the warhead reentered the atmosphere, thereby confusing and overwhelming any defensive system. It was a small theoretical jump to go from uncontrollable "penaids" onboard a missile to independently targetable warheads instead. Solving the technical problems of guidance, lift weights, warhead yields, and so on was a very attractive challenge for the technical community.

The inner dynamic of the technical community was greatly facilitated by the diffusion of technical information among executive arena technical agencies, corporate-managerial arena defense contractors, and academic-professional arena scientists and engineers. Ted Greenwood comments:

> By 1963 the need for both improved penetration capability and more warheads was widely felt in the technical community dealing with strategic missiles. By then, too, technical advances in a variety of areas made the idea of a maneuvering bus seem readily feasible to many people in that community. Because of the extensive mobility of individuals and the rapid diffusion of information and ideas within the technical community each specialist was aware of developments and needs in related areas. The penetration people who were busy designing decoys and deployment mechanisms for multiple warhead and decoy system knew the prognostications about guidance and warhead size, and the weapons and guidance people understood the problems faced by the decoy designers.[46]

With this high level of regularized contact among decision makers from different arenas concerned with strategic missiles, Greenwood concludes that

> MIRV was originally conceived by the technical and industrial community that supports the service missile organizations and was suggested to these organizations and to DDR&E by this community. Because it was not viewed as a new weapon system, but only as an improvement of one that was already authorized or being planned, it was able to advance quite far in conceptual design without receiving explicit authorization from either the services or DDR&E. Unlike a new bomber or a new missile system which requires substantial funding and the Secretary's authorization before it advances very far, MIRV moved through its early stages purely on the initiative of the technical community.[47]

Coordinating and overseeing the activities of both Air Force and Navy technical agencies was the Director of Defense Research and Engineering. DDR&E served as the chief liaison between the technical agencies within the services and the political leadership, especially the secretary of defense. Its responsibilities included the general oversight of weapons research and development activities throughout the Pentagon, giving political leadership to the technical agencies and technical advice to the political leaders. DDR&E was deeply involved in the MIRV programs of both the Air Force and the Navy.

MIRV played a different set of roles at the civilian leadership level at the Pentagon, where strategic and domestic political considerations dominated purely technical ones. Secretary of Defense Robert McNamara favored MIRV because it met both sets of objectives so well. At the strategic level, MIRV technology offered both a way of responding to potential Soviet ABM developments and of giving U.S. forces an enhanced capacity to target Soviet military installations. On the domestic side, MIRV served two functions, too. On the one hand, it offered the secretary of defense an inexpensive way of expanding the U.S. nuclear arsenal without having to approve costly new missile systems. It also helped the secretary to resist efforts by the armed services to obtain greater funding for new strategic forces; the Air Force had strongly resisted the Pentagon's decision to limit the deployment of Minuteman missiles. Ronald Tammen summarizes the domestic political pressures facing McNamara:

> The administration had rapidly overbuilt the U.S. strategic force as confirmed by the more reliable satellite estimates of Soviet deployments. Yet the pressure for more land-based missiles continued for parochial and "worst case" reasons. The secretary of defense, with his emphasis on effectiveness and his back door battle against additional Minuteman deployments, seized on MIRV as the technological solution to domestic military and political pressures.[48]

Tammen then goes on to discuss the domination of domestic over strategic concerns in the MIRV decision:

> In a real sense, MIRV was seen as an arms control device, not vis-à-vis the USSR, but as an alternative to domestic pressures for more armaments. Little or no thought

was given to the long-range effect of MIRV deployment. It was time-urgent and solution-wise. Even at the policy level, the guiding forces were domestic rather than international.[49]

Tactical and strategic considerations, such as responding to specific Soviet actions, actually played a minimal role in the early decisions to develop MIRV. As Tammen has noted: "The engineering origin of MIRV was only remotely related to specific Soviet intentions or capabilities."[50] Indeed, the strategic arguments offered by MIRV's supporters—from the secretary of defense to the defense contractors to the scientific and technical communities—changed over time as the public debate shifted. At one point or another, MIRV was defended as the best possible response to a potential Soviet antiballistic missile defensive system, as an excellent hard-target killer, and as the most economical way to expand the U.S. strategic arsenal, among others. Tammen concludes:

> Repeatedly one is drawn to the two facts that most characterize MIRV: that it was justifiable by a wide set of circumstances and that it was responsive to domestic pressures. The lesson for defense planners is to design a weapons system that will change with the times and possess great versatility politically and militarily. The lesson for arms controllers may well be to concentrate on bureaucratic and domestic factors as determinants of weapon system development, rather than on the programs of potential adversaries.[51]

The evidence is clear that the origins of the idea of placing several independently targetable warheads on a single missile can be traced to several ongoing strategic projects scattered within the technological community, none of which was specifically trying to invent MIRV. In effect, as Greenwood notes, "MIRV was 'invented' almost simultaneously in several places within the technical community."[52] When the advances made in these other programs were brought together, the technical community saw the possibility of MIRV. And when that technical possibility was joined to a host of organizational, political, and strategic aims being pursued by many individual decision makers scattered throughout the government, defense contractors, and the technological community, the MIRV program took on its seeming inevitability.

The Strategic Defense Initiative

Our second case study focuses on the Strategic Defense Initiative, a very ambitious research and development program intended to discover if it is possible to defend the United States against Soviet ballistic missiles. A multi-billion-dollar program, SDI involves the development of a whole host of exotic space-based technologies—laser beams, particle beams, pumped x-ray lasers, rail-guns, and others—which has led the media to dub the program "Star Wars," after the very popular science fiction motion picture. If SDI succeeds—in fact, even if it is pursued and ultimately fails—the program portends the most significant change in superpower strategic relations since the invention of atomic weapons.

SDI differs from other cases because it was established as a research program, not a development and deployment program. Its goals are to develop and evaluate technologies potentially useful to a future ballistic missile defense; thus, the effort is exploratory rather than operational. This is in recognition, even by SDI's strongest supporters, that the major technologies needed for ballistic missile defense are still on the drawing boards and that a great deal of technical development will be needed before any weapons system can be declared worthy of actual prototype development or testing.

Unlike the MIRV, SDI is a weapons system—more accurately, a whole series of weapons systems—that received its impetus from the political arena rather than the technical community. The decision to proceed with the Strategic Defense Initiative appears to have been made very nearly exclusively by one person, President Ronald Reagan, and over the scientific and technical doubts of many of his national security staff. Jonathan B. Stein details many of the technical reservations voiced by some of the leading defense specialists inside and outside the administration. The president, however, sought a fundamental change in U.S. strategic policy:

> The principal Reagan defense advisors have from the first been hostile to MAD, SALT, and all the accompanying acronymic concepts brought forth by the age of offense-dominated deterrence. They shun MAD because, under its terms, one must accept parity (strategic equivalence) with Moscow. The 1980 Republican platform called for a resurgence in military spending to attain America's long-lost strategic superiority. In the nuclear era, however, there is only one way for either side to achieve meaningful superiority—through developing the means, if feasible, to defend one's territory and military forces against opposing nuclear weapons.[53]

Although Reagan was elected in 1980 by a stunning landslide, the average person in the United States did not share some of the Reagan administration's early readiness to act belligerently toward the Soviet Union. Indeed, administration officials' calm discussions of possible "nuclear warning shots" in Europe should the Warsaw Pact invade, plus the administration's obvious distaste for continued arms control negotiations with the Soviets, led to a ground swell of public concern and fear. In response, the administration toned down its harsh rhetoric about the USSR being an "evil empire." Still, as Stein continues:

> ...many of the top appointees [in the Reagan administration] did not relinquish their longer-term objective of regaining superiority. As uncomfortable as ever with MAD...the Reagan national security officials could turn only to BMD [Ballistic Missile Defense] as the preferred alternative to building more MAD systems, with increasingly limited support, or engaging in sustained arms control negotiations that ultimately reinforce nuclear parity and undermine the nation's will to pursue strategic defense.[54]

President Reagan's idea of launching the Strategic Defense Initiative produced quite a stir among defense and national security specialists, in large measure because it flew directly in the face of the dominant theory of nuclear deterrence: the doctrine of mutually assured destruction (MAD). According to MAD, both superpowers agree to leave their civilian populations vulnerable to nuclear attack, while their respective nuclear arsenals are to be protected from preemptive attack. In this reversal of traditional military strategy, each side is deterred from launching a surprise first strike against the other by the certain knowledge that the victim would still be able to launch a terribly destructive counterattack, regardless of how intense the first strike was. The tremendously destructive nuclear weapons in each arsenal means that both sides would be devastated in a nuclear war; there could be no victor and no victory for attacker or attacked.

Adam Garfinkle finds some additional motives for the Reagan decision: SDI served to divert public attention and split popular support for the rapidly spreading nuclear freeze movement in the United States, as well as the growing anti-nuclear movement in Western Europe, to bypass the endless debates in Congress over the MX missile, and to blunt criticisms of Reagan administration hostility toward arms control.[55]

Stein tells us that, while there had been a continuous small-scale research program in BMD, many within the defense community were caught unawares by Reagan's dramatic SDI proposal. Many scientists and engineers familiar with the existing technologies and with reasonable projections of where those technologies might be in the near-term, felt that the president's goal of making ICBMs "impotent and obsolete" was unrealistic. Indeed, some within the Pentagon began almost at once to tone down the president's ambitious goals. They began speaking of BMD that would be used not to protect population centers, cities, and so on, but would protect missile sites, thereby adding assurance to the missiles' survivability and ability to retaliate. This led the president and his advisers, especially Secretary of Defense Casper Weinberger, to publicly repudiate the "protect the missiles" approach. This, after all, would amount to a reaffirmation of MAD, a strategic doctrine the president wanted to abandon.

The SDI program split the academic-professional arena, with many scientists, at well-known, prestigious universities signing pledges refusing SDI funding for their research. However, the program promised a very large increment in federal funding for basic and applied research, and, as Jeff Hecht notes, "One thing is clear: money is a powerful lure for grant-hungry scientists. Some of those who initially sneered at the program have begun to change their tune, publicly at least."[56]

Indeed, in 1985, universities and university-managed laboratories received more than $34 million in SDI funding. However, nearly half of that amount actually went to three off-campus facilities that regularly work for the military: Lawrence Livermore National Laboratory ($2,085,000) and Los Alamos National Laboratory ($3,046,000), both operated by the University of California, and the Lincoln Laboratory ($10,200,000), operated by the Massachusetts Institute of Technology.[57] Among the universities, the big winners were the University of Texas, which received $5.1 million; Georgia Institute of Technology, $4.5 million; and Utah State University $2.4 million.

If the universities lined up for SDI monies, they still do not compare with defense contractors. Members of the corporate-managerial arena have sought SDI funding eagerly, as Fred Hiatt and Rick Atkinson relate: "Inside the arms industry, strategic defense—Star Wars—is now tacitly viewed as the greatest prospect for profit ever."[58]

Here we have a clear example of the dominant configuration at work, forming the required cross-arena relationships needed to institutionalize the SDI program. As Hiatt and Atkinson note:

> The military-industrial complex, as President Dwight D. Eisenhower called the peculiar marriage of public and private defense interests, has in the past 30 months cobbled together a miniature replica of itself—a kind of Star Complex—complete with Star War lobbyists, Star Wars newsletters and Star Wars division vice presidents. As Star Wars is intended to shield the United States from enemy warheads, so the Star Complex hopes to defend this new business opportunity against any threat, including political potshots, technical naysayers and irksome arms-control agreements.[59]

Many of the largest defense contractors have sought, and received, substantial SDI contracts (see Table 7-1), and are eager to see that the program is continued. They work together to influence policymakers, especially in Congress, to maintain—better, to increase—federal funding. What they hope to do is to create a mobilized constituency supporting SDI, a constituency made up of the scientists and engineers whose jobs are at stake, of the communities where SDI funding would occur, of labor unions interested in gaining lucrative contracts, and, ultimately, of members of Congress dedicated to protecting important spending programs in their districts. As SDI critic John E. Pike comments: "It [SDI] hasn't yet become a jobs program. It will become a jobs program, but you have a couple of years to debate it on the merits."[60]

The corporate-managerial arena is interested in SDI not only for the direct profits it promises for defensive technologies. It is also interested for the potential commercial spinoffs the program will generate. One estimate of the total commercial potential for SDI technologies ranges between $5 trillion and $20 trillion in private-sector sales.[61] No one can tell this far in advance what kinds of scientific and technological breakthroughs will result from the program, but many expect to see innovations in ceramics, computers, miniaturization, radar, lasers, particle beams, and a dozen others. For corporate-managerial decision makers, these kinds of potential technical innovations are simply too attractive to pass up.

By tying SDI to local employment and federal contracts and to foreign nations as technological partners, and by emphasizing the potential commercial spinoffs, supporters of SDI hope to institutionalize their cause to such an extent that no future president could sensibly cancel the program. Pike voices a concern of SDI opponents: "The ultimate question is whether this develops such a constituency that it leaves the realm of sensible discourse so that by the time we have a new president, it's too late."[62] Harvey Brooks expresses similar sentiments:

Table 7–1
Top Star Wars Contractors as of 1985 (in millions of dollars)

Company	SDI Contracts Awarded
Teledyne Brown	$237.1
Boeing	211.8
Rockwell International	204.4
McDonnell Douglas	199.0
Lockheed	195.8
TRW	186.8
LTV Aerospace	114.3
Hughes	98.3
AVCO Corporation	77.2
BDM Corporation	62.0
Aerojet General	51.9
Honeywell	43.3
General Research	42.7
Science Applications	37.9
RCA	35.7
Martin Marietta	33.8
Litton Systems	33.3
Grumman	32.1
Nicols Research	30.1
General Dynamics	27.9
Ford Aerospace	25.7
General Motors	24.3

Source: Fred Hiatt and Rick Atkinson, "Space: The Defense Contractors' Final Frontier," *Washington Post National Weekly Edition,* November 4, 1985, p. 10.

The size and duration of the SDI effort imply the creation of enormous vested interests against program changes and the necessity for a continuous political selling job on the part of several successive administrations. The possible effects of this high-pressure salesmanship on the American political process are troubling. *Recent worries about the political influence of the military-industrial complex may pale beside what will be generated by SDI.*[63]

Just as in the past, the dominant configuration has worked to protect established weapons technologies and to work out acceptable, if competitive, relationships for defense contractors, today these same arena decision makers are trying to construct a protective zone within which they may continue to compete for SDI funding.

These efforts, while successful enough during the Reagan years, have not succeeded as well under the Bush administration. While President Bush continues to support the Strategic Defense Initiative and to recommend robust funding for the program, the Congress has been reluctant to appropriate as much money as the President wants.

Three factors seem to have undermined support for SDI in Congress. The end of the Cold War, symbolized by the fall of the Berlin Wall in 1989, and the continued turmoil inside the Soviet Union, have made SDI seem less urgent. The crippling size of the federal deficit makes massive funding for programs like SDI harder to justify, when domestic programs are facing cuts. And, finally, the eagerness of SDI supporters to put some version of Star Wars into space before the program is killed outright by Congress, has led to charges that SDI's managers have skimped on testing the system's components. Following the Challenger disaster, the problems with the Hubble Space Telescope, and other recent mechanical failures of high-ticket scientific equipment, Congress is unwilling to be rushed into funding SDI programs before they are fully tested. Without a threatening enemy to defend against, facing the need for substantial federal spending cuts, and challenged with cutting corners in testing, the Dominant Configuration supporting SDI may be unable to protect the program from its opponents.

CONCLUSIONS

The interactions of many arena decision makers are constrained by some important limitations that directly affect the amount of influence the various arenas have in final decisions. For instance, the coordination of the efforts of literally thousands of individual scientists, engineers, technicians, and bureaucrats over the several years, or even decades, required to bring a new weapon concept to fruition can create a considerable amount of program momentum, as years of work and personal careers hinge on the successful completion of the different stages of project developments. The expenditure of so much effort, resources, talent, and money cannot stop easily or quickly.

Indeed, as a specific weapons project develops and grows, members of the affected military services and civilian bureaucracies gradually come to see the project as necessary, whether for the sake of agency funding and mission or for personal reasons. To obtain continued support for the project, they subtly help shape the alternatives presented to higher level policymakers, moving them to see the project as necessary and inevitable. By the time the decision arrives at the highest levels of government, considerable consensus may already exist pushing policymakers to fund and deploy the system.

Although the strategic concerns of the elected government—the president and Congress—continue to be important in weapons development—the SDI case is the best recent example—that importance is diminished. Often, the real source of ideas for new weapons and the rationale for adopting them come from within the technological community, reflecting the interests of the contracting corporations and scientific and technical personnel as much as those of the military services. The MIRV also illustrates this point.

The truly important decisions about new weapons must be made many years before the conditions for the need and use of such weapons are clearly known, and are often made first by lower echelon officials who then work to convince higher ranking people to support their decisions. Thus, the role of major policymakers is often reduced to selecting from a list of prepackaged options presented to them by technological communities committed to continued weapons development.

The realities of the arms race have been called "an intranational action-reaction phenomenon."[64] This suggests that the real arms race may occur within the technological communities of each nation, with scientists, engineers, and technicians on each side extrapolating from the latest scientific findings to potential technical advances conceivably available to the other side and then trying to find ways of countering such possible breakthroughs. In a perverse way, the technological communities on both sides may race against their own technical projections as much or more than they race against the actual steps taken by the other side.

The arms race, thus, is deeply embedded within the technical communities of both sides, as both try to survey the possible technical breakthroughs the other might be working on. The combination of the technically possible and the bureaucratically and/or politically useful provides the "technological exuberance" that pushes the arms race along. The strongest incentives are for individual technological decision makers to remain within the dominant configuration that has benefited them so well, despite periodic internal squabbles and public displeasure. The close, working relationships among corporate-managerial defense contractors, laboratories and universities, Pentagon procurement offices, and legislators, have by now become so well known to all the players that there is little reason to seriously challenge the arrangement.

ENDNOTES

1. JEROME SLATER and TERRY NARDIN, "The Concept of a Military-Industrial Complex," in *Testing the Theory of the Military-Industrial Complex*, ed. Steven Rosen, (Lexington, Mass.: Lexington Books, 1973), pp. 27–61.

2. MARC PILISUK and THOMAS HAYDEN, "Is There a Military-Industrial Complex?" in *The Military-Industrial Complex*, ed. Carroll W. Pursell, Jr. (New York: Harper & Row, 1972), pp. 51–81.

3. SAM C. SARKESIAN, ed., *The Military-Industrial Complex: A Reassessment* (Beverly Hills, Calif.: Sage Publications, 1972).

4. WILLIAM H. BAUGH, *The Politics of Nuclear Balance: Ambiguity and Continuity in Strategic Policies* (New York: Longman, 1984).

5. RALPH E. LAPP, *Arms Beyond Doubt: The Tyranny of Weapons Technology* (New York: Cowles, 1970), p. 7.

6. HERBERT YORK, *The Advisors: Oppenheimer, Teller and the Superbomb* (San Francisco: Freeman, 1976), p. ix.

7. ROBERT S. MCNAMARA, "The Dynamics of Nuclear Strategy," *Department of State Bulletin*, 57, October, 1967, p. 450.

8. YORK, *The Advisors*, p. 11.

9. LAUREN H. HOLLAND, and ROBERT A. HOOVER, *The MX Decision: A New Direction in U.S. Weapons Procurement Policy?* (Boulder, CO: Westview Press, 1985), pp. 20–21.

10. GRAHAM T. ALLISON, "What Fuels the Arms Race?" in *Contrasting Approaches to Strategic Arms Control*, ed. Robert L. Pfaltzgraff, Jr. (Lexington, Mass.: Lexington Books, 1974).

11. GORDON ADAMS, *The Iron Triangle: The Politics of Defense Contracting* (New York: Council on Economic Priorities, 1981), pp. 132–133.

12. Ibid., p. 77.

13. Ibid., p. 79.

14. BOB ADAMS, "Revolving Door Seen as Open to Conflict," *St. Louis Post-Dispatch*, April 19, 1983, p. 1.

15. Ibid., p. 12.

16. DONALD R. HALL, *Cooperative Lobbying: The Power of Pressure* (Tuscon: University of Arizona Press, 1969), p. 54.

17. ADAMS, *The Iron Triangle*, p. 157.

18. Ibid.

19. Ibid., p. 169.

20. Ibid., p. 131.

21. Ibid., p. 117.

22. BOB ADAMS, "Congressmen Who Can Help Get Helped," St. Louis Post-Dispatch, April 18, 1983, p. 8.

23. Ibid.

24. ADAMS, "Revolving Door," p. 12.

25. Ibid., p. 1

26. BOB ADAMS, " 'Butter-On-Toast' Subcontracting Creates Pop-up Lobbyists," St. Louis Post-Dispatch, April 21, 1983, p. 1.

27. Ibid.

28. WARREN F. DAVIS, "The Pentagon and the Scientist," in *The Militarization of High Technology*, ed. John Tirman (Cambridge, Mass.: Ballinger) p. 159.

29. JOEL PRIMACK, and FRANK VON HIPPLE, *Advice and Dissent: Scientists in the Political Arena* (New York: Basic Books, 1974).

30. JACQUES S. GANSLER, "The Defense Industry's Role in Military R&D Decision Making," in *The Genesis of New Weapons: Decision Making for Military R&D*, ed. Franklin A. Long and Judeth Reppy (New York: Pergamon Press, 1980), p. 43.

31. Ibid., p. 44.

32. Ibid., p. 43.

33. MATTHEW EVANGELISTA, *Innovation and the Arms Race: How the United States and the Soviet Union Develop New Military Technologies* (Ithaca, N.Y.: Cornell University Press, 1988).

34. MARY KALDOR, *The Baroque Arsenal* (New York: Hill and Wang, 1981), pp. 22–23.

35. GANSLER, "The Defense Industry," pp. 44–45.

36. Ibid., p. 50.

37. CHRISTOPHER PAINE and GORDON ADAMS, "The R&D Slush Fund," *The Nation*, January 26, 1980, p. 72.

38. Ibid.

39. Ibid.

40. Ibid., p. 75 (emphasis added).

41. Ibid., p. 74.

42. Ibid., pp. 74–75.

43. T. GREENWOOD, Making the MIRV: A Study of Defense Decision Making (Cambridge, Mass.: Ballinger, 1975) pp. 14–15.

44. Ibid., pp. 20–21.

45. ALLISON, "What Fuels the Arms Race?" p. 468.

46. GREENWOOD, *Making the MIRV*, p. 28.

47. Ibid., p. 35.

48. RONALD L. TAMMEN, *MIRV and the Arms Race: An Interpretation of Defense Strategy* (New York: Praeger, 1973), p. 138.

49. Ibid.

50. Ibid.

51. Ibid., pp. 139–140.

52. GREENWOOD, *Making the MIRV*, p. 14.

53. JONATHAN B. STEIN, *From H-Bomb to Star Wars: The Politics of Strategic Decision Making* (Lexington, Mass.: Lexington Books, 1984), p. 67.

54. Ibid.

55. ADAM GARFINKLE, "The Politics of Space Defense," *Orbis* (Summer 1984), 241.

56. JEFF HECHT, "Star Wars—An Astronomical Bribe for Scientists," *New Scientist*, June 20, 1985, p. 14.

57. KIM MCDONALD, "Universities Received $34 Million for Research on Star Wars," *The Chronicle of Higher Education*, October 30, 1985, p. 5.

58. FRED HIATT and RICK ATKINSON, "Space: The Defense Contractors' Final Frontier," *Washington Post National Weekly* November 4, 1985, p. 10.

59. Ibid.

60. Ibid. p. 11.

61. MALCOLM W. BROWNE, "The Star Wars Spinoff," *New York Times Magazine*, August 24, 1986, pp. 19–73.

62. HIATT and ATKINSON, "Space...," p. 10.

63. HARVEY BROOKS, "The Strategic Defense Initiative as Science Policy," International Security, 11 (2), p. 181 (emphasis added).

64. ALLISON, "What Fuels the Arms Race?," p. 468.

Chapter 8

The Environmental Challenge

For a long time in the United States, science and technology were nearly universally applauded as vehicles of social and economic progress. The authors of the Constitution were imbued with the scientific spirit of the Enlightenment and were committed to the growth and the application of scientific knowledge for the improvement of society. They included language in the Constitution providing for legal patenting of new inventions, and the early presidents, especially Thomas Jefferson, actively sought to expand scientific knowledge. In the 200 years since, the United States has led the world in developing and using new technologies undreamt of by Benjamin Franklin or Jefferson. With ample natural resources and a generally hardworking, literate work force, American science and technology undergird our standard of living, and our prosperity, our way of life and has made us literally the envy of the entire world.

Today, even as we enjoy the wonders, amenities, and conveniences from what historian Thomas Hughes calls "a century of invention and technological enthusiasm,"[1] we discover that we face an array of problems largely unseen by the proponents of science and technology-based advancement. Modern industrialized manufacturing produces the thousands of consumer products that make ordinary life in America richer by far than the wealthiest of royalty in feudal times, but it also produces air, land, and water pollution that threaten not merely the pleasures of life in the technological society but even the possibility of life itself. Concerns about human damage to the environment pose frontal challenges to the cultural notion that more science and more technology automatically mean more progress.

In addition to ease and convenience, a mass-consumption, throw-away economy produces literally mountains of garbage and waste, much of it lethally toxic. The freedom of the highways is purchased at tremendous costs to nature, as millions of automobiles clog the roads and disgorge noxious fumes into the air we breathe. So profligate are we that scientists tell us that we now, for the first time in the 4.5 billion-year history of the planet, have the potential to do irremediable environmental harm to the entire biosphere. We hear that human refuse is found regularly in some of the most remote locations on the planet, at both the North and South polar regions and on the high seas. At the same time, aggressive development is destroying critical components of the world's environment—the tropical rain forests, for example—upon which all life on the planet relies. Resolving these problems continues to grow in importance even as our abilities to respond effectively seem to diminish.

ARENA PARTICIPANTS

Dealing with complex issues such as these inevitably involves politics, with all the conflicts and compromises always found in political decision making. In our case, environmental politics pits one set of desirable goals against another: economic growth and prosperity, on the one hand, and a livable, nontoxic habitat in which to enjoy the fruits of prosperity, on the other. These issues involve decision makers in all of the technological decision-making arenas and entangles us deeply in the problems of technological flexibility and political gridlock discussed in Chapter 1.

Corporate-Managerial Arena

As we have seen in earlier chapters, it is a mistake to treat all decision makers in the corporate-managerial arena as though they all thought the same way and reacted in the same manner. However, when it comes to environmental issues, differences among the various members of the corporate-managerial arena are less significant than the common features of the marketplace facing all decision makers in this arena, regardless of the kind of corporation in which they must make decisions. There are some elementary features of free market capitalism that make it difficult for decision makers in this arena voluntarily to take special precautions against environmental damage, regardless of how any individual technological decision maker may feel.

As we saw in Chapter 3, for most large-scale, standardized product manufacturers, the chief focus of competition in the market is the shelf price of the finished product. Everyone already knows what a light bulb is, what toothpaste is supposed to do, what standardized industrial chemicals are expected to be. With such products, there is little competitive advantage to be gained from modifications in the general features of the product. Customers, in fact, may depend heavily on a product having precisely predictable characteristics, and any variation from the norm may be disadvantageous to the people who use the product. To compete on price, a manufacturer must keep production costs as low as possible, and hence the interest standardized manufacturers have in new manufacturing process innovations that can allow them to fabricate their commodity more economically and thereby gain a competitive edge in the market.

However, anything that increases the costs of production makes the manufacturer less competitive when compared to another firm that does not have the same increase in costs. Labor costs are one such potential rate increase, as would be changes in the prices of raw materials or energy. For many corporate-managerial decision makers, rigorous environmental regulation constitutes a major increase in production costs, affecting their ability to compete in the marketplace. We do not have to assume that corporate-managerial decision makers are uniquely or inherently uncaring about the environment (although, like any group of people, some will be); we need only remember that many decision makers in the corporate world resist any attempts by outsiders to levy competitively disadvantageous costs on them.

The central theoretical problem with protecting the environment in a capitalist system is that environmental values—clear air, drinkable water, nontoxic land—are "common goods," in economic terms. This means that while there is a demand for them, for all practical purposes they cannot be produced at a profit. The reason that common goods cannot be produced at a profit is that, once produced, it is very difficult or impossible to separate those who obtain them by paying for them from those who obtain them for free. If the product can be had for free, why would anyone willingly pay for it?

Clean air is an excellent example. Suppose you invented a machine that could rid the air of all industrial pollutants. How would you get anyone to pay you for doing that? Once you began to clean it, anyone in the area is free to enjoy the unadulterated air simply by breathing. Unless you posit some bizarre conditions, such that everyone must wear some kind of breathing apparatus into which you put your mechanically cleaned air, there is no practical way for you to get compensated for your invention, at least in the marketplace. Clean air, like other common goods, becomes available to everyone as soon as it is available to anyone.

This is one of the reasons that we have been so careless for so long with the environment, a process called the "tragedy of the commons."[2] Since the environment is held in common and belongs to everyone equally, no one has had an incentive to protect it. In fact, each person in the marketplace, acting quite rationally, has a perverse incentive *not* to contribute to protecting the environment. Suppose that you are a civic-minded manufacturer who is concerned that your factory, along with all the others in your region, is pumping dangerous and noxious pollutants into the air. You go to the other manufacturers, urging each to take steps, such as installing expensive smokestack scrubbers, to reduce or eliminate the air pollution each contributes.

Suppose further that each of the other manufacturers refuses to join your clean air campaign. What can you do? You cannot coerce them to join you. You could go ahead with the installation of expensive pollution abatement equipment in your factory, but this will cost you a lot of money, and even if you fully eliminated all of the air pollution coming from your factory, such a reduction might not even be noticeable if the other factories continue to pollute. You would have spent a great deal of money for an effort that, in the end, makes no noticeable difference in the problem. Moreover, by adding expensive pollution abatement equipment in your factory, you will greatly increase the cost of producing the products you sell and might actually help your still-polluting competitors drive you out of business altogether.

Small wonder that decision makers in the corporate-managerial arena are slow to take unilateral steps to protect the environment. It simply makes no business sense to take on such added expenses alone. This example, of course, assumes a corporate-managerial decision maker filled with civic consciousness. While many decision makers in the corporate-managerial arena do care about their communities, certainly there are just as many who do not. For them, there is even less incentive to pay attention to issues thought irrelevant to competitive advantage and profitability.

The problem in our example is how to get everyone to install pollution abatement equipment at the same time, so that no one can gain a market advantage by still using the air, water, and land as a bottomless sink for the inevitable garbage produced in manufacturing. As long as the environment is held in common, with no one responsible for its protection, it will not be protected. The ordinary operation of the competitive market will see to that. Supporters of government environmental programs argue that only the government can provide the protection we all want but cannot seem to obtain solely in the marketplace. Opponents claim that government regulations will not only *not* clean up the environment, they will actively harm the economy, to boot.

Accommodating new environmental protection regulations can be quite difficult for manufacturers, that use very specialized, expensive, and highly inflexible manufacturing equipment. Production machinery of this type cannot easily or cheaply be modified to meet new or changing pollution standards. Thus, manufacturers often have fought against government regulations that require them to modify the kinds of pollutants they dispose of in the air and water, as well as regulations affecting worker health and safety. They also complain that regulatory arena decision makers constantly change the terms of specific environmental regulations, sometimes in response to unwarranted public scares instigated and fanned by overzealous groups in the popular mobilization arena. Even if the changes in regulatory requirements do not derive from what corporate-managerial decision makers believe to be false and misleading scare tactics, it is difficult for them continually to adjust to each alteration in regulatory decision making. They also complain that regulatory arena decision makers take far too long to make some critical decisions, leaving the business community unable to plan rationally for future expenses or investments.

Some corporate-managerial decision makers simply choose to close older, polluting factories altogether, rather than bear the costs of expensive retrofitting with the latest in what seem to them to be an ever-changing array of environmental protection equipment. They, of course, know that merely hinting at the closure of older, noncomplying plants can be a very effective tool in motivating elected representatives to fight against new regulations or to seek exemptions or exceptions for the affected facilities. Few events generate more excitement in a representative's office than the threat of losing several hundred jobs in the home district.

Again, it is not necessary to assume that decision makers in the corporate-managerial arena simply do not care about environmental degradation or about worker injury (although this may be true in some cases) in order to understand their resistance to new or expanded programs in these areas. Repeated, mandated changes in environmental regulation disrupt manufacturing processes, impose new, unexpected costs that threaten competitiveness, and violate the general expectation within the corporate-managerial arena that only members of this arena should be allowed to make such important decisions. Corporate-managerial resistance will be all the greater if they are in direct competition with foreign manufacturers that do not face such stringent regulations in their own country.

Executive Arena

For the most part, environmental issues have been important within the executive arena to the extent that specific presidents have made those issues central to their policy goals. Thus, Theodore Roosevelt took upon himself the task of protecting the American wilderness and creating the National Park System. Later presidents would continue the policies of those who had come before them, but often with little personal attention or leadership. Protecting nature, of course, is a "motherhood and apple pie" issue, and any sensible politician will be foresquare in favor of conserving resources, wildlife, and wilderness areas. But this is often not much more than symbolic politics, not reflecting the real concerns of most administrations. Still, individual presidents, if they place enough emphasis on environmental concerns, can bring about important changes in policy.

On the other hand, when there is widespread public concern about pollution, toxic wastes, and endangered species, as during the late 1960s, 1970s, and, despite the Reagan years, throughout the 1980s, very few presidents will be willing to stand against the tide. It is clear, for instance, that President Richard Nixon, during whose administration most of the recent environmental legislation was passed, personally opposed many of the new programs. Nonetheless, he signed the legislation as it arrived on his desk, and made speeches praising the programs he would just as soon have scuttled. The only recent president who clearly identified himself with antienvironmental concerns was Ronald Reagan, and he suffered political setbacks because of it.

While individual presidents may choose to associate themselves or not with environmentalism, depending on their individual policy agendas, the rest of the executive arena cannot be so flexible. Many executive arena agencies, such as the Departments of Interior and Agriculture, the National Forest Service, and the National Parks Service, are responsible for the administration of the environmental legislation and programs, and are thus required by law to be attentive and active in these areas. Yet, as we will see when we review the activities of agency appointees in the Reagan administration, individual technological decision makers within the executive arena can make critical differences in how policies are interpreted and implemented. Ideology matters a great deal when an administration takes on the tasks of environmental protection.

Legislative Arena

For some members of Congress, environmental concerns are central to the legislative agenda they pursue, while for others, environmentalism is of secondary importance. And for some legislators, opposition to specific environmental programs is crucial to their constituents, as we will see when we examine the congressional struggles over the Clean Air Act, hazardous waste disposal, and the problem of acid rain. Thus, one conclusion we can draw immediately is that there is no single, unified legislative arena response to the issues of environmental protection.

When local constituent interests, usually corporate-managerial interests, oppose environmental regulations, the elected representative will be expected to work to prevent, delay, or obstruct new restrictions and regulations or to help the affected interests obtain clearances, variances, exemptions, and the like. Thus, representatives who have automobile manufacturing facilities in their districts will predictably oppose auto emission standards opposed by the automobile industry and to work to see that stricter standards are not implemented. So, also, representatives from districts having coal-burning electrical generating plants will oppose the demands of environmental groups and others that expensive scrubbers be installed on the smokestacks in those plants. Such interests may be so important to the local economy that no representative could afford to support such environmental restrictions, even if he or she privately understood the need for such actions. To do so would be political suicide. Other members, not so vulnerable to local demands, will be more amenable to political pressures, bargaining, and logrolling.

As noted in Chapter 5, the environmental movement has become well established in Washington and well connected on Capitol Hill. Several members of Congress regularly speak for the movement's goals and have developed national reputations as committed environmentalists. Nonetheless, environmental issues face competition from many other problems and concerns pressing on decision makers in the legislative arena. When the national economy is prosperous, members feel freer to pursue environmental policies even if they impose added costs upon the corporate-managerial arena. When the economy is ailing, when voters express growing fears about job losses, factory closings, and international competitiveness, legislators are just as willing to set environmental issues on a back burner, a fact never forgotten by decision makers in the environmental movement. We can therefore also conclude that legislative interest in and support for environmental issues shifts with the changes in the larger agenda of national politics.

Regulatory Arena

Decision makers in this arena are often at the center of the political storms surrounding environmental issues. Because the existing array of environmental legislation invariably requires active implementation by the government, the burden of turning legislative intent into practical realities falls to decision makers in this arena. As such, regulatory decision makers are the focus of intense pressure from those who support and those who oppose environmental regulations.

Regulatory decision makers might be able to avoid these political struggles if the legislation they are required to implement contained clear and unambiguous instructions; however, most often such instructions are absent. Instead, regulatory decision makers often must interpret the language of the law and congressional intent, making many discretionary decisions each of which may become the focus of contention. The specific decisions they make, the logic and rationale behind those decisions, and the consequences for competing interests become the focal point of many political battles.

As Walter Rosenbaum[3] notes, the substantive and procedural provisions of environmental legislation quite intentionally differ from most federal regulatory programs. The pro-environmental forces in the legislative arena, joined by environmental interest groups, pressed hard for alterations in traditional regulatory schemes as the environmental programs were taking shape. For example, most environmental programs mandate that "scientific and technological determinations must be one, and sometimes the only, standard by which substantive regulatory decisions affecting environmental quality are reached."[4] These programs integrate scientific analysis into regulatory decision making in new and important ways, separate from and in addition to the common economic and political factors used to determine acceptable trade-offs in policy decision making.

In addition, the framers of the new environmental agencies took steps to prevent "regulatory capture," the tendency seen in other regulatory programs for the interests (usually corporate-managerial) ostensibly being regulated gradually to acquire such influence in the agency that those interests, in effect, "capture" the agency intended to regulate them. Thus, for instance, early agency staffing decisions guaranteed a strong pro-environmental bias from the outset.

Also, the legislation creating the environmental agencies often contained "action-forcing" provisions: strict compliance deadlines and procedural timetables intended to restrict the degree of bureaucratic discretion available to agency decision makers. To prevent cozy regulatory and corporate-managerial relationships from developing, the environmental programs contained clear-cut provisions for citizen participation and, most importantly, explicit citizen standing to sue the agency in federal court, should it fail to live up to the obligations imposed by the law.

In sum, the framers of the new environmental legislation anticipated that regulatory arena decision makers would be at the eye of the political storms surrounding environmental issues and took steps to ensure that antienvironmental forces, predominantly from the corporate-managerial arena, would be unable to dominate or unduly influence the kinds of decisions emanating from inside the regulatory arena. As we will see, those efforts have produced mixed results, at best.

Popular Mobilization Arena

The political clout of the environmental groups within this technological decision-making arena remains one of the enduring developments in modern American politics, as noted by Helen Ingram and Dean Mann:

> The rise of the environmental movement in the 1970s and its staying power through the 1980s is one of the major alterations in the landscape of American politics. The movement has become one of the major forces in the political system, capable of altering the political agenda and winning significant victories against the dominant industrial and commercial interests of the United States.[5]

The environmental movement has become fully institutionalized, as seen in the number of professional associations devoted to environmental values, university-level academic programs in environmental engineering, economics, politics, and so on, and the creation of public agencies charged with protecting the environment. As Ingram and Mann conclude: "The environmental movement has grown from a cause to an accepted set of institutionalized American values."[6] However, we must remember, as we saw in Chapter 5, that for all its political clout, the environmental movement is fragmented among various groups that pursue different agendas, and that decision-making influence for the movement as a whole depends heavily on the willingness of its constituent groups to form effective coalitions, with each other and with sympathetic outsiders. Lacking this willingness to pull together, the movement's power and influence decisions made elsewhere dwindle dramatically.

There has been considerable change in the organization and strategies adopted by environmental groups over the past 20 years, as the movement has evolved from crusading political outsiders to respected political insiders. Where once the predominant line of advance was through confrontational political tactics, public protests, and publicity campaigns focused on the most recent "crisis," in recent years environmental groups have begun to adopt more conventional insider tactics. This change stems in part from the maturation of environmentalism and the broad public acceptance of general environmental values, as well as from some transient political circumstances.

With political maturity has come the recognition that the tactics so useful in the early days of the movement may not contribute to the resolution of contemporary problems. Instead, some groups have begun consultations and cooperative efforts with executive, regulatory, and corporate-managerial decision makers, attempting to resolve environmental disputes without the bitter divisiveness of earlier years.

These same organizations have also begun a change in leadership style, moving away from charismatic leaders to professional managers. The organizations have become quite large, with professional staffs, major headquarters, sophisticated computerized direct-mail capabilities, and the like, and they feel the need to shed the backpacking, granola-eating images they enjoyed in the past. They have become insider players in Washington, and need organizational structures and leaders who know how to play the game effectively.

Naturally, such evolution, while predictable, dismays some within the movement, who feel that cooperation with "the enemy" amounts to co-optation by the enemy. Thus, some more radical environmental groups steadfastly refuse to enter into the pluralist bargaining game, even if this means that they remain marginal to policymaking. Some, sometimes called "eco-guerrillas," have even resorted to civil disobedience and violence to make their points.

Individual decision makers in leadership positions must make critical choices about when, where, and how to apply their organizations' inevitably limited resources. To select an unwinnable fight or unsuccessful tactics would dissipate those resources uselessly. In the end, the movement's leaders will have to find mechanisms to sustain their policy influence, including how to maintain membership levels now that the Reagan/Watt/Buford era has passed, how to keep up sufficient funding, and how to select appropriate organizational and policy priorities. There are bound to be differences, perhaps bitter differences, among the leadership of environmental groups on all of these issues.

Academic-Professional Arena

Legislative requirements that regulatory arena decision makers base their decisions upon scientific and technological information, instead of or in addition to the usual economic and political considerations, has thrust members of the academic-professional arena directly into the spotlight in environmental policymaking. This unaccustomed policy centrality has left some members of academe unsettled and uneasy about how their expertise can contribute to resolving environmental disputes and concerned that by being dragged into hotly contested political battles, the special position of science in America may be placed in jeopardy.

In point of fact, modern science often is simply unable to provide the clear policy guidance on many of these issues that the framers of the legislation hoped they could. In many cases, the scientific community cannot answer unequivocally the policymakers' questions, and when they try to respond with professionally careful conditions and reservations, the scientists find themselves charged with hidden political biases by all sides.

In fact, all sides in environmental disputes find the use of scientific evidence to their advantage, so much so that we can legitimately wonder if they would really welcome definitive scientific findings in any dispute. As long as scientists remain divided in their conclusions, as long as legitimate doubts exist about the reliability of test results, of dose-response experiments with animals, with carcinogenicity assessments, and so forth, all sides in the dispute can continue to struggle. What is more, they are likely to be able to find some scientific evidence supporting their positions.

The scientists, however, find their work and even their professional reputations challenged before regulatory hearings and in the all too frequent litigation that follows. Their practices and procedures become the fodder for lawyers, as each side attempts to undermine the scientific validity of the other side's experts.

Professional and even personal disputes are aired in public, and the policy-relevant cognitive authority of science diminishes with each fight. Of course, often there are disputes within the scientific community, both professional and personal, just as there are many cases where findings are challenged in the professional literature and conclusions eventually withdrawn in the face of countervailing evidence. Scientists are accustomed to this kind of contention; it is the very stuff of science. However, these kinds of interactions usually occur within the sympathetic confines of the academic-professional arena, not in public hearings and courtrooms. To air the dirty laundry of the scientific community in this manner leaves many scientists worried.

Judicial Arena

Judicial arena decision makers are often at a disadvantage when dealing with the technical or scientific components of environmental issues. As we saw in Chapter 4, federal courts have varied in their willingness to accede to the judgments of technically responsible agencies, sometimes willing to take a hard look at agency decision-making procedures and at other times deferential to those agencies.

For popular mobilization decision makers, who believe that they are politically outgunned when compared to the influence of corporate-managerial interests in the legislative and executive arenas, the resort to litigation has been a tactic of some efficacy. So convinced of the utility of judicial review were the framers of environmental programs that, as we have seen, they included specific provisions for citizen or environmental group access to the courts if they believe that federal agencies are failing to live up to the requirements of the law. In recent years, corporate-managerial interests have also had recourse to litigation to achieve their ends, with each set of interests about equally effective in obtaining the kinds of judicial decisions they desire.

BACKGROUND OF THE ENVIRONMENTAL MOVEMENT

Concern for the general environment reached its peak in modern America during the 1960s and 1970s, when more than 25 major pieces of environmental legislation were enacted by Congress. However, worry about the impact of human beings on nature predates the modern environmental movement by several decades.[7] The conservation and preservationist movements of the early years of this century saw such achievements as the creation of the National Parks System and the National Forest System, along with the organization of some of the oldest and still active environmental interest groups. While conservationists and preservationists often fought each other bitterly over whether wildlands should be maintained in their pristine state or wisely managed for their natural resources (a difference that still marks the environmental movement, as we saw in Chapter 5), their collective activities helped to sensitize many Americans to the natural threats created by modern industrial development. Many notable Americans, including Theodore Roosevelt, John Muir, and Gifford

Pinchot, led the first wave of conservation and environmental activists. However, in the immediate post–World War II era, general concern for the environment faded before the demands of economic prosperity. What forms of environmental damage that actually made the news, such as smog in Los Angeles or Pittsburgh, were seen as local problems, rather than national issues.

The event that probably did more to recatalyze public concern about environmental degradation was the publication in 1962 of Rachel Carson's *Silent Spring*, in which she documented the deleterious effects of massive use of pesticides on the environment. Suddenly, the public was mobilized over these issues, seen now as major national problems. Responding to the growing ground swell of demands for energetic government responses to the "environmental crisis," Congress enacted the tremendous spate of new laws, four major pieces of legislation in both 1972 and 1977 alone.

There was strenuous and persistent opposition to this legislation from the corporate-managerial arena, which complained of the costs and burdens these new programs placed on business. Nonetheless, the federal government created a whole panoply of regulatory programs and agencies, established strict time-tables for corporate-managerial compliance, imposed "technology-forcing" requirements, and encouraged the creation of similar programs and agencies at the state level.

Nor was the issue partisan. Although the Republican officials often resisted environmental legislation and Democrats supported it, the largest array of major programs was enacted during the Nixon/Ford years. What is more, repeated public opinion polls show that very large majorities of Americans remain supporters of strong environmental protection programs, even if they entail increased costs in other areas.[8] This is a set of issues that transcends the temporary enthusiasms that are so characteristic of American politics.

This history makes the more recent developments in environmental politics so remarkable. Although the movement rode high during the 1960s and 1970s, it suffered an important political eclipse during the eight years of the Reagan administration, from 1981 to 1988. The "Reagan revolution" began with calls for major changes in how the federal government dealt with the rest of society. President Reagan called for the rollback of government regulations on economic activity, not simply in environmental areas, but across the board. Getting the "government off our backs" became a rallying cry for the new administration, a clarion to which an overwhelming majority of voters responded with enthusiasm.

The Reagan administration took its electoral landslide in 1980 as confirmation of the public's approval of its "regulatory relief" agenda and began quickly to appoint to important posts in the regulatory arena individuals who were closely associated with corporate-managerial interests and opposed the government's role in health, energy, consumer, and environmental policies. James Watt, the incoming secretary of the interior, Anne Buford, EPA administrator, and Rita Lavelle, head of the "superfund" toxic clean-up program at EPA, were only the most notable appointments. The administration's plan, according to Norman Vig, included four elements:

1) Personnel policies designed to change the ideological orientation of the agencies; 2) governmental reorganization intended to facilitate centralized White House

control over policy and to institute changes within departments and agencies that would help to further the president's policy agenda; 3) budgetary cutbacks to force the agencies to operate more "efficiently" and to reduce their regulatory activity; and 4) imposition of more detailed regulatory oversight to ensure implementation of the president's economic and regulatory relief goals.[9]

Personnel changes were used "with a vengeance" to eliminate the "environmental zealots" the Reagan team was sure filled regulatory posts. Virtually all important posts were given to political appointees who had strong connections with the corporate-managerial arena and were committed to rolling back the regulatory efforts of the Carter administration. Agencies and their subunits were reorganized, consolidated, or simply abolished. In the Executive Office of the President, the entire staff of the Council on Environmental Quality was sacked, and the now much smaller organization was demoted. The task of the CEQ was to provide direct, independent advice to the president, a function the new administration thought it could do without. At the Department of the Interior, Watt greatly reduced the size of the Office of Surface Mining, responsible for overseeing the strip mining program, and Anne Buford greatly reduced the size of the enforcement and inspection units at EPA. Both steps signaled to the corporate world that the probability of getting caught and punished for violating environmental statutes was greatly reduced. The Reagan administration also used budget cuts to alter the regulatory process, by so greatly reducing the budgets of enforcement and research units that they had virtually no chance of actually fulfilling their tasks.

Finally, the Reagan administration imposed significant new centralized control of regulations by requiring review of any new environmental regulations by the Office of Management and Budget, and by issuing Executive Order No. 12291, mandating cost-benefit analysis for all new major regulations. These changes allowed the president to pursue his regulatory rollback without having a public fight in Congress:

> This process was designed to slow agency rule making and enhance the influence of the president and OMB in regulatory policy....Unable to move regulatory reform legislation through the Democratic House, the administration depended on OIRA (Office of Information and Regulatory Affairs—OMB) to carry out deregulation by executive means, believing that Congress would accept the fait accompli.[10]

By slashing specific program budgets, reducing or transferring personnel, dropping or delaying proposed regulations, softening enforcement procedures for existing regulations, granting special exceptions and exemptions, and other easements, the Reagan team within the regulatory arena could effect significant changes in environmental policy without having to engage in highly public fights in Congress. Of course, there would be outcries from affected groups because of these regulatory changes, but it is difficult for outsiders to affect substantially the internal operations of federal bureaucracies. By defending such changes in terms of economic efficiency, bureaucratic costcutting, and enhancements in American international competitiveness, the administration hoped to split public reaction to its activities and keep its critics on the defensive.

CASE STUDIES

A key feature of environmental politics over the past decade has been political gridlock, largely produced by the combination of assaults to the environment with inflexible and expensive-to-modify technological decisions. The economic interests that have invested in those inflexible technologies strongly resist efforts by people concerned about environmental degradation to impose new costs on them. Indeed, during the early 1980s, when an administration sympathetic with corporate-managerial concerns came to power in Washington, industrial and commercial interests launched a major effort to roll back the environmental regulations enacted during the preceding decade. The results of the political battles during the 1980s were frequent stalemate and inaction.

Of course, as commentators have noted for generations, American politics is often marked by just such stalemates, not merely in environmental areas or even scientific and technological issues generally. The separation of powers, a bicameral Congress, the complexities of the legislative process, staggered elections, and competitive political parties, are ready-made for policy immobilism, if contending forces are unable or unwilling to reach consensus on issues. Michael Kraft points out that policy gridlock

> derives from the tension between two competing expectations for the policy process. One emphasizes prompt and rational problem solving; the other stresses representation of pertinent interests and policy legitimation. From the first perspective, gridlock is a needless, and possibly dangerous, blockage of sensible policy making. Dire consequences are foreseen unless immediate action is taken to institute preventive measures. From the second perspective, it is essential to improve understanding of the problems faced and to formulate policies that are broadly acceptable to the diverse interests affected by governmental action.[11]

We have already discussed the tension Kraft mentions, described as the difficulties in finding policies that are, at one and the same time, technologically responsible and democratically responsive. We will return to this theme in Chapter 11.

In both of the cases we will review, environmental policies during the 1980s suffered from extended and pernicious political gridlock (while, we should note, other environmental policies were successfully resolved). Both of these cases involve the conflicts that emerge when corporate-managerial decision makers seek to protect themselves against what they see as unneeded and expensive regulations, while environmental groups and their allies strive to force regulatory and technical changes in the name of cleaning the air, water, and land.

Reauthorization of the Clean Air Act

By all accounts, the Clean Air Act of 1970 and the 1977 amendments to that act constitute the most complex environmental program ever enacted by the legislative arena. The act's legislative authorization expired on September 30, 1981 (although still enforced, on a year-to-year basis, pending formal congressional reauthorization), and for nearly a decade, government decision makers were stalemated in renewing the act. This is a classic example of political gridlock at its most pernicious.

The goal of the Clean Air Act (CAA) is "to protect the public from dirty air. But to achieve that seemingly simple goal, the law costs American industry billions of dollars each year and affects nearly all industrial, energy production, transportation and real estate activities in this country."[12] Everyone agrees that CAA has achieved some of its goals. For instance the emission of particulates (dust and other particles from industry and fuel consumption) has declined by more than a third, while sulfur dioxide has dropped by nearly one fourth.

Still, there remain troublesome pockets of air pollution, most often associated with congested urban areas. According to the bipartisan National Commission on Air Quality, by 1981, millions of Americans lived in areas with air dirtier than national standards, and locales such as Los Angeles, Houston, New York, and Boston might never meet national ozone standards and Denver might never meet standards for carbon monoxide.[13] In total, more than 100 million Americans in at least 81 urban areas endure levels of ozone and carbon monoxide that exceed legal air quality standards.[14] While some important progress has occurred, it has not been uniform. What is more, there are growing concerns about new problems, such as acid rain and potentially carcinogenic forms of air pollution. Clearly, more work needs to be done (see Tobin[15]).

Many people had complaints about the stringency of CAA and its amendments, most often, but not exclusively, these complaints coming from the corporate-managerial decision makers. This was surely inevitable, given the complexity of the law. Critics argue that EPA has been too slow to approve state implementation plans and has been too intrusive in the local handling of pollution problems. The law further impedes the construction of major sources of new pollution unless existing sources can reduce their emissions enough to compensate. Since many existing facilities are older, using technologies that are inflexible and very expensive to modify, this amounts to a prohibition on new plants and factories, critics assert. Or it induces corporate-managerial decision makers simply to close down older facilities, thus increasing unemployment.

Moreover, the law imposed firm restrictions on new sources of air pollution in areas that currently enjoy clean air, such as in many places in the West. Developers complain that the restrictions impede useful economic growth for the sake of preserving air quality standards substantially higher than imposed in older urban areas. Because the law forbids regulatory arena decision makers from considering the costs of implementing clean air regulations, many in the corporate-managerial arena protest that compliance with existing regulations is economically harmful. Many in the corporate-managerial arena also complain that there is little relation between the rising costs of compliance with air quality regulations and any resulting social benefits.

As the reauthorization debate began, a sizable array of corporate-managerial interests were lined up in opposition to CAA, especially to the discretion it gave to regulatory decision makers to impose emission regulations as well as the specific technologies on plants and facilities:

> Coal, oil, automobiles, chemicals, paper, utilities, steel and mining companies and their trade associations have thrown bountiful resources into the conflict. Some of them have been doing homework on the law for as long as two years. Now their pulses have been quickened by the scent of a government more sympathetic to business.[16]

Corporate-managerial interests commissioned volume after volume of industry-sponsored research and analysis to buttress their complaints against the legislation, the way it had been implemented, and the scientific evidence on which those regulatory decisions are made.

Because CAA is such a broad and encompassing piece of legislation, affecting so many different industries, the corporate-managerial lobbying efforts varied from industry to industry, to some extent weakening the total impact decision makers in this arena had in Congress. One approach, primarily supported by oil, chemical, coal, and wood products industries (and the building trades unions of the AFL-CIO), downplayed highly confrontational tactics, stressing a more cooperative approach to lobbying in the legislative arena during CAA reauthorization. Rather, business interests should align themselves with the general goals of CAA, while seeking modifications advantageous to industry. Some environmental decision makers acknowledged that this "soft-sell" approach offered serious political challenges: "To some extent, one might consider [the "soft sell" approach] more dangerous from a political point of view than the groups that are more outrageous in their public statements."[17]

Other corporate-managerial organizations, such as the Business Roundtable, advocated more radical changes in the law. Specific industry trade associations also pressed for changes beneficial to particular industries, such as the Motor Vehicle Manufacturers Association, Chemical Manufacturers Association, American Paper Institute, American Petroleum Institute, American Mining Congress, and Edison Electric Institute, among others. Even individual companies engaged in lobbying, seeking out their local representatives about specific problems with the law.

Environmental groups and their allies also marshalled their resources for the upcoming fight. Many in the popular mobilization arena feared that, given the antagonistic tenor of the incoming Reagan administration and the Republican capture of the Senate, there was a serious chance that major elements of CAA might be greatly weakened or eliminated altogether. Their public posture was to favor modifications in the law that would expedite the extensive paperwork required by the law, asserting: "We're not for red tape."[18] But they were determined to prevent radical changes in the existing framework of the act. They hoped to obtain support from non-environmental groups as well, such as the League of Women Voters, various labor unions, and western ranchers concerned about coal mining and synthetic fuels development.

Like the corporate-managerial interests, environmental groups also gathered together their own complement of technical and scientific experts. While much of the CAA reauthorization debate would involve traditional economic and regional interests and conflicts, each side in this debate knew that scientific evidence and conclusions would serve as important political assets.

Decision makers in the labor arena were sharply split on CAA reauthorization. Some unions, such as the United Steelworkers and the Oil, Chemical, and Atomic Workers, generally sided with the environmentalists. They feared that if corporate-managerial interests succeeded in changing the conditions of CAA, they might be able to make similar radical changes in health and safety legislation too. On the other hand, trade unions associated with construction, such as the Building and Construction Trades Department of the AFL-CIO, sympathized with business, as did the United Mine Workers and the United Auto Workers, for different reasons.

Thus, the setting was ripe for potentially significant changes in CAA during the reauthorization process in 1981: The newly inaugurated Reagan administration had pointedly criticized CAA as an example of regulatory excess, the Republican-controlled Senate was primed to follow the Reagan lead, and corporate-managerial interests were massing their considerable resources to strike at this opportune moment. A series of political missteps, however, combined to rob the Reagan administration and its corporate-managerial allies of the opportunities for the legislative arena victory they hoped to achieve. Richard Tobin[19] notes three errors made within the executive arena: misreading public opinion, overestimating Congress's willingness to accept fundamental changes, and the administration's inability to develop and present proposals for change.

The Reagan landslide in the 1980 election, plus the Republican capture of the Senate, led decision makers in the executive arena to assume widespread and prevailing public approval for all of the policy objectives defended by Reagan during the election. Yet public support for environmental programs remained high even during the Reagan years. Public opinion polls showed clearly that nearly eight out of ten Americans thought that existing air pollution laws were either "just about right" or "not protective enough."[20] The public might agree with Reagan's call to "get the government off your back," but they also wanted the air cleaned up. The Reagan administration mistook the public's rejection of the Carter years as wholesale approval for the Reagan regulatory agenda.

They also overestimated the willingness of decision makers in the legislative arena to make deep changes in CAA. When CAA was reauthorized during the bitter 1977 debates, Congress created a nonpartisan National Commission on Air Quality (NCAQ) to undertake an in-depth assessment of the law and to advise Congress concerning needed changes in 1981. Many in the legislative arena, hoping to avoid the divisiveness of the 1977 experience, and not just a bit overwhelmed by the complexities of the law itself, intended to use the NCAQ findings to guide their decisions.

Unfortunately for the corporate-managerial position, NCAQ found that CAA as amended in 1977 did not significantly inhibit economic growth, had not been an important obstacle to energy development, and that, while some marginal modifications would help with certain inefficiencies, radical changes were not needed. The commission also called for further attention to air pollution problems to meet the goals of the act.[21] Those members of the legislative arena not already ideologically committed to radical changes in CAA, and aware of the polling results about air pollution, could use the NCAQ results to justify leaving the act largely unchanged.

Lastly, the Reagan administration was slow in coming forward with specific legislative proposals for altering CAA. Part of the delay was due to the hold-up in Anne Buford's approval as head of the Environmental Protection Agency and part from the administration's preoccupation with economic issues, tax and budget cuts. Also, pro-environmental forces in Congress procured draft copies of various changes under consideration by the administration:

> The drafts called for things such as the elimination of national air quality standards, the application of cost-benefit analysis to the setting of standards, the elimination of federal sanctions for localities not achieving standards, and elimination of the requirement that pollution-control devices on automobiles be maintained in proper working order.[22]

While the administration claimed that the recommendations were preliminary and not under serious consideration, the publicity that followed the disclosure hurt the administration's case.

The result of these errors was that the executive arena lost the legislative initiative on CAA and eventually found itself reacting to others' decisions: "By failing to provide specific proposals in a draft bill, the administration and EPA relinquished an opportunity to play an influential role in the revision process. Without its own bill, the administration had nothing with which it could lobby or negotiate."[23] Conservative members of Congress introduced a bill of their own, with the backing of such corporate-managerial mainstays as the Business Roundtable, National Association of Manufacturers, U.S. Chamber of Commerce, and Motor Vehicle Manufacturers Association. While the Reagan administration backed the bill, the combined pro-environmental forces were able to deadlock legislative action in divisive and bitter debate.

With the 1982 off-year election, more pro-environmental Democrats entered the legislative arena, reducing even further the possibility that the Reagan administration would achieve its changes through the legislative process. This change in legislative arena personnel, accompanied by the growing controversies involving Buford, Lavelle, and Watt, contributed to the ability of the pro-environmental forces in Congress to resist further efforts by the Reagan administration to legislatively alter CAA. While environmental forces could effectively block the Reagan administration's efforts to weaken CAA, the Reagan forces were also able to block any efforts to enhance or strengthen the act. Indeed, for the next seven years, the legislative arena was unable to complete the reauthorization of CAA, a nearly decade-long case of political gridlock.

But this did not mean that there were no alternate routes open to the Reagan administration to accomplish its goals with regard to the Clean Air Act. The administration simply shifted its efforts out of the legislative arena and into the regulatory arena. The 1977 amendments were often vague, giving the EPA administrator considerable bureaucratic discretion:

> The administrator can decide, for example, which air pollutants should be regulated and how strictly. Similarly, the administrator can establish deadlines, grant waivers from these deadlines, and determine what constitutes compliance with regulations. In short, the complexity of the amendments and the need for literally hundreds of implementing regulations provide any administrator with wide latitude.[24]

The Reagan administration used this latitude to relax, revise, or eliminate many regulations imposed by the Carter EPA. In 1981, the EPA sought to relax previous limitations on lead in gasoline for small oil refiners, and only recanted when faced with stiffened legislative resistance.

The administration was more successful in other areas, however, in delaying the imposition of emission standards for diesel-powered vehicles, for example. The Reagan EPA also delayed establishing emission standards for various hazardous air pollutants until compelled to by court order and fell far behind its own schedule for determining new source performance standards. Delay proved to be nearly as useful and beneficial to corporate-managerial allies of the administration as the unsuccessful legislative changes they had sought in CAA. Indeed, the discretionary activities of Anne Buford, the administrator at EPA, contributed importantly to the intense public controversy that surrounded her tenure at the agency, and eventually led to her resignation and to the indictment of her deputy, Rita Lavelle, who headed the "Superfund" program. Rosenbaum notes a major complaint about Buford:

> One procedure widely criticized was the repeated use by EPA administrators of irregular or secret meetings with representatives of regulated industries to decide regulatory policies affecting them. These meetings, lacking public notice, public comment, or other procedural arrangements normally required for such agency deliberations, seemed highly irregular and suspiciously biased. Critics charged that the meetings were cloistered caucuses where the agency's administrators resolved sensitive issues in close consultation with interests to which they were strongly sympathetic and without interference from environmentalists or other groups.[25]

Thus, the Reagan administration's regulatory arena appointees willingly used the discretion granted by CAA and other environmental programs to eliminate popular mobilization arena decision makers, along with their legislative arena allies, from participation in important regulatory decisions.

By the middle of Reagan's second administration, the balance of forces focused on the still unfinished CAA reauthorization had changed radically. Following the 1986 off-year election, the Democrats regained control of the Senate, at least in part because of growing public discontent with how the Reagan administration had handled environmental issues. Pro-environmental forces, emboldened by the election results and the continued strong public support for environmental values, launched its own effort to strengthen, rather than weaken, CAA.

The tactics adopted by the opposing sides thus neatly reversed. During the first Reagan administration, when corporate-managerial forces were strongest, environmental groups and legislative allies argued that CAA was fundamentally sound, needing only modest improvements rather than the radical alterations proposed by the administration, while the Reagan team and their corporate-managerial allies insisted that the law was deeply flawed. Environmental forces used stall and delay tactics in Congress to prevent the Reagan initiatives from being enacted.

During the second term, as pro-environmental ranks grew, it was the Reagan administration and its corporate-managerial allies who argued that "the Clean Air Act as it is written now is working,"[26] while various Democrats in the legislative arena asserted that the act needed radical changes, including more stringent pollution standards. Now it was the Reagan administration and the business community that tried to delay legislative action, to prevent the environmental initiatives from moving forward.

In both cases, of course, political gridlock was the result. For nearly a decade, from 1981, when CAA authorization expired, through the end of the Reagan administration in January 1989, decision makers in the responsible government arenas, executive, legislative, and regulatory, were unable to fashion a coherent consensus on national air pollution policies. At best, the opposing sides were able to stalemate each other, neither powerful enough when ascendant to obtain the desired decisions from the relevant decision makers, yet each able to block and obstruct the other.

The sources of the stalemate are clear. Each side in the CAA reauthorization debate entered the contest with its position firmly set. Years of corporate-managerial resistance and opposition to environmental programs of all kinds led environmental forces to anticipate a tough and demanding battle over the terms of the law. Corporate-managerial interests, often having invested in relatively inflexible production technologies and facilities, depicted the costs of pollution abatement regulations as harmful to necessary business-related decision making and in need of substantial change. The unexpected Reagan landslide and Republican capture of the Senate provided a political "window of opportunity" that corporate-managerial interests hoped to exploit. While some within the business coalition urged a soft-sell, ostensibly cooperative approach, they were unable to disguise the extent and depth of changes they wanted in CAA.

The pro-environmental coalition was just as determined that the corporate-managerial strategy would not work and took steps to ensure that end. The complexities, openness, and constituent sensitivity of American legislative politics ensured that both sides would have many opportunities to press their demands and to blunt the efforts of their opponents.

However, most uncommitted legislative arena decision makers, uncertain of the real impacts of so complex a law as CAA, and attentive to the persistence of general popular support for clean air programs, were looking for ways to justify their decisions without offending the electorally powerful Reagan administration and its important corporate-managerial supporters or antagonizing their worried constituents, were only too happy to use the recommendations of non-partisan NCAQ to guide their specific decisions. This meant that the demands for radical reforms of CAA faced an uphill fight, despite Reagan's personal popularity. Combined with contingent factors, such as the administration's failure to make specific legislative proposals, the premature disclosure of some proposed changes being considered within the administration, and the delay in confirming Buford as EPA administrator, environmental forces were able to stall action in committees and on the floor of Congress.

When the tables turned during the second Reagan term, as pro-environmental legislators entered Congress, it was the turn of the Reagan administration and its corporate-managerial allies to use stall and delay tactics, this time to prevent what they saw as an undesirable strengthening of CAA. The end result of all these machinations was that a central piece of national environmental policy was held hostage to political and ideological battles pursued by opponents largely unwilling to compromise. Political gridlock, linked to inflexible technological choices driven by the special requirements of the corporate-managerial arena, has meant that a politically responsible reaction to a set of pressing environmental problems was simply beyond the capacity of our national political institutions.

On June 12, 1989, the administration of George Bush came forward with another set of CAA reauthorization proposals. After yet another year of stalemate, the logjam finally broke: Congress enacted the reauthorization of the Clean Air Act on October 27, 1990. Although Congress changed the Bush proposals significantly, with executive arena leadership instead of obstruction, both sides in this decade-long policy gridlock compromised enough to bring forth a successful bill. Regional conflicts between "dirty" coal-burning states in the Midwest and Eastern regions suffering from acid rain were resolved, as were disputes over auto emission standards between smog-ridden cities and workers in automobile factories. Neither the corporate-managerial nor the environmental decision makers embraced the bill wholeheartedly; both complained that they had had to make significant sacrifices. Still, after ten years of wrangling, the environmentalists could claim success, as Representative Henry Waxman (D-Calif.) said: "In almost every title we have provisions stronger than those we were advocating through the years."[27]

Pesticides Policy

This second example of political gridlock derived from the combination of ecological injury and inflexible technological decision making involved efforts to reauthorize the 1972 Federal Insecticide, Fungicide, and Rodenticide Act (FIFRA), the major regulatory program through which EPA regulates the use of pesticides in the United States. The reauthorization struggle began in 1981 and continued through the end of the decade.

The reauthorization of FIFRA promised a political battle characterized by "a grass-roots campaign by dozens of environmental, health and labor organizations seeking to make the law more protective, and a well-organized push by a coalition representing pesticide producers, applicators and users who oppose any changes."[28] Predictably, the rival sides in the FIFRA fight presented diametrically opposing views of the impacts of pesticide use. Environmentalists asserted that pesticides can cause cancer, birth defects, and neurological damage, among other evils. Average citizens are exposed to potent and dangerous pesticides in their food, water, and air and in their homes. Moreover, decision makers in the regulatory arena, they claimed, were too sympathetic with chemical companies and too slow to complete needed toxicity testing of existing and new pesticides. As one environmentalist asserted:

> Most Americans probably assume that all pesticides have been carefully examined by EPA and have passed rigorous health and safety tests. This is simply not true. At least 84 percent of pesticides now in use have never been adequately tested to determine whether they cause cancer.[29]

Corporate-managerial representatives, through such industrial associations as the National Agricultural Chemicals Association, Southern Agricultural Chemicals Association, National Pest Control Association, National Cotton Council, National Forest Products Association, among others, cited the many benefits of pesticide use, including tremendous gains in farm productivity at lower costs, reduced food costs to consumers, and the eradication of dangerous, disease-bearing pests. The kinds of reforms of FIFRA sought by the environmentalists, they argued, would impose millions of dollars of added production costs on producers and users while generating no real social benefits.

A great deal was at stake in the reauthorization debate. The pesticide industry is a $4 billion enterprise, and pesticides have become critical to most of American agricultural production. On the other hand, repeated public opinion polls showed clearly that there was a growing awareness and worry about pesticides among average citizens:

> People who found out a couple of years ago that their Betty Crocker cake mixes might have EDB in them now discover that the pesticides don't just wash off their apples. These are people whose houses are treated with Chlordane. They are sitting up and taking notice, and they are going to have a big effect on Congress.[30]

In a manner similar to the Clean Air Act reauthorization fight, the early phase of the FIFRA battle saw corporate-managerial forces, joined by a sympathetic Reagan administration, pursuing significant revisions of the act that would benefit industry: "In 1982, pesticide makers and users sought changes to keep states from imposing controls stricter than federal ones, and to keep the public from getting information on the health effects of pesticides, information that pesticide makers considered to be trade secrets."[31] Just as in the CAA battle, corporate-managerial decision makers

> perceived the coming of Reagan as a golden opportunity for favorable policy change. Environmentalists seemed in disarray, whipsawed between an EPA

suddenly displaying suspicious orientations and a Congress of uncertain loyalties. The Reagan philosophy on deregulation and the wisdom of market forces seemed preeminent both in the executive and legislative branches, even among those traditionally regarded as friends of the environment.[32]

Seeing themselves on the defensive, pro-environmental forces in the legislative arena sought to have FIFRA reauthorized in its existing form, without the weakening amendments desired by industry. Environmental organizations also knew that, unlike air pollution problems, pesticide controls carried little weight with the general public.

However, the public scandals at EPA and the results of the 1982 congressional elections saw a dramatic shift in political power on Capitol Hill. Environmental forces, no longer willing simply to protect FIFRA as it stood, launched a more aggressive approach to reauthorization, demanding new amendments to strengthen EPA's ability to remove dangerous pesticides from the market, to allow citizen lawsuits to force regulatory arena action, forcing greater public disclosure of health risks associated with specific pesticides, to provide greater protection against groundwater contamination, and so on. Just as in the latter stages of the CAA reauthorization struggle, corporate-managerial interests and the Reagan administration now began to *defend* FIFRA as it stood, abandoning their own efforts at making radical changes in the law. The political tide had turned, with each side swapping political strategies and tactics.

Both sides used the scientific complexities of pesticide use to their political benefit. As we discuss in more detail in Chapter 9, on dealing with risk assessment, there is a great deal of controversy even within the academic-professional arena about the precise levels of human health risks posed by various substances. There can be considerable room for disagreement among acknowledged experts in toxicology, immunology, and public health about the conclusiveness of laboratory test results and what, if anything, decision makers in the regulatory arena ought to do about controlling human exposure to various chemical elements.

Many within the environmental movement argue that FIFRA as written is far too easy on chemical companies and that decision makers at EPA have been too lenient on the use of dangerous pesticides. They see themselves as blocked from influencing regulatory arena decision making not only by the existing terms of FIFRA but also by the administrative tactics used by Reagan administration appointees. As Christopher Bosso notes:

> ...the agency through 1983 systematically sought to reduce, if not eliminate, whole sets of FIFRA provisions objected to by the chemical industry. The agency in 1982, for example, proposed broad changes in pesticides regulation, including almost total devolution of enforcement (but not standards) to the states, more lenient data requirements for registration, and voluntary compliance with EPA testing protocols....The OPP [Office of Pesticide Programs] in early 1983 also tightened public access to health and safety data....Environmentalists, labor unions, and many farm organizations complained bitterly that these restrictions severely undermined independent data verification...[33]

Once again we can see a similarity to the CAA reauthorization struggle. When ultimately stalemated in the legislative arena, the Reagan administration also employed the considerable bureaucratic discretion provided by the statute to effect changes administratively that it had been unable to effect through the legislative process.

Environmentalists did enjoy an important political advantage over corporate-managerial decision makers, however, in their ability at least periodically to engage public fears about exposure to pesticides. Sheila Jasanoff[34] illustrates how effectively environmental groups used the public media to bring intense pressure to bear on regulatory arena decision makers in the case of Daminozide, a chemical sprayed on apples. Although Daminozide, under the brand name Alar, is a known carcinogen, EPA was hampered in removing it from the market because EPA's Science Advisory Panel disagreed with the definitiveness of the research data the agency was using to determine the risks of continued use of Alar.

To spur EPA to action, the Natural Resources Defense Council (NRDC) in 1989 announced in a press conference that its own scientific analysis of the chemical showed that those who consume large quantities of apples sprayed with Alar, especially small children, were at significantly increased risk of cancer. When the news media picked up the story, the public became highly agitated, as thousands of parents refused to purchase apples in supermarkets and schools removed apples from lunchrooms. Although EPA, the Surgeon General's office, and representatives from the chemical industry and the apple industry argued that the results of laboratory tests were inconclusive, and that the amount of Alar on store-bought apples was negligible and posed no health risks, these efforts came to naught. Once terrified by what looked like independent—and thus more credible—scientific analysis, the public was not going to accept government or industrial assurances. Eventually, the chemical company producing Alar promised to remove it from the market "voluntarily," while the apple industry, frightened by the rapidly spreading apple boycott, promised to stop using the substance altogether.

The lesson of the Alar case is that, while corporate-managerial decision makers may enjoy a "privileged position" in American politics, effective mass mobilization—the chief weapon of popular mobilization arena decision makers, after all—can still be very potent weapon, at least from time to time. However, while powerful, public outrage most often cannot sustain entry into decision-making circles for popular mobilization arena decision makers. With legislation as complicated and controversial as FIFRA, public fears about a particular chemical are not likely to provide the political force necessary to overcome the organized resistance of a determined corporate-managerial coalition.

While the executive and legislative arenas eventually worked out a compromise reauthorization of FIFRA before the end of the second Reagan term, the bill enacted was seen by all as a stripped-down compromise in which most of the controversial issues were deferred for future fights. Concerns about limiting pollutants in groundwater, extending the patent life of pesticide products, and protecting farm workers from exposure were removed from the compromise. Many within the environmental movement have begun to despair of ever achieving a comprehensive rewrite of FIFRA and have started talking about making changes one at a time, in smaller revisions sometimes added to other pieces of legislation. Clearly, the experience of nearly a decade of struggle and conflict in Washington demonstrates that environmental issues heavily laden with both scientific uncertainty and high economic costs often prove beyond the capacity of both executive and legislative arena decision makers to resolve.

CONCLUSIONS

We should begin by acknowledging that not every environmental issue faced by the federal government displays the kinds of political gridlock seen in both of these cases. And we should reiterate that political stalemate can be found in many other policy domains, and is not an exclusive property of either environmental policy in particular or of science and technology policy in general. The potential for gridlock exists in large part because of the structure of our government, deriving from the constitutional architecture created more than 200 years ago by leaders who lived in a small, fragmented, and largely pre-industrial society located along the Atlantic coast of North America.

The ultimate result of the gridlock examined here is that the responsible decision-making bodies of government for many years proved unable to deal forthrightly and directly with major environmental issues. Instead, they found themselves caught up in seemingly endless wrangling from entrenched and inflexible pressure groups, each determined to have its own way in critical policy areas or, failing that, to obstruct their opponents for as long as possible.

What lessons can we draw from this experience?

First, with the exception of environmental groups within the popular mobilization arena, environmental issues are always secondary to other concerns. They are clearly not central to corporate-managerial decision makers, for whom they too often represent merely one more obstacle in the way of efficient and profitable manufacturing and marketing of products. They are also secondary within both the executive and legislative arenas, although specific decision makers within those arenas can help to elevate their significance. Others can make environmental issues more salient and pressing for both executive and legislative arena decision makers, however, by emphasizing obvious connections between one's dedication to environmental values and internal pressures within each arena—electioneering, campaign contributions, threats of job losses, public scares about health, and so on.

Second, we can see that one's position on a specific environmental problem is directly affected by the pressures and constraints of the decision-making environment in which one must operate. Thus, definitions of what counts as an environmental problem and what looks like a workable solution are directly related to the technological decision-making arenas in which individual technological decision makers dwell and which color their perceptions, values, and goals. Adversaries in environmental disputes often seem to talk past each other rather than to or with each other, in large measure because each decision maker approaches the problem from the specific vantage point of his or her decision-making environment. Often, they seem to be unable, or at least unwilling, to look at the issue from the other side's perspective, except to the extent that doing so contributes to more effective political tactics.

Third, it is also clear that specific decision makers can and do make a major difference in how an environmental issue develops and whether it is ever resolved. While technological decision-making arenas constitute a general decision-making environment surrounding decision makers, that environment conditions but does not wholly determine the kinds of decisions made. The impact of Reagan administration appointees on regulatory arena decision making is one very visible example of how important individual technological decision makers are, as is the impact of changes in leadership posts in the legislative arena.

Fourth, we can see that when dealing with environmental problems, issues of scientific credibility and technological effectiveness very often mingle with nonscientific and nontechnological concerns, especially with economic interests. Rarely, if ever, does an environmental controversy hinge simply and directly on laboratory results or engineering designs. Instead, these elements are marshalled by groups whose major goal lies elsewhere. Science and technology very often are merely weapons used in a battle fought for quite different ends.

Fifth, there is striking evidence that once a controversial environmental issue erupts within the legislative arena, the contending sides will stake out such rigid and uncompromising positions that relatively rapid resolution of the issue may well be beyond the capacity of the government. Interest groups have become so sophisticated, so well organized and financed that they often seem able to bring paralyzing pressure to bear on vulnerable legislators. Those legislative arena decision makers beholden to corporate-managerial or popular mobilization arena interests are adept at using the labyrinthine procedures of Congress, minimally to frustrate the efforts of their opponents to make the legislative changes they desire. Too often, stalemate and gridlock appear more attractive to opponents than does resolution on somewhat undesirable, compromised terms.

As long as legislative arena decision makers remain vulnerable to election pressures, it is unreasonable to expect them to risk loss of their offices by neglecting important constituent interests. Members of Congress are neither stupid nor unconcerned about making effective and responsible policy decisions. But, unless they can gain some kind of insulation from organized interest groups (see the discussion in Hamlett[35]), we can reasonably predict that they will continue to behave as they have in the past. What is more, as Kraft[36] notes, just over the horizon are a number of additional pressing environmental issues still needing resolution.

As we have seen, it is often at the renewal or reauthorization stage for major environmental programs where political gridlock is likely to occur, as the opposing sides use the opportunity presented by a major review of an existing program to push for modifications they find desirable. Finding effective and safe ways to dispose of mountains of solid and hazardous wastes may prove to be just as intractable as renewing the Clean Air Act or reauthorizing FIFRA, with corporate-managerial and environmental forces just as inflexibly opposed to each other's positions.

Then there are the international environmental issues of global climate change, acid rain, deforestation, demands for reduced consumption of fossil fuels and carbon emissions, and the like, that present many of the same features that lead to political gridlock: "...the issues become more complex, scientific evidence remains inconclusive, economic costs and social impacts are perceived to be great, there are unresolved regional inequities, and public opinion is divided."[37] When all this is coupled with weak executive arena and legislative arena leadership (or outright opposition) and the increasing ability of well-organized interests to block coalition building and frustrate compromise, the stage seems amply set for continued policy immobilism and political stalemate.

We may well wonder whether there are ways to keep opposing sides in environmental disputes from digging in their heels in rigid, inflexible positions. Is there some way to ensure that opposing sides in these kinds of issues—and in other scientific and technological disputes as well—resist the seemingly irresistible tendency to see the conflict from the narrow perspective of their respective decision-making environments? We return to this question in the concluding chapter.

ENDNOTES

1. THOMAS P. HUGHES, *American Genesis: A Century of Invention and Technological Enthusiasm, 1870–1970* (New York: Viking Press, 1989).

2. GARRETT HARDIN, "The Tragedy of the Commmons," *Science*, 162 (1968), 1243–1248.

3. WALTER A. ROSENBAUM, "The Bureaucracy and Environmental Policy," in *Environmental Politics and Policy: Theories and Evidence*, ed. James P. Lester (Durham, N.C.: Duke University Press, 1989).

4. Ibid., p. 213.

5. HELEN M. INGRAM and DEAN E. MANN, "Interest Groups and Environmental Policy," in *Environmental Politics and Policy: Theories and Evidence*, ed. James P. Lester (Durham, N.C.: Duke University Press, 1989), p. 135.

6. Ibid.

7. HENRY P. CAULFIELD, "The Conservation and Environmental Movements: An Historical Analysis," in *Environmental Politics and Policy: Theories and Evidence*, ed. James P. Lester (Durham, N.C.: Duke University Press, 1989).

8. RILEY E. DUNLAP, "Public Opinion and Environmental Policy," in *Environmental Politics and Policy: Theories and Evidence*, ed. James P. Lester (Durham, N.C.: Duke University Press, 1989).

9. NORMAN J. VIG, "The President and the Environment: Revolution or Retreat?" in *Environmental Policy in the 1980s: Reagan's New Agenda*, ed. Norman J. Vig and Michael E. Kraft (Washington D.C.: CQ Press, 1984), p. 87.

10. Ibid., p. 89.

11. MICHAEL E. KRAFT, "The Politics of Environmental Gridlock," in *Environmental Policy in the 1990s: Toward a New Agenda*, ed. Norman J. Vig and Michael E. Kraft (Washington D.C.: CQ Press, 1990), p. 105.

12. KATHY KOCH, "Coming Clean Air Debate Will Reflect Traditional Costs vs. Benefits Quandry," *Congressional Quarterly Weekly Report*, February 7, 1989, p. 267.

13. Ibid., p. 268.

14. GEORGE HAGER, "Bush Sets Clean-Air Debate in Motion with New Plan," *Congressional Quarterly Weekly Report*, June 17, 1989, p. 1464.

15. RICHARD J. TOBIN, "Revising the Clean Air Act: Legislative Failure and Administrative Success," in *Environmental Policy in the 1980s: Reagan's New Agenda*, ed. Norman J. Vig and Michael E. Kraft (Washington D.C.: CQ Press, 1984), p. 227.

16. "Industries Mass for Clean Air Debate...Environmentalists on the Defensive," *Congressional Quarterly Weekly Report*, February 7, 1981, p. 272.

17. Ibid.

18. Ibid., p. 273.

19. TOBIN, "Revising the Clean Air Act."

20. Ibid., p. 233.

21. KATHY KOCH, "National Commission Report Starts Congressional Debate on Renewing Clean Air Act," *Congressional Quarterly Weekly Report*, March 7, 1981, pp. 423–424.

22. TOBIN, "Revising the Clean Air Act," p. 227.

23. Ibid., pp. 233–234.

24. Ibid., 235.

25. WALTER A. ROSENBAUM, *Environmental Politics and Policy* (Washington D.C.: CQ Press, 1985), p. 210.

26. ROCHELLE L. STANFIELD, "Punching at the Smog," *National Journal*, March 5, 1988, p. 600.

27. ALYSON PYTTE, "A Decade's Acrimony Lifted In the Glow of Clean Air," *Congressional Quarterly Weekly Report*, October 27, 1990, p. 3592.

28. JOSEPH A. DAVIS, "House Members Rush Pesticide Law Changes," *Congressional Quarterly Weekly Report*, June 8, 1985, p. 1107.

29. Ibid., p. 1108.

30. ROCHELLE L. STANFIELD, "Legalized Poisons," *National Journal*, May 2, 1987, p. 1066

31. DAVIS, "House Members Rush Pesticide," p. 1108.

32. CHRISTOPHER J. BOSSO, *Pesticides & Politics: The Life Cycle of a Public Issue* (Pittsburgh: University of Pittsburgh Press, 1987), p. 218.

33. Ibid., p. 211.

34. SHEILA JASANOFF, "EPA's Regulation of Daminozide: Unscrambling the Messages of Risk," *Science, Technology & Human Values*, vol. 12, no. 3 & 4, 1987.

35. PATRICK W. HAMLETT, "A Typology of Technological Policy Making in the U.S. Congress," *Science, Technology & Human Values*, Spring 1983, vol. 8, no. 2, pp. 33–40.

36. KRAFT, "The Politics of Environmental Gridlock," *op. cit.*

37. KRAFT, "The Politics of Environmental Gridlock," *op. cit.*, p. 120.

Chapter 9

Risk
in the Technological
Society

In this chapter we will probe one of the most complex, urgent, and bitterly disputed areas of technological politics: how we deal with the many risks—to our health, personal safety, the environment in which we all live—created by modern technology.

Technological risks raise profound issues that often have thorny scientific, political, economic, and cultural components. Determining what risks exist, who is exposed to them and at what sacrifice, and what if anything, can be done to alleviate the hardship those risks impose have become very complicated problems. What is more, these problems often require the services of technical experts to measure. This, in turn, brings up the debate about democratic control of decision making, since the average person cannot easily understand the language, methods, or conclusions used by the experts, yet must perforce live with the results.

Moreover, the very complexity of risk issues that leads to the experts' involvement often means that the experts themselves disagree about the existence, degree, and costs of various dangers and hazards. Lacking technical consensus on these points, risk issues too often end up being resolved through political pressures rather than scientific rationality.

HOW DANGEROUS IS THE TECHNOLOGICAL SOCIETY?

Is it true, as most people believe, that technological society is more dangerous today than it was in the past? It does seem that the news is filled with headlines warning of new cancer-causing foods and chemicals, yet another toxic waste dump leaking into the environment, airplane crashes, radiation scares, birth-defect–inducing air and water pollutants, dioxin, saccharin, intrauterine devices, the chlorofluorocarbon destruction of the protective ozone layer in the atmosphere. Certainly, these are scary stories, and it is understandable that people are concerned and report that in their view modern life has become more perilous and fraught with risks.

153

Yet as William Lowrance tells us, "Mankind is in many ways safer today than ever before."[1] Lowrance reminds us of the kinds of hazards faced by people in, for example, New York City as recently at 1900: formaldehyde at high concentrations, lead arsenate–based pesticides, lead chromate as a food additive, adulterated medicines, coal soot, 150,000 horses and the resultant manure, kitchen slops, cinders, and so on, in the streets, and recurrent waves of diphtheria, pneumonia, influenza, and tuberculosis.

Modern life is unquestionably safer, healthier, and more pleasant today than it was in decades or centuries past. For example, many diseases that scourged previous generations are virtually unheard of today. Our diets, at least in the industrialized world, are more bountiful than ever before in history and actually healthier (despite the ready volume of high-sugar, high-salt, high-fat fast foods). Modern medicine promises longer, more robust lives, and a panoply of medical procedures to repair our bodies undreamt of in earlier centuries. And a plenitude of technologically intricate machines has made our work—in factories, offices, and homes—easier and safer as well. If this were not enough, new forms of machine-based entertainment, travel, and leisure activities enhance our lives.

Despite all these advances, it is also clear that we face an array of new and unfamiliar hazards, from unsafe products, radiation, toxic wastes, and even global ecological threats. Not only do the threats seem novel, the consequences of exposure to some of the new risks seem catastrophic and irreversible, as in worries about irradiation or recombinant DNA accidents. Moreover, many risks are invisible, and thus involuntary. It is one thing to ride motorcycles without helmets or to go skydiving, we assume that people who do those dangerous things have freely chosen to expose themselves to possible harm. But when the danger comes in unknown food additives, tasteless water pollutants, or in the very air we breath, we feel that we cannot control many of the risks we take; indeed, often we do not even know the risks we take.

THE POLITICS AND ECONOMICS OF RISK

The matter of risk in modern society is deeply embroiled in political and economic struggles. The technical problems associated with risk issues are used by all sides in these conflicts to attack the positions of others and to justify each side's preferred outcome.

Risk Assessment and Risk Management

In order to isolate the political from the scientific and technical aspects of technological risk analysis, regulatory arena decision makers and other risk analysts often employ a distinction between risk assessment and risk management. **Risk assessment** is intended to be strictly objective and scientific, whereas **risk management** explicitly involves political influences and judgment. Risk assessment includes both the identification of risks and estimation of the probability and severity of harm associated with them. Estimation involves determining the probability of occurrence of certain events and the severity of negative consequences of those events; the negative consquences may be economic or property loss, injury, disease, premature death, or damage to environmental quality.[2]

The assessment phase is supposed to be based on the best state-of-the-art scientific procedures, providing a value-free, impartial, and politically neutral factual basis for policymakers. Once the assessment phase is completed, the more complicated and politically responsive risk management phase begins. With the factual basis of the risk issue resolved, it is up to the policymakers and the political process to decide how acceptable various possible levels of risk are, what steps, if any, the government should take to lessen the risk, and how the costs and benefits of such actions should be distributed among the parties affected.

Several commentators assert that this neat, two-staged process is too simplistic to be accurate. They assert that there often are significant difficulties in separating fact from value in the assessment stage, that too often the technical nature of the risk is unknown, and that the model often reverses the actual order of assessment and management. Albert Nichols and Richard Zeckhauser comment:

> In practice, however, the line between risk assessment and management is blurred. Fundamental gaps in knowledge make risk assessment extraordinarily imprecise, requiring many choices to be made among competing models and assumptions. In the absence of firm data or scientific consensus, many of these nominally technical decisions end up being implicit choices about values and policies, though they are not acknowledged as such. This obscures the true character of the choices being made and reduces political accountability.[3]

Indeed, we shall see that most of the risk battles are fought in the risk assessment rather than the risk management phase.

Technological risk questions are often major battlegrounds involving all of the technological decision-making arenas, but especially the corporate-managerial, the regulatory, and the popular mobilization.

Corporate-Managerial Arena

Risk problems are crucially important to members of the corporate-managerial arena, especially for those that develop, produce, sell, and use potentially hazardous materials. Companies may have massive investments in the product that it needs to protect; indeed, whole corporate careers may hinge on the successful development and marketing of a possibly harmful product. Pharmaceutical firms, for instance, may have spent millions of dollars developing a new medicine. Both the company and the company's officers who sponsored the new product have a lot riding on the competent merchandising of the drug. Public utilities may have invested heavily in new energy technologies and need several years of operation to pay back the investment.

Consumer product firms may operate on relatively small profit margins across their product lines and need to move large quantities of goods to market if they are to stay in business. Public questions about the safety or risk potential of these goods and products can play havoc with corporate plans and pursuits.

The consumers of such materials and products have a stake in risk issues, too. For some industries, there simply are no available substitutes for the raw materials that go into their products; if one or another of those important raw materials were banned or severely restricted by regulatory action, the industry may face a very grim future. Even if substitutes are available for the suspect material, the substitute may be significantly more expensive to obtain, thereby increasing the shelf price of the final product, or the substitute may not perform as well as the restricted material, thereby reducing the marketability of the end product.

Recalling our earlier distinction between product and process innovators among corporate-managerial decision makers, we know that for manufacturers of high volume, mass-produced products, any significant change in the production process can be very expensive. A regulatory finding of unacceptable risk—to workers from the existing production methods or materials or to customers—may require very costly changes in manufacturing plant and facilities. For some companies, such mandated changes might be so expensive that the company may choose to close its doors or to move its production facilities overseas, where such regulatory impositions may be absent.

Academic-Professional Arena

Because modern technological risks are so complex, members of the academic-professional arena play a critical role in defining and measuring risk and in proposing solutions. Such is the respect for the expertise of academic-professional participants that we assume they must have precise and unquestionable ways of measuring risk and safety for the rest of us. The reality, as any good scientist will acknowledge, is quite different. Many of the risks posed by modern technology are, quite literally, on the cutting edge of scientific knowledge, making unequivocal, definitive scientific judgments very difficult. Often, equally competent scientists can look at the same data and come to dramatically different conclusions. As Walter Rosenbaum cautions us, there are several formidable problems facing scientists in assessing risk:

Missing data. Many risks are so new that scientists have only just begun to study them. The effects of new pollutants, industrial chemicals, or consumer products cannot easily be measured. Experts, lacking adequate data, must extrapolate from fragmentary information. Conclusions drawn from such incomplete data often become the basis of disagreements among experts.

Late or latent effects. A number of risky substances do not produce immediate health effects in people exposed to them. Instead, consequences may appear only after many months, years, or even decades, as is often the case with cancer. With such delays, many other potential risk causes may have to be factored in, making clear, unequivocal cause-and-effect judgments very hard to reach.

Animal experiments. Scientific analyses of the potential dangers of new chemicals, pollutants, and products have the additional problem of being unable to use experiments with human beings, for ethical reasons. Instead of testing such materials on people, scientists use animal studies to measure the toxicity or carcinogenicity of a chemical. However, animal metabolism differs from human metabolism in important ways. Substances that produce, for instance, cancerous tumors in rabbits may leave laboratory mice unaffected. Which animal most closely resembles the human response? How many animals must be used to obtain reliable human projections? Rosenbaum tells us: "To demonstrate conclusively with 95 percent confidence that a certain low-level dose of some substance causes less than one case of cancer per million subjects would require a 'mega-mouse' experiment involving 6 million animals."[4] Studies of this dimension are prohibitively expensive; instead, researchers use far fewer animals, but much larger doses, and then apply a mathematical dose-response model to predict human reactions. Unfortunately, different models produce substantially different predictions, sometimes ten orders of magnitude higher than other models. One observer notes:

> Because experiments to determine which model is more accurate cannot be done with today's knowledge and techniques, the choice among the models thus becomes a policy choice. A "conservative" model risks over-prediction of potential cancers; a "liberal" model risks underprediction. The choice depends more upon value judgments than science.[5]

Thus, a great deal may hinge on which specific dose-response model is employed.

Epidemiological studies. These studies examine the impact of known human exposures to hazardous substances and then project statistical relationships between different levels of exposure and whatever adverse effects are observed in the population. Again, the models involve assumptions that can be questioned by other specialists, adding to the controversy.

Especially with latent effects, it becomes very difficult to filter out other factors that may affect the results. For example, if exposure to an industrial chemical is thought to be carcinogenic, but tumors only appear a decade or more after exposure, how can we know positively that the substance actually caused the cancer? What if, in the meantime, the victim was exposed to other potential carcinogens? What if the victim smoked cigarettes? These, and many other possible factors, complicate greatly the conclusions different scientists may draw from the same case studies.

A feature common to risk disputes is the use of science by both corporate representatives and consumer/environmental activists to bolster and rationalize their diverse positions on specific risk issues. One source of science's privileged standing in modern society is the popular perception that science is uniquely disinterested and objective in its judgments about physical reality compared to other social institutions. Moreover, academic-professional decision makers work to protect the image of the scientist as disinterested, nonpolitical, and objective and to ward off competing claims to science's status.

Since each side in these disputes seeks to enlist science as an ally in its arguments, it must perforce attack the scientific arguments presented by the other side; after all, both sides cannot be correct simultaneously. In effect, scientists within the academic-professional arena find themselves, their professional work and reputations used as weapons in risk battles. There are two connected, and ironic, reasons for this. Science, because of the tangible successes it provides and the high popular esteem it enjoys, occupies a unique place in our society as an arbiter of certain kinds of disputes about the physical world. Yet many of the technological risks we face in modern society remain beyond the reach of contemporary science to resolve. This opens the door to the political exploitation of science.

For academic-professional decision makers, serving as battering rams for both sides in risk disputes poses some important political dangers, as Sheila Jasanoff tells us

> The authority of science is seriously jeopardized when scientists are called upon to participate in policy-making. Administrative decision-making often requires a probing of the areas of greatest indeterminacy in science. Regulation of risks to health and the environment, in particular, involves issues at the frontiers of current scientific knowledge, where consensus among scientists is most fragile.[6]

When scientists get involved in risk policymaking, the essentially adversarial and juridical style of administrative procedures between contending parties brings out and emphasizes the usually hidden disagreements, disputes, and doubts that exist—as a normal part of how science operates—among various researchers and risk specialists. Gary Bryner comments:

> In the adversary process there is some tension between the search for truth and the representation of the parties involved. Participants in the adversary proceedings have incentives to emphasize the differences between the parties involved, to conceal information damaging to their positions, even though it might help resolve differences or increase the quality of the eventual decision, and to use delaying tactics to slow down administrative action.[7]

It is a critical step in administrative hearings to challenge the credibility of one's opponents' arguments; bringing forth well-known experts who will call those arguments into question is a time-honored tactic. Jasanoff's point is that the airing of such scientific disputes and the sight of noted experts publicly disagreeing undermine science's social and political standing.

Regulatory Arena   12291 - Reagan

During the late 1960s and throughout the 1970s, the U.S. government created a wide array of environmental and health and safety regulatory programs, in large measure through the efforts of popular mobilization and labor arena decision makers and over corporate-managerial objections. Under the provisions of these enactments, regulatory bureaucracies are required to review and approve or disapprove specific materials that may be introduced into the general environment or into a specific workplace or factory. What is more, such regulators are empowered to order removal of products or materials deemed injurious to human health and safety.

Legislative decision makers realize all too well that they are not equipped to make the highly technical judgments required by the laws they pass. Not only are members of Congress not technically trained in such fields as immunology, genetics, or medicine, but they face a large array of other issues requiring legislative attention, and thus cannot devote the time and effort to master these topics even if they wanted to.

Instead, Congress usually delegates to the regulatory arena a substantial degree of **bureaucratic discretion:** "the delegation of broad, policy making powers to administrative agencies."[8] Bureaucratic discretion is a well established tenet of representative government, usually exhibited in the issuance of "rules" that govern the implementation of laws by bureaucratic agencies. Such rules have much of the impact of formal legislation upon the people and organization affected.

Indeed, from some perspectives, bureaucratic discretion is both essential and inevitable in order to allow necessary flexibility and adaptability in the implementation of law, to bring expertise and professionalism to bear on public problems, and to encourage the diffusion of political conflict. Because regulatory agencies are often given multiple, complex problems to resolve, having the capacity to make policy decisions without having to get advance approval from Congress is imperative. Bryner tells us: "Laws cannot be written to anticipate and address all of the possible situations within an agency's jurisdiction. They must permit a consideration of economic, regional, cultural, personal and other differences among those who fall within the agency's regulatory reach."[9] This is all the more important when, as in most public safety and health issues, the scientific basis of regulatory decisions is incomplete or uncertain.

In those risk areas where the data and knowledge base are incomplete or uncertain, regulatory arena decision makers often find that they cannot always justify their specific decisions by referring to universally accepted scientific findings. Inevitably, such decisions include some subjective policy elements, regardless of how "objectively" they may be expressed. These subjective policy decisions, of course, are often the focus of political battles between corporate-managerial and consumer and environmental decision makers. Just how much independence and discretion regulatory decision makers ought to have, and how they should exercise that discretion, are especially contested issues in the area of technological risk.

When there is scientific disagreement concerning various aspects of risk policy, such as whether substances that cause cancer in animals will also trigger cancer in humans, whether there is some kind of "threshold" exposure limit below which an potentially dangerous substance may be considered safe, or whether tests performed on laboratory animals are good predictors of harm for humans, regulators must often choose which opinions to use in making their decisions. Many corporate-managerial decision makers claim that regulatory arena decision makers systematically side with the preferences of consumer and environmental groups, in effect imposing political values onto a decision process that should be based on science. They protest that regulators too often use their bureaucratic discretion to impose the scientifically unproven values and beliefs of the popular mobilization arena on regulatory decisions, all the time cloaking those decisions with the prestige of "objective" science.

On the other hand, members of consumer and environmental groups complain that regulatory decision makers are too much influenced by the corporate-managerial arena. And, once again, the use of bureaucratic discretion by regulators is the focus of their grievances. Among the kinds of discretionary decisions made by regulators are choices about what specific risk to address. Since no regulatory agency ever receives sufficient funding to take on all possible risks, administrators must continually set priorities, taking action on some fronts while ignoring others. What risks to deal with and which can be ignored, are decisions of great importance to members of the corporate-managerial arena.

Consumer and environmental decision makers complain that, under pressure from the corporate-managerial arena, regulatory agencies too often steer clear of certain public risks, all the time justifying their actions on the basis of limited resources. Echoing the complaints of the corporate-managerial arena, consumer and environmental groups accuse regulators of systematically siding with corporate-managerial interpretations of risk issues, camouflaging overtly political decisions as "science."

As necessary and inevitable as bureaucratic discretion is, regulatory arena decision makers do not have a completely free hand in making the rules that control how risk programs are implemented. There are, in fact, a number of legal and institutional limitations on the use of bureaucatic power. Over the years Congress has enacted legislation that addresses the use of bureaucratic discretion, either directly, as in the 1946 Administrative Procedure Act, or as part of regulatory programs, such as the Occupational Safety and Health Act and others, which contain restrictions on the use of bureaucratic discretion. In addition, the regulatory arena decision makers must employ a number of in-house review steps to ensure that high-level agency officials have carefully monitored the development and handling of the entire process. Also, outside groups may gain access to the agency materials, records, and data, to assist them in preparing responses to the proposed agency action.

All of these steps, which can take three to four years to complete, may then be followed by external reviews in either or both the legislative arena and the judicial arena. Congressional committee investigations also impose bounds on bureaucratic discretion, as regulatory arena decision makers may be required to explain their actions to sometimes hostile legislators.

The involvement of the federal courts in administrative rule making began with the passage of the Administrative Procedures Act right after World War II, intended to allow legal recourse for any person "suffering legal wrong because of agency action, or adversely affected or aggrieved by agency action." The courts have reviewed both the procedures used by regulatory arena decision makers, as well as the substance of those decisions. Finding that some agencies' procedures were inadequate, the courts now require more formal guidelines guaranteeing greater access on the part of affected persons, as well as loosening the conditions needed for judicial standing. Substantively, the courts have also reviewed the content of rules decisions, requiring a fuller record explaining how and why the regulatory arena decision maker reached a particular decision. The courts have also tried to give clearer interpretations to the sometimes ambiguous legislative language contained in regulatory laws.

Executive arena actions can also impose limitations upon the decisions taken by members of the regulatory arena, although formal changes in the laws imposing the regulations would require the agreement of Congress. In recent years, the Office of Management and Budget has assumed increasing control of regulatory actions taken by executive branch agencies.

Thus, while bureaucratic discretion continues to play a very central role in technological decision making concerning risk within the regulatory arena, there are several kinds of restraints upon that discretion imposed by members of other technological decision-making arenas. The Administrative Procedures Act, plus specific procedural requirements contained in individual regulatory statutes, legislative arena interventions in regulatory decisions, judicial arena reviews of both the procedures and substance of regulations, and executive arena impositions all serve to restrain bureaucratic discretion. Such restraints serve

> to legitimize administrative discretionary and regulatory power. It assuages the concern that administrative power be constrained and checked. It provides the constitutional due process prequisite for the administrative taking of liberty and property. It serves as a check on the fusion of legislative, executive, and judicial powers that are central to the regulatory process. It rests on the perceived virtues of the adversary process—the opportunity it provides for protagonists on both sides of an issue to present their cases and the ability the process has to discover the "truth" from this competitive framework.[10]

What is more, all of these points of leverage on individual decisions and decision makers within the regulatory arena are the sites of important political battles among individual technological decision makers from all of the affected technological decision-making arenas. Moreover, the existence of so much scientific uncertainty and controversy over the origins and causes of various risks only adds to the highly charged political atmosphere surrounding risk questions.

Labor and Popular Mobilization Arenas

Eliminating or controlling technological risks has been a prime objective of participants from both of these arenas. For organized labor, workers' safety is a major focus of contract negotiations and political action. The labor arena strongly supported the creation of the Occupational Health and Safety Administration (OSHA), and often criticizes the regulatory arena decision makers for failing to take steps to eradicate unsafe shop floor conditions. Labor unions have also sought restrictions on worker exposure to potentially hazardous industrial chemicals.

A great many consumer and environmental groups have struggled with risky technologies, including civilian nuclear energy, air, land, and water pollution, toxic wastes, unsafe consumer products, food additives, and many others. Such groups have been especially effective in mobilizing public concerns about such risks and in pressuring the legislative arena to pass stringent laws to address them. They have also made extensive use of the courts as leverage on corporate-managerial decisions.

Legislative Arena

As an institution, Congress is not well suited for resolving highly technical issues. While it does have impressive in-house technical staff support—the Office of Technology Assessment (OTA), General Accounting Office (GAO), Legislative Research Service, Library of Congress (LRS-LOC), and Congressional Budget Office (CBO)—and has access to outside scientific experts, Congress itself remains a wholly political institution. Political pressures make it very difficult for the legislature to make policy decisions based on scientific rationality.

Not only is Congress usually unwilling to give detailed direction to risk programs, assess the quality of existing scientific knowledge about risk, or know when to commission new studies, the legislative arena often ducks politically controversial risk issues by transferring the issue into the regulatory arena for resolution. When Congress does this, it often encodes in the law the compromises and bargains that are part and parcel of the legislative process. The result too often is legislation containing unclear and vague provisions. Rosenbaum notes some of the consequences of legislative ambiguity:

> Different substances are often regulated according to different standards. The same agency may have to use as many as six or seven standards depending upon which substances, or which laws, are involved. The same substance may be subject to one regulatory standard when dumped into a river and another when mixed into processed food. Statutory risk standards are commonly vague and sometimes confusing; congressional intent may be muddled, often deliberately. Agencies must, nonetheless, render from this confusion defensible judgments.[11]

Rosenbaum lists five different statutory formulas required by different laws for determining permissible exposure levels to various risks:

1. *No-risk criteria*. Some laws permit no risks to human health from the use of a substance. Moreover, regulators are forbidden to consider costs when setting standards. The Delaney amendment to the Food, Drug and Cosmetic Act of 1938 is an example of this kind of standard.
2. *Margin-of-safety criteria*. Under this criterion, regulatory agencies set exposure standards that contain an additional margin of safety. The Clean Air Act of 1970 contains this kind of standard.
3. *Cost-regarding criteria*. Congress requires or permits regulatory agencies to consider both the costs of regulation along with the benefits. There are two varieties of cost-regarding criteria:
    A. *Cost-sensitive criteria*. Under this direction, agencies are allowed but not required to balance the benefits of a specific regulatory standard against the costs of enforcement. The Occupational Safety and Health Act of 1970 is an example of this kind of criterion.
    B. *Cost-benefit criteria*. In this, agencies are required to balance the costs and benefits of standards for exposure to a substance. The Consumer Product Safety Act of 1972 contains this requirement.[12]

See Table 9-1 for a list of decision-making criteria for regulatory agencies in health and safety.

In effect, regulatory arena decision makers must balance sometimes conflicting social and political values in their decisions. How much health protection is worth how much economic cost? How much should we as a society be willing to "pay"—in jobs, in new investment, and in other opportunity costs—to protect lives? Clearly, such questions are beyond science's ability to answer; indeed, they are not about science at all, but about philosophy. By including such nebulous expressions as "an adequate margin of safety," "in the judgment of the Administrator," "most adequately assures," "to the extent feasible," "on the basis of the best available evidence," or "the benefits expected from the rule [must] bear a reasonable relationship to its costs," the legislative arena virtually guarantees that regulatory agencies will enjoy a considerable degree of freedom in determining if their actions meet these standards. At other times, however, when it wants to place explicit limits on bureaucratic discretion, Congress will load a statute with so many criteria of risk assessment that the regulatory arena decision makers find it very difficult to comply with the law.

Executive Arena

The executive arena can significantly alter the policymaking environment within which regulatory arena decision makers operate. For instance, in February 1981, President Ronald Reagan signed Executive Order 12291, requiring that all federal agencies prepare a cost-benefit analysis for all "major" regulations prior to issuing those regulations. Although Executive Order 12291 does not apply to all regulatory agencies, nor does it override specific procedures that may be mandated in the statutes implemented by specific agencies, does represent an important effort

Table 9-1
Decision-Making Criteria for Health and Safety Agencies

Agency\Program			Criteria for Regulatory Actions
EPA	Clean air	Statutory sources	Avoid risk: provide "an ample margin of safety to protect public health."
		Mobile sources	Balance risk with available technology: standards to reflect the greatest degree of emission reduction achievable through technology available."
	Clean water	Toxic pollutants	Balance risk with the available technology: "provide an ample margin of safety," based on best available technology economically achievable.
		Safe drinking water	General balancing: protect health "to the extent feasible (taking costs into consideration)."
	Hazardous wastes		Avoid risk: take action "necessary to protect human health and the environment."
	Toxic substances		General balancing: "protect adequately against such risk using the least burdensome requirement."
	Pesticides		General balancing: Avoid "unreasonable adverse effects" meaning "unreasonable risk to man or the environment taking into account the economic, social and environmental costs and benefits."
CPSC			General balancing: standards to "be reasonably necessary to prevent or reduce an unreasonable risk of injury," benefits expected from the rule (to) "bear a reasonable relationship to its costs."
OSHA			Balance risk with available technology: standards to "adequately assur(e) to the extent feasible that no employee will suffer material impairment of health or functional capacity."
FDA	Food	Additives	Avoid risk: ban if substance shown to be carcinogenic.
		Contaminants	General balancing: take action "necessary for the protection of public health."
	Drugs		General balancing

Source: Gary C. Bryner, *Bureaucratic Discretion: Law and Policy in Federal Regulatory Agencies* (New York: Pergamon Press, 1987), p. 45.

by the executive arena to impose controls on the kinds of technological decisions reached by members of the regulatory arena.

And, as we have seen, executive arena decision makers can directly influence regulatory arena decisions by making personnel changes within regulatory agencies, altering budgets, shifting organizational burdens, and the like.

Judicial Arena

The courts are directly involved in risk issues whenever injured parties seek damages for their injuries through lawsuits, the traditional way we handle risk in our society. But courts are also involved in administrative law, in which they assess how well regulatory agencies do or do not fulfull the obligations of the law. This has been a major site for conflict among the corporate-managerial, the popular mobilization, and the regulatory arenas.

Because Congress has, in a sense, delegated its oversight authority to the courts by including appellate review provisions directly in regulatory legislation, the role of the judicial arena has grown larger. Thomas McGarity tells us:

> To the extent that the courts, in exercising their review function, reduce the discretionary power of the agencies, then, they enhance their own power. Because the exercise of judicial discretion is limited by the very statutory words that define the limits of agency discretion and because the judges interpret those discretion-limiting statutes, the judiciary is, in a very real sense, at large when it divides power between itself and the agencies.[13]

McGarity goes on to note that while a judge cannot compel a regulator to exercise greater discretion or take on more authority, "an appellate court's power to limit discretion is constrained only by the court's own self-restraint and by the possibility of Supreme Court review."[14] As McGarity notes, all sides in court reviews of regulatory risk decisions understand the wide power the court enjoys, as seen in the hectic efforts of contending lawyers to file cases before appellate judges thought to be sympathetic to their clients' interests.

The courts must usually review three aspects of the use of bureaucratic discretion: how accurately the regulatory agency interpreted its authority to act in the case at hand, how well the agency abided by the constraints and limitations of relevant administrative law, and the substantive decision reached by the agency, examining the agency's records and reasonings to determine if the action was "arbitrary and capricious."

Aside from questions about the courts' competence in judging highly technical issues, there are worries in some quarters that the courts have often drifted far away from judicial self-restraint:

> Examination of the appellate court decisions over the past fifteen years has left more than one observer with the impression that the courts are guided not so much by neutral rules of judicial review as by individual judges' opinions about the social value of a particular agency's goals.[15]

Thus, we can conclude that for the foreseeable future, the judicial arena will continue to play a central role in resolving risk issues.

ARENA INTERACTIONS

To review: We are exploring the ways in which individual technological decision-makers attempt to bring their specific technological projects to successful completion and how they very often must obtain needed decisions from decision makers in other technological decision-making arenas. To obtain these decisions, they must find ways to influence the pressures, constraints, limitations, ambitions, and so on that characterize the general decision-making environment of the arena from which the specific decision is needed.

In some areas we have explored, relations among members of different technological decision-making arenas, although sometimes antagonistic, have become largely routine, predictable, and even cooperative. Not so in the area of technological risk. Here decision makers from the various concerned arenas engage in often tough, acrimonious struggles. This is in part because there is so much money at stake in these conflicts and in part because there is such a difference of opinion, of philosophy, among the participants as to how we should deal with the problems of potentially dangerous technologies.

In risk issues, there are a large number of decisions to examine, from corporate-managerial choices to develop and market new technological products, processes, or materials, to legislative arena decisions about new regulations or other risk-related statutes, to regulatory arena decisions about the general riskiness of new or existing products or substances and their susceptibility to regulatory control, to recurring popular mobilization arena actions challenging regulatory arena determinations, to judicial arena findings concerning the legal applicability of specific ordinances and the administrative procedures followed, among others. There are, indeed, a great many sites for technological decision-making arena battles about risk. Moreover, it is characteristic of these battles over risk that, as Aaron Wildavsky notes, all sides claim the validity of science for their position: "Almost all participants in the risk debate...claim a respect for facts and attempt to legitimate their policy preferences by reference to canons of scientific inquiry."[16] Indeed, members of the academic-professional arena often find that their professional reputations and the very code of scientific investigation that is to guide their research are used as political weapons by the contending parties in risk issues.

Rule Making in Cancer Policy

While there are hundreds, even thousands, of different technological risks we could examine, delving into government policies toward cancer gives us an excellent view of a crucial area of risk and of how the various technological decision-making arenas respond to the problem.

Popular concerns about cancer reached a peak in 1971, with the public declaration of a "war on cancer" by President Richard Nixon and the passage of the National Cancer Act, greatly enhancing federal support for cancer research. In addition, during the same decade a number of environmental, workers' health, and consumer protection laws contained explicit provisions requiring federal bureaucracies to monitor and control human exposure to potential carcinogens. Regulatory arena decision makers sit directly at the center of cancer policy, as Jasanoff notes:

> The most distinctive feature of the cancer policies developed in the United States is their assumption that gaps between science and policy should be bridged by means of administrative rules. Formal statements about how to test carcinogens and interpret these tests proceed from a belief that, when all the scientific evidence is in, regulators will still be confronted by numerous uncertainties and expert conflicts. Science alone will not be sufficient to dictate the correct policy choice. In order to make policy in a publicly accountable manner, regulators should therefore state principled rules for overcoming the expected omissions and conflicts in the scientific record.[17]

Indeed, the Environmental Protection Agency, Food and Drug Administration, and Occupational Safety and Health Administration were each given important responsibilities in this area. How well these regulatory agencies meet those responsibilities regarding cancer has been the focus of considerable political strife among decision makers in the corporate-managerial, popular mobilization, and the regulatory arenas.

In the beginning, regulatory arena decision makers dealt with carcinogens covered by the various statutes on a case-by-case basis, exercising substantial bureaucratic discretion. As Jasanoff tells us, "The agency has resorted to ad hoc procedures and arguments in interpreting scientific evidence so as to reach results consistent with a politically acceptable regulatory outcome."[18] However, popular mobilization arena decision makers objected to the informal procedures used by regulatory agencies and began using lawsuits in the judicial arena to pressure the agencies to change their decisions. In addition, members of consumer and environmental groups used decisions made within the legislative arena for the same purpose. Thus, the passage of the Federal Environmental Pesticide Act (FEPA) of 1972 and the later Toxic Substances Control Act by Congress reflected the rising popular concerns about possible cancer causing substances and increased pressures on regulatory arena decision makers to discover, measure, and control those substances for the public health. FEPA especially, with its mandatory 90 days for final decisions in pesticide-cancellation proceedings, forced EPA to find ways for streamlining its often drawn-out proceedings.

One response was EPA's effort to develop generic rules that the regulator would use in decisions about carcinogenicity. As Mark Rushefsky tells us: "The purpose of generic guidelines is to create uniformity and consistency in decision making either within an agency or across agencies."[19] What the regulators sought to do was review the scientific literature on carcinogenicity and draw the best supported conclusions into a clearly stated list of decision principles. Such generic rules, it was hoped, would settle once and for all various general questions about how to determine the carcinogenicity of a suspect substance, so that as EPA dealt with individual decisions, it would not have to reconsider, and reargue, those general issues over and over again.

As these first attempts at generic rule making regarding cancer were promulgated, corporate-managerial decision makers took strong exception to the specific terms those rules imposed. Chemical companies especially questioned the scientific validity of EPA's approach. It was important for the corporate-managerial decision makers to raise objections to EPA's rules because they would be applied not just to the specific case in question, but across the board in cancer cases generally. Indeed, under corporate-managerial pressure, EPA gradually softened the specific rules it adopted.

The Occupational Safety and Health Administration (OSHA) also moved to develop generic rules governing its cancer decisions, this time more because the agency needed to overcome its public image as an overzealous regulator given to issuing trivial standards. By taking up cancer issues one at a time, the agency had already dealt with asbestos, vinyl chloride, arsenic, coke oven emissions, and acrylonitrile. Nevertheless, the agency continued to take criticism from the labor arena for the slowness of its cancer policy determinations.

OSHA hoped that its cancer policy would resolve definitively many of the issues that continually reappeared in individual regulatory proceedings involving specific carcinogens: the correctness of bioassays using animals, methodological rules for such tests, and how to evaluate epidemiological tests. By debating these issues in one detailed rule-making process, surveying the best and latest scientific data, and coming to specific conclusions on each issue, OSHA hoped to simplify and speed up regulatory proceedings concerning specific substances. Jasanoff describes the very substantial effort OSHA went through to reach its conclusions:

> Issued as a final rule in January, 1980, OSHA's cancer policy covered almost 300 pages in the Federal Register, of which more than half were devoted to the agency's analysis of specific scientific issues. The publication capped more than three years of regulatory development, distilling the views of at least fifty-four experts in the field of carcinogenesis and summarizing a total record of over 250,000 pages. At least on the surface, there could be no question that OSHA had fully complied with the dictates of good administrative practice. The agency had listened to experts from government, industry and independent institutions. The decision-making record carefully described their conflicting viewpoints and justified the agency's decision to accept one or another position.[20]

Despite this herculean effort, OSHA's cancer policy also met with hostility from the corporate-managerial arena. The chemical industry immediately filed suit in federal court against the agency and its cancer policy. The industry's complaint was that, given the uncertainties surrounding cancer issues, OSHA was encoding into its cancer guidelines positions on important controversies based more on the policy preferences of the regulators than on solid science. This, they argue, is an abuse of bureaucratic discretion.

Clearly, corporate-managerial decision makers have a vital stake in how members of the regulatory arena derive cancer policy decisions. Should the regulatory arena adopt generic procedures and standards showing a consistent bias against corporate-managerial interests, this would constitute a major setback to specific technological projects pursued by industry. That the corporate-managerial arena reacted to OSHA's cancer policy by appealing to the judicial arena rather than by trying to influence OSHA's decision makers directly indicates that corporate representatives felt unable to manipulate the pressures and constraints that operate within OSHA as they had done at EPA. Instead, they hoped to induce the judicial arena to make a decision that would leverage a change in OSHA's standards.

There are grounds to accept at least some of the corporate-managerial objections to the OSHA policy. As Rushefsky notes, there are many legitimate questions about any cancer policy. Such a policy must address and answer questions such as these:

> What kinds of evidence are needed to demonstrate carcinogenicity? What is the role of bioassays (animal studies) in demonstrating carcinogenicity in humans? What role is given to positive versus negative studies? How are conflicting studies weighed? How are benign and malignant tumors counted? What are appropriate dose levels? What kinds of mathematical extrapolation models are used? How are thresholds treated in risk assessments? Is the distinction between initiators and promoters used? Is the distinction between genotoxic and epigenetic carcinogens used?[21]

While these questions appear to require scientific answers, science, as yet, is unable to answer them conclusively.

Regulatory decision makers, however, do not have the luxury of long times or endless resources to resolve these questions. They must come to decisions within the time frames imposed by law, even if that means making decisions without firm answers to such controverial issues. Thus, the regulator must often make choices between contending perspectives on these questions, choices that, in the last analysis, cannot be justified by science, but are policy choices.

Rushefsky suggests that there are at least two attitudes in how these kinds of questions are answered: a risk-averse or a risk-tolerant bias. The risk-averse perspective seeks the greatest safety from potential harm and will consistently impose stiffer standards on suspect carcinogens, even if doing so inflicts economic costs on the manufacturer, wholesaler, or consumer of the substance. In general, the risk-averse position will presume that a potential carcinogen is dangerous until proven safe. Popular mobilization and labor arena decision makers uniformly adopt a risk-averse position on cancer issues.

The risk-tolerant perspective, on the other hand, wants to weigh health risks against other values, especially economic costs, and is likely to impose less stringent standards than the risk-averse position. This perspective is apt to argue that a suspect carcinogen should be considered safe unless and until it is definitively proven dangerous. Corporate-managerial decision makers regularly defend the risk-tolerant outlook, as have a number of executive arena officials during the Reagan administration. It is important to note that, while both sides typically cite scientific evidence to back their arguments, neither position can claim scientific validity; each is really a policy preference.

The corporate-managerial critique of OSHA's cancer policy asserted that the agency had chosen answers to these questions that exhibited a systematic bias opposed to industry interests, and that it had ignored or dismissed counterarguments raised by industry scientists. Since such a bias cannot be justified on scientific grounds, they charged, it must represent a subjective and basically political agenda. More generally, the corporate-managerial arena maintained that the regulatory arena had too often adopted the risk-averse policy preferences of consumer and environmental decision makers as its own and then tried to dress those preferences in the garb of legitimate science.

OSHA responded that, as the record clearly shows, it had exerted great effort in consulting with the finest cancer specialists and in combing the scientific literature in its massive effort to resolve the remaining questions about cancer. OSHA had carefully considered all of the corporate-managerial arguments about each of the major issues and simply found those arguments unconvincing. Indeed, it asserted, it was the corporate-managerial arena, having "lost" the debate on scientific grounds, that was trying to introduce unsubstantiated policy preferences under the guise of "good" science. Jasanoff summarizes the regulatory arena's quandary in cancer policy:

> Entrusted with increasingly complicated tasks, and working under stringent timetables and the ever present threat of litigation, agencies like OSHA and EPA find more and more attractive the possibility of simplifying the issues in dispute and, if possible, permanently foreclosing debate on some of them. But as the examples of high-dosage testing and negative epidemiological studies show, agencies may have to engage in arbitrary exercises of discretionary power in carrying out such simplification.[22]

In effect, she asserts, in order to enhance regulatory arena values and practices, such as policy uniformity, continuity, and predictability, regulators have employed bureaucratic discretion to adopt simplified decision-making rules that may sometimes fly in the face of the changing scientific knowledge base that ought to underlay highly technical regulatory decisions. Members of affected arenas take objection to such rules, especially if those rules lock in a series of future decisions inimical to their interests.

Corporate decision makers argued for a reinvigoration of the distinction mentioned earlier between risk assessment and risk management. They wanted a formal separation between the processes of risk assessment, to be based exclusively on science, and of risk management, to be based in larger measure on regulatory policy choices. Their complaint was that OSHA's generic guidelines blurred this distinction, allowing policy preferences to penetrate into what should be an objective, disinterested risk assessment process.

However, Jasanoff alerts us to the real purpose of the corporate-managerial objections: "In industry's political agenda, however, the demand for formal risk assessment was part of a larger strategy to remove risk assessment from the control of agency scientists and bureaucrats, whom industry regarded on the whole as captive of pro-regulatory interests."[23] The chemical industry wanted to create a formal risk assessment mechanism away from the regulatory agencies, by delegating the task of completing risk assessments to a panel of independent scientists, such as the National Academy of Sciences (NAS). In effect, the corporate-managerial participants wanted to shift the risk assessment process completely away from the regulatory arena and to the academic-professional arena.

Using our decision-making framework, we see that the corporate-managerial decision makers found themselves unable to shape the kinds of specific cancer guidelines they wanted from within the regulatory arena, and thus tried a variety of tactics to hem in or limit those decisions by influencing decisions made in other arenas— thus the initial resort to litigation when OSHA's policy was announced. And the corporate-managerial arena won an important victory in a case brought against OSHA's proposed standard for benzene, a known cause of leukemia. The U.S. Supreme Court invalidated the agency's proposed rule because the agency had failed to perform a quantitative risk assessment for benzene before issuing its proposed standard.

Next, the corporate-managerial arena hoped to remove even marginally scientific issues and the interpretation of technical information from the control of the regulatory arena by shifting the responsibility to the academic-professional arena, where they counted on having more influence. In the end, however, NAS rejected the industry's proposal for a separate, single central board for regulatory risk assessment, stating:

> If risk assessment as practiced by the regulatory agencies were pure science, perhaps an organizational separation could effectively sharpen the distinction between science and policy in risk assessment and regulatory decision-making. However, many of the analytic choices made throughout the risk assessment process require individual judgments that are based on *both scientific and policy considerations....* Given the inherent mixture of science and policy in risk assessment, organizational separation would simply move risk assessment policy into a different organization that would then have to become politically accountable.[24]

Thus, the corporate-managerial arena's effort to shift the decision from the regulatory arena to the academic-professional arena ultimately failed, as the scientists themselves acknowledged that all but a handful of the analytical steps involved in cancer risk assessment inevitably involved a mixture of science and policy.

However, the struggle between the corporate-managerial and the regulatory arenas over cancer policy was not over. Corporate-managerial decision makers tried again to impose limitations on the kinds of regulatory decisions emerging from agencies such as OSHA and EPA, this time, however, by using members of the executive arena. Corporate-managerial decision makers were deeply involved in the election campaign of Ronald Reagan, in large measure because of Reagan's public and long-standing antiregulatory positions, especially in the areas of safety, health, and the environment.

With Reagan's land-slide election in 1980, industry decision makers could reasonably hope for greater efforts from the executive arena to impose limits on bureaucratic discretion within the regulatory arena. And, as we have already noted, in February 1981, Reagan did indeed sign Executive Order 12291, imposing cost-benefit analysis requirements on all new regulations and allowing for substantial review of new regulations by the Office of Budget and Management. More than this, though, corporate-managerial decision makers hoped to see the president use his appointment powers to name specific decision makers who also shared his antiregulatory perspective, and place them in important decision-making positions throughout the federal bureaucracy.

Among the more controversial appointments were James Watt, as secretary of the interior and Anne Burford as director of the Environmental Protection Agency. These were the most public of Reagan's appointments, but others were also given important decision-making slots at lower levels in several federal agencies, including John Hernandez, EPA deputy administrator, and John Todhunter, EPA's assistant administrator for toxic substances, in the Office of Toxic Substances. These last two were deeply involved in a controversial attempted shift in regulatory cancer policy.

In October 1979, two major chemical companies, Monsanto Chemical Products and the Celanese Chemical Company, let EPA know that recent studies suggested that the chemical formaldehyde may be carcinogenic for laboratory test animals. Formaldehyde is widely used in industry for adhesives, insulating materials, plastics, paper, textiles, rubber, certain agricultural products, drugs, and vaccines. We can see that the chemical industry and the many end users of formaldehyde had a great deal at stake should this very useful product prove to cause cancer in humans. Thus, EPA faced deciding on the risk formaldehyde may present to public health, and of what steps, if any, the regulatory agency should take to restrict or eliminate this substance. While considering the initial evidence of carcinogenicity, as well as additional information, the 1980 election intervened, with the subsequent changes in personnel at EPA. The new EPA leadership, then, inherited the formaldehyde problem from the Carter administration.

The new leadership at EPA quickly signaled important changes in risk policy when Deputy Administrator John Hernandez initiated a series of three "science forums" to review the data on formaldehyde. However, the only participants in these meetings were Hernandez, EPA staff scientists, and representatives of the chemical companies and of the Chemical Industry Institute of Toxicology. Rushefsky tells us:

No public notice of the meetings was made, nor transcripts kept.... The science forums were apparently intended to provide industry with an opportunity to critique the scientific evidence in front of top EPA decisionmakers. There were few outside observers (by the last meetings there were no outside observers) and apparently no attempt to seek outside and independent review of industry critiques. Hernandez relied heavily upon those meetings in his decision.[25]

The existence of the meetings was inadvertently discovered by a congressional aide, whose notes constitute the only written record of any of the meetings.

These clandestine meetings were followed by a memorandum prepared by John Todhunter, detailing why formaldehyde did not warrant EPA consideration, even though the holdover Carter administration appointees had recommended such consideration. Although Todhunter, and several other Reagan appointees, previously had criticized EPA and other regulatory agencies bitterly for what they saw as a misuse of bureaucratic discretion, Todhunter made extensive use of those discretionary powers in reaching the conclusions detailed in his memorandum. Jasanoff summarizes: "In building his case on formaldehyde, Todhunter exercised the US administrator's privilege of picking and choosing from the scientific record those bits of data that best supported his policy decision."[26]

The Todhunter memorandum varied from earlier cancer guidelines because it abandoned the risk-averse perspective and systematically adopted the significantly more risk-tolerant position in dealing with potential carcinogens favored by the corporate-managerial arena. Rushefsky summarizes how Todhunter differed from earlier cancer guidelines:

> The Todhunter memorandum was different from previous statements in several ways. First, it stated that a proof of carcinogenicity required positive results in two rodent species and both sexes. It also supported the initiator/promoter distinction which would permit the establishment of a threshold and effectively allow greater exposure to formaldehyde than would previous risk assessment assumptions. For example, the memorandum states that promoters required repeated exposures; that low levels of substances, especially promoters, posed not signficant risk; and that low levels of exposure allowed reversibility of potentially carcinogenic effects.[27]

Rushefsky tells us that there were two other cancer policy documents issued in the early years of the first Reagan administration—additional cancer guidelines from EPA and a set of risk assessment principles prepared by the White House Office of Science and Technology Policy (OSTP)—that also adopted a more risk-tolerant perspective than the existing regulatory guidelines. For example, the EPA additional guidelines proposed a modified form of the "no observable effects level" (NOEL) model for quantitative risk assessment, instead of the more common linear model used in other guidelines. The NOEL model posits that there may be certain thresholds below which a potential carcinogen ceases to pose a health hazard, while the linear model assumes that the risk a substance poses exists at all possible exposures. Thus, NOEL would permit concentrations of possible carcinogens 10 to 369 times greater than the linear model would allow.[28]

All three of these regulatory documents were subjected to severe criticism from many members of the academic-professional arena. A number of noted cancer scientists, including Bernard Weinstein of Columbia University, testified before Congress that, in their opinion, there were no grounds, no new research, to justify the kinds of cancer policy changes suggested in the Todhunter memorandum and the other documents.[29] Norton Nelson, of New York University, criticized Todhunter for a misuse of bureaucratic discretion, calling his memorandum "[t]he sort of document that one would not expect an objective scientist to produce."[30] Nelson agreed that federal cancer policy needed revision and updating, but that such changes should be undertaken by an accredited scientific body, such as the National Academy of Sciences, rather than by actions of appointed bureaucrats.

CONCLUSIONS

Unquestionably, the general notion of risk marks one of the most important points where the American political decision-making process intersects with the technologies that underpin life in modern society. It is equally clear, especially from the cancer policy case study, that finding policy consensus on how to deal with technological risks remains one of the most difficult tasks facing government in a high-tech society. This is because, unless we decide simply to let people take their chances willy-nilly, any political response invariably creates "winners" and "losers," groups and individuals who either benefit from efforts to ameliorate risk or who must pay for those steps.

If those who fear that they may be required to pay for what they think are expensive and unnecessary risk policies can convince crucial decision makers that no risk exists, or that it is negligible, or that the benefits of the source of the risk greatly outweigh its costs, or that those exposed to the risk do so voluntarily or in some other way "deserve" the exposure, or that they have already taken sufficient steps to ameliorate the risk, or whatever, they may evade the costs of a stiff risk-reduction or risk-elimination decision.

On the other hand, those who fear the risk must convince those same decision makers that the risk is indeed real, severe, and involuntarily imposed upon its victims. Thus, the focal point of risk politics is the specific decisions reached by very real decision makers: regulators, legislators, judges, presidential assistants, and the leaders of interest groups. The political dynamic of risk policymaking, then, often involves groups in conflict over how to measure or determine whether a specific technology poses any risk at all and what, if anything, can or should be done about the risk.

Quite often, the hidden agenda of risk disputes involves how to levy the costs of responding to the risk—that is who should pay to remove or ameliorate the consequences of continuing to use the risky technology. The contending sides, predictably, propound answers to these questions that advance their interests, citing whatever available scientific evidence can be found to substantiate their claims. Because of the myriad scientific uncertainties that are acknowledged by everyone involved, especially by the scientists, each side can frequently mount reasonably coherent science-based arguments in favor of their positions.

All too often, scientific "findings" become pliable weapons in political struggles. Each side, knowing the importance of science as a rationale for political decisions, often exaggerates the conclusions it draws from scientific evidence, while attacking the reliability of the other side's evidence and the neutrality of the other side's specialists. Often it seems that each side's experts are on hand merely to debunk the claims of the other side's experts.

Each side commonly paints the other in the most extreme, venal, and irrational terms, hoping thereby to discredit their opponents in the eyes of the public and of important decision makers in other arenas. Thus, corporate-managerial decision makers frequently accuse environmental and consumer groups of gross distortion and exaggeration in risk disputes, and often suggest that such groups secretly want to undermine the free market and other "un-American" activities. By the same token, environmental, consumer, and labor groups often depict corporate-managerial decision makers as unscrupulous and mercenary servants of power and wealth who simply do not care about the harm and damage they do. It is not surprising that the public quickly loses the ability to judge the validity of each side's position, given the clamor and din of claims and counter-claims that mark risk disputes.

The case of cancer policy illustrates all of these characteristics.

Cancer policy has involved a large number of technological projects, some involving specific products or substances, such as formaldehyde, others focused on regulatory arena efforts to establish generic rules to guide decisions about specific substances. In each of these cases, decision makers from opposing arenas have fought to bring their contradictory technological projects to successful completion by inducing other decision makers to make the kinds of decisions they want. The politics of risk can be seen in these rival campaigns.

Unfortunately for the corporate-managerial participants, decision makers in the regulatory arena were experiencing considerable pressures from the popular mobilization, labor, legislative, and judicial arenas to do something dramatic and concrete about cancer. Since the chemical industry believed that most members of the regulatory arena had been already "captured" by consumer and environmental activists, and thus were already predisposed against corporate-managerial interests, they largely abandoned efforts to influence regulatory arena decisions directly.

Instead, they sought to induce decision makers from other arenas to force the regulators to change their generic cancer policies. Thus, we see the appeals to the judicial arena through lawsuits, the attempt to strip the regulatory arena's jurisdiction over cancer risk assessment by establishing an independent risk assessment mechanism under the aegis of presumably the more compliant academic-professional decision makers, and finally the effort to change regulatory arena decisions by first campaigning for and electing a more pro-corporate-managerial executive arena, who would then appoint more sympathetic decision makers within the regulatory agencies. The new personnel in turn would alter regulatory arena decisions to favor industry interests.

However, the corporate-managerial arena's effort to alter the kinds of decisions being made within the regulatory arena by working to change regulatory personnel seems to have largely failed. Ironically, this defeat came through the highly critical comments of members of the academic-professional arena, the very site to which the corporate-managerial arena had earlier tried to shift decision making about cancer. When that effort fizzled, the corporate-managerial decision makers tried to reshape regulatory arena decision making by changing regulatory appointments and then by using bureaucratic discretion to redirect cancer policy. This tactic was to be frustrated by cancer scientists, who accused the bureaucrats of the very manipulation of administrative authority that the corporate-managerial decision makers themselves had complained of so often.

Our point here is neither to cheer nor mourn the frustrations of the corporate-managerial efforts to dominate cancer policy, but to use this struggle as an illustration of risk politics in an advanced technological society with political institutions like ours. Technological risks pose very real social, economic, and ecological challenges that are often entangled with relatively inflexible technologies. Together, this leads to the all too typical pathologies of political decision making: loss of technical and scientific objectivity and of public confidence in political decision making, endless procedural challenges and delays, intransigent and polarized political demands, and, ultimately, policymaking paralysis. Unless we can make organizational and procedural changes in how we handle technological risk, we are likely to see this pattern reappear with numbing regularity.

ENDNOTES

1. WILLIAM W. LOWRANCE, *Of Acceptable Risk: Science and the Determination of Safety* (Los Altos, Calif.: William Kaufmann, 1976), p. 3.

2. MICHAEL E. KRAFT, "The Political and Institutional Setting for Risk Analysis,"in *Risk Evaluation and Management*, ed. Vincent T. Covello (New York: Plenum Press, 1987), p. 414.

3. ALBERT L. NICHOLS and RICHARD J. ZECKHAUSER, "The Perils of Prudence: How Conservative Risk Assessments Distort Regulation," *Regulation*, 10, no. 2 (1986), p. 14.

4. WALTER A. ROSENBAUM, *Environmental Politics and Policy* (Washington, D.C.: CQ Press, 1985), p. 88.

5. THOMAS O. MCGARITY, "Judicial Review of Scientific Rulemaking," *Science, Technology & Human Values*, 9, no. 1 (Winter 1984), p. 99.

6. SHEILA S. JASANOFF, "Contested Boundaries in Policy-Relevant Science," *Social Studies of Science*, 17, (1987), 197.

7. GARY BRYNER, "Assessing Environmental and Health Risks in Regulatory Agencies," paper presented at the annual meeting of the Midwest Political Science Association, Chicago, April 10–12, pp. 5–6.

8. GARY C. BRYNER, *Bureaucratic Discretion: Law and Policy in Federal Regulatory Agencies* (New York: Pergamon Press, 1987), p. 1.

9. Ibid., p. 5.

10. BRYNER, "Assessing Environmental and Health Risks," p. 5.

11. ROSENBAUM, *Environmental Politics*, p. 90.

12. Ibid., pp. 90–91.

13. McGARITY "Judicial Review of Scientific Rulemaking," p. 97.

14. Ibid.

15. Ibid., p. 94.

16. AARON WILDAVSKY, *Searching for Safety* (New Brunswick, N.J.: Transaction Books, 1988), p. 2.

17. SHEILA JASANOFF, *Risk Management and Political Culture: A Comparative Study of Science in the Policy Context*, Social Research Perspectives: Occasional Reports on Current Topics 12 (New York: Russell Sage Foundation, 1986), p. 10.

18. SHEILA JASANOFF, "Science and the Limits of Administrative Rule-Making: Lessons from the OSHA Cancer Policy," *Osgoode Hall Law Journal*, 20, no. 3 (1982), p. 541.

19. MARK RUSHEFSKY, "Assuming the Conclusions: Risk Assessment in the Development of Cancer Policy," *Politics and the Life Sciences*, 4, no. 1 (1985), p. 33.

20. JASANOFF, "Science and the Limits," p. 549.

21. MARK RUSHEFSKY, *Making Cancer Policy* (Albany, N.Y.: State University of New York Press, 1986), p. 40.

22. JASANOFF, "Science and the Limits," p. 555.

23. JASANOFF, "Contested Boundaries," p. 210.

24. National Academy of Sciences, *Risk Assessment in the Federal Government: Managing the Process* (Washington, D.C.: National Academy Press, 1983), p. 143. (emphasis added).

25. RUSHEFSKY, *Making Cancer Policy*, p. 49.

26. JASANOFF, "Contested Boundaries," p. 206.

27. RUSHEFSKY, *Making Cancer Policy*, p. 38.

28. Ibid., p. 39.

29. U.S. House of Representatives, Committee on Energy and Commerce, Subcommittee on Commerce, Transportation and Tourism. *Control of Carcinogens in the Environment*. 98th Congress, 1st Session, March 1983, p. 7.

30. Ibid., p. 71.

Chapter 10

The Biotechnology Revolution

Perhaps the most exciting scientific and technological innovation occurring today is the field of biotechnology. Encompassing a whole array of techniques and procedures derived from the manipulation of genetic materials, biotechnology has grown with explosive force in the last two decades. One of the reasons the field is so exciting, aside from the expansion of human knowledge, are the sizable personal fortunes that have been made by several scientist-entrepreneurs and the lure of yet more profits in the future.

Biotechnology is touted by many as the new technology for a new industrial revolution, greater even than the computer in shaping a new age, as we see in the following quote from two informed observers:

> Few scientific breakthroughs have been the subject of more overstatement in terms of what can *now* be accomplished. Yet if we attempt to look into the future, around the corner of a new century less than twenty years away, it is impossible to exaggerate the potential of genetic engineering for good and, if misused, for evil.[1]

ECONOMIC POTENTIAL

Biotechnology, many say, can restore the American economy. Indeed, the potential economic applications of biotechnology are staggering, from new pharmaceuticals to specialty and commodity chemicals, food, agriculture, and many others. While estimates vary, and are sometimes subject to overstatement, Edward Sylvestor and Lynn Klotz forecast that existing or prospective discoveries in genetic engineering will produce multi-million-dollar changes in a wide variety of industries. For example, in medicine, biotechnology promises new and improved vaccines, antiviral medicines, artificially created hormones and enzymes (such as human insulin and human-growth hormone), blood proteins (such as factor VIII, lack of which causes hemophilia), and natural painkillers like endorphins and enkephalins. Perhaps the most exciting medical possibility comes from work with interferon, a natural antiviral agent, which may be a natural cancer-fighting agent. Bulk pharmaceuticals, such as vitamins and antibiotics—which is well over a $500-million-a-year industry—could be radically changed through the introduction of biotechnological processes as well.

Similarly, in industrial chemicals, biotechnology bids well to revolutionize organic chemistry. Stable catalysts and enzymes (such as glucose isomerase, used in manufacturing high fructose corn syrup) can dramatically reduce feedstock costs in several industries, replacing some feedstocks currently derived from expensive and unreliable petroleum sources. In addition, genetic engineering may help to relieve problems associated with sewage, landfill garbage, and agricultural waste disposal (as well as provide a cheap source for methane gas, currently valued at $12.57 billion).

But the most promising area for the application of biotechnological processes is in genetic farming. Improved strains of existing grains, fruits, vegetables, and other cash crops are on the horizon, as are genetically improved cattle and poultry. At the most optimistic, researchers look to the day when wholly new, genetically altered animal stocks may be introduced. Even if these dreams are never realized, it is clear that the techniques collectively called biotechnology promise very great returns for those clear-sighted enough to have invested in it.

PERCEPTIONS OF PERIL

Despite the promise of medical, industrial, and agricultural profits, many people —including many of the scientists actively involved in the work—are worried about the potential dangers of this kind of technological activity. Altering the genetic structure of living organisms is something human beings have never done before, and it is much harder than usual for new technologies to anticipate all of the consequences of such activities. No one, not even the specialists involved, can predict precisely what would happen to, say, a genetically altered bacterium once it entered the general environment. Nonspecialists—including average citizens— naturally worry that such bacterium might pose a lethal threat to humans who were haplessly exposed to it. Some even fear a plague, as humans may have no resistance to new bacterial strain. There are many examples of isolated populations, succumbing to "new" diseases. A case in point is that of native Hawaiians who suffered mass deaths when exposed to the completely new germs and diseases carried by European explorers. The introduction of the kudzu vine into the southern United States and of rabbits into Australia are other examples of plant and animal "experiments" that went awry and caused significant social and economic problems.

Even more ominous is the thought of human genetic research, associated in the minds of many with the notorious Nazi medical experiments of World War II. Efforts to map the human genome—essentially, to create a full and complete map of the 100,000 human genes—raise concerns about possibly misguided efforts to create a superman through genetics.

Others are concerned that biotechnological experimentation will not be carried out with maximum safety precautions if done by for-profit organizations. Private corporations are in the business of making money, and many fear they would cut corners on safety in their efforts to be first with a new medicine. Also, corporate control of genetic engineering would needlessly impede the free exchange of new information and discoveries, the heart of the scientific process, in the name of proprietary technologies.

Some observers take a different tack, worrying that private corporations might be overly hesitant to bring out new, valuable medicines, lest they be sued by persons who are injured by taking the medicine. Liability lawsuits have increased dramatically, and many are afraid that people will suffer needlessly from corporate trepidation.

ARENA PARTICIPANTS

Major participants in the biotechnology field are located in the corporate-managerial, regulatory, legislative, executive, academic-professional, and judicial arenas, and thus decisions about this new technology are influenced by the pressures and limitations that are found in those arenas.

Corporate-Managerial and Academic-Professional Arenas

When probing progress in biotechnology, we must look at both the corporate-managerial and the academic-professional arenas as the domains where most of the action goes on. Nowhere else in modern technology are these two arenas more closely joined, adding many troubling questions to the debate about biotechnology.

The modern biotechnology industry has involved a much closer relationship between universities, their research faculties, and their research staffs and facilities with private corporations than any other recent technology. Many of the scientific and technical breakthroughs in gene splicing, monoclonal antibodies, protein synthesis, and the like came from university laboratories, as Martin Kenney notes:

> Perhaps the most stunning aspect of the rapid growth of genetic engineering has been the absolutely critical role of university professors.... All of the earliest genetic engineering companies were founded by professors. The initial research was undertaken in university laboratories, and even when the companies secured laboratory space some of the professors did not resign their university positions. Rather, professors chose to remain faculty members and work for their companies.[2]

Often, following a laboratory breakthrough, the researchers have tried to commercialize their discoveries by forming private R&D corporations, led by the scientists themselves, now operating as both researcher and entrepreneur. Many such small-scale R&D firms begin with venture capital investments, often from insurance companies, corporate pension funds, private institutions, or wealthy individuals. In other cases, public stock offerings are used to raise funds.

There have been close relationships between universities and corporations for many years in a variety of fields; thus, such connections are not a new development. However, as Nicholas Wade notes:

> ...the commercialization of molecular biology is a unique case. First, the scale of the enterprise is unprecedented: never has a whole discipline, or at least the vast majority of its leading practitioners, become involved in commercial ties. Second, the separation that usually exists between the making of a discovery and its reduction to a salable commodity is almost completely absent in molecular biology.[3]

In a number of other cases, established chemical, energy, or pharmaceutical corporations have invested in new biotechnology firms, sometimes contracting with the firm for research the larger corporation wants done but will not or cannot do in-house.

Considerable controversy accompanied the commercialization of biotechnology, focusing on the contradictions between a university scientist's professional obligations to the wider scientific community and that scientist's growing interest in the profitability of the R&D company with which he or she is associated. Within the wider science community, the scientist's chief obligation is to the search for scientific truth, which includes living up to certain disciplinary demands. Among the most important of these demands is for the free and rapid sharing of new information, usually through publication in professional journals, so that the rest of the scientific community can become aware of the latest developments in the particular field of research. Free communication of procedures, materials, and findings, however, is the last thing a commercial organization wants. It is the possession of proprietary knowledge and skills that often means success or failure in a for-profit company; the thought of freely sharing one's hard won discoveries with commercial rivals is simply unthinkable for the entrepreneur.

As university-based scientists experienced commercial success in biotechnology, a number of university administrations were unprepared for the sudden growth of the biotech industry. University administrators responded in several different ways to the financial opportunities the new biotechnology industry presented. Some universities have created their own biotechnology R&D firms, although some of the most prestigious universities decided not to, after considerable controversy and criticism. Other public and private universities have formed special relationships with private corporations in which the corporation provides a designated amount of funding of research done in university laboratories, in exchange for first rights to commercialize the results. So lucrative have the promises of biotechnology become that, as Kenney critically reports:

University administrators across the United States are actively seeking opportunities to link their institutions and faculty members with the private sector. State legislators are allocating special monies to encourage university-industry partnerships. There is an increasing acceptance of industrial ethics in the university as scientists become entrepreneurs and students are viewed as hired employees.[4]

In other cases, rather than develop basic biological research laboratories of their own, some chemical and pharmaceutical corporations have invested directly in university research. Usually established for limited time periods, such investments, joint ventures, and major grants move the research efforts in directions useful to the corporation. While the university usually keeps the right to patent the research results (or has the first right of refusal), the corporation will have the first right to license and develop any patentable products. Corporate sponsors, naturally, prefer to hold the patent rights to research results themselves, especially in biotechnology where patents become obsolete quickly.

These university/industry arrangements develop on a case-by-case basis through negotiations between the corporate sponsor and the university. However, as Dorothy Nelkin notes, "[T]he nature of the developing university-industry agreements varies widely, often depending not so much on the needs of the negotiating parties as on their bargaining strength."[5]

Executive Arena

The involvement of the executive arena in biotechnology arises from the concerns, expressed by both expert and nonexpert groups, that many of the techniques used and products produced in this field may be hazardous to human beings. The most important executive arena participant in this area is the Office of Management and Budget, which is responsible for coordinating and orchestrating the federal government's regulatory response to the growth of genetic engineering. OMB's concerns are mixed and, to an extent, contradictory: It wants to support and encourage the commercial development of biologically engineered products and processes, while also imposing sufficient regulatory protections for public health and safety.

Also involved are the National Institutes of Health (NIH), which have been involved in setting safety standards for practicing geneticists, microbiologists, and other scientists actually involved in laboratory experimentation. Although not formally a regulatory agency, NIH (along with the National Science Foundation and the National Cancer Institute) is a major source of federal funding for genetic engineering research and uses its control of grants to impose laboratory containment requirements on grant recipients.

NIH (and NSF and NCI, for that matter) faces certain contradictory pressures, because the agency has one foot in the executive arena and the other in the academic-professional arena. It is formally a member of the executive branch, but is staffed by scientists, researchers, and others whose training and first loyalty are to the academic clients they serve. As Sheldon Krimsky notes:

NIH's bureaucratic structure was a known entity, and scientists had good working relations with NIH officials. The peer-review structure for evaluating research grants enhanced confidence, and most scientists viewed NIH more as their advocate than their adversary, even when its role included regulation.[6]

It serves the dual role of representing the scientific community to the administration and representing the administration to the scientific community—not an easy task.

Regulatory Arena

Regulatory arena participation in biotechnology came relatively late. As we will discuss in more detail, in the initial phases of the public controversy about gene splicing and genetic engineering, the scientists directly involved sought to develop internal regulatory procedures within the scientific community to deal with the potential dangers of biotechnology. Only later did the formal regulatory agencies of the federal government get involved.

At present, the regulatory environment surrounding biotechnology is in flux, reflecting the rapidly changing state of the industry and of the government's role in it. The major regulatory agencies involved in biotechnology are the Environmental Protection Agency, U.S. Department of Agriculture, Occupational Safety and Health Administration, and Food and Drug Administration. None of these agencies is empowered to regulate all aspects of biotechnology; instead, each operates within a relatively clearly delimited area under specific laws. For instance, the Food, Drug, and Cosmetic Act requires FDA approval for certain drugs, medical devices, biologic substances, and so on, whereas OSHA is responsible for worker safety. EPA administers the Toxic Substances Control Act, through which it regulates chemical substances used in industry. Also, the Federal Fungicide and Rodenticide Act requires EPA approval for pesticides. USDA administers a variety of enactments, including the Federal Plant Pest Act and the Noxious Weed Act. These permit the agency to regulate any living stage of any exotic parasitic plant. As Thomas McGarity reminds us, while it is unclear precisely how these statutes will apply to the newer forms of biotechnology products and techniques, these agencies do have substantial authority in areas critical to the development and commercialization of biotechnology.[7]

Popular Mobilization Arena

A variety of consumer and environmental groups have expressed considerable concern about biotechnology techniques and products. For instance, among the groups protesting the NIH guidelines for rDNA research were the Federation of American Scientists, Natural Resources Defense Council, Friends of the Earth, Environmental Defense Fund, Sierra Club, and the Boston chapter of Science for the People. While these groups had a diversity of goals, they were united in their desire to see the decision-making process concerning rDNA research opened to nonexpert, nonscientist participation.

They were especially concerned that the decisions about biotechnology had been too heavily dominated by scientists and by the drug company representatives who were themselves interested parties and whose sensitivity to public worries about the dangers of genetic engineering was suspect. Clearly, the kinds of incentives and constraints thought by the scientists and corporate executives as sufficient to protect the public were not convincing to participants from other arenas.

ARENA INTERACTIONS

The biotechnology industry is only about 15 years old. The key to gene splicing, genetic engineering, and similar techniques was the cracking of the genetic code by James Watson and Francis Crick in the 1950s. However modern, industrial biotechnology did not emerge until the early 1970s, when geneticists perfected laboratory techniques for separating and combining segments of DNA from different organisms.

The First Fight over rDNA Regulation

The first concerns expressed about recombinant DNA (rDNA) research came not from the public, or the government, or environmental groups. It came from the scientists themselves. The biologists and geneticists involved in the new rDNA techniques were concerned because most of the laboratory work was done with the *Escherichia coli* (*E. coli*) bacteria, which is found inside the human intestine. The initial fear was that a genetically altered form of *E. coli* might accidentally escape from the lab and colonize in people, possibly creating new, lethal infections. In one of the most remarkable examples of public-spirited concern by members of the academic-professional arena, microbiologists around the world voluntarily suspended the most potentially dangerous rDNA research projects until the dimensions of the possible biohazards could be assessed.

The Asilomar Conference In February 1975, a now-famous conference was held in Asilomar, California, attended by 86 American and 53 foreign scientists to deal with the issues of rDNA dangers. After four days of sometimes difficult debate, the conference participants adopted a provisional set of experimentation guidelines for rDNA work. The guidelines established, among other things, certain laboratory containment procedures to protect against accidental release of genetically altered organisms, along with a recommendation that specially weakened forms of *E. coli* be used, strains of the bacteria that were intentionally designed not to survive outside laboratory conditions. The conference also recommended that a special Recombinant DNA Advisory Committee (RAC) be created within the National Institutes of Health in order to provide continuous enforcement of safety guidelines.

Thus, the first decisions about rDNA research were made almost entirely within a single technological decision-making arena: the academic-professional arena. Even the creation of NIH guidelines, technically done within the executive arena, was informally controlled by members of the academic-professional arena. NIH is an agency for funnelling federal research grants to scientists, not a regulatory agency with statutory responsibilities, and the agency is dominated by scientists and researchers.

Maintaining Scientific Autonomy   In addition to concern about potential public hazards from rDNA research, there were other reasons why the scientists at Asilomar and NIH were greatly concerned about what kinds of decisions were made in controlling this research field. Members of the scientific community prize above all the professional autonomy they enjoy in establishing their own research agendas and in determining what kinds of laboratory techniques they will use, and they resist intrusions by nonscientists into their internal decision making. Scientists devoutly believe that no one can monitor or control how science is done better than scientists themselves. Indeed, the scientific community's claim that it alone is qualified to police scientific research is basic to how the scientific community sees itself, and participants in the academic-professional arena try to avoid doing things to undermine public confidence in science's self-correcting capabilities.

Having decided among themselves that rDNA research actually did pose some possible hazards, and that there was a need for some kind of research regulation, it was critical for the academic-professional arena to maintain control of the issue, to keep the problem "all in the family," as it were. If the scientists who first raised the issue of biohazards should appear unable to devise workable safety procedures, they risked inviting nonexpert groups into the decision process, with unknown and unpredictable results.

Strategies for Keeping the Issue Under Control   The Asilomar scientists knew that their ability to ensure continued scientific control of rDNA research, while allowing that research to go on, depended on three things: their ability to come up with regulatory guidelines to contain the potential hazards that research posed, finding incentives from within the academic-professional arena to ensure compliance with those guidelines by the research scientists involved, and continued public regard for the scientific community's ability to resolve the issues.

1. *Defining the issue.* One step the scientists at Asilomar took, as Krimsky notes, was in defining the problem as fundamentally technical, not political, in nature and thus most appropriately left to the scientists themselves for resolution:

> In this first stage of debate, the controversy was interpreted as a technical, in contrast to a public policy, issue. Resolution was expected to remain with scientists and scientific advisers of the principal funding agencies.... The Asilomar conference perpetuated the assumption that analysis of risk was narrowly technical in nature. In this context, broad public and scientific input into the process was not considered.[8]

Defining a problem or issue as technical rather than political is a tactic used by decision makers eager to restrict access to the decision process, since such a definition establishes an expertise threshold for participation most nonspecialists cannot pass. Only those with the proper credentials can legitimately claim the right to participate in making decisions about the problem. Such a technique will work only under certain conditions, however. The experts designated to resolve the issue must do so relatively quickly and must display at least general agreement about the steps needed to do the job. If the experts cannot produce a solution rapidly, or if they reveal significant disagreement within their ranks, nonexpert groups or individuals may seek to join the decision process, breaking the control over the issue held by the authoritative specialists.

2. *Limiting participation.* The Asilomar scientists also limited the number of scientists invited to the conference, hoping thus to come to a consensus position quickly on rDNA research regulations. Indeed, the organizers of Asilomar were later criticized for limiting the participants. Krimsky tells us that many observers

> complained that this major area of risk-assessment was closed to many scientists who had important contributions to make. Only a smattering of infectious disease experts, clinical microbiologists, and public health personnel had contributed to the decisions at this historic meeting, for papers on risk-related aspects of the research were presented by invitation only and there was no general call for papers by key professional societies. Also absent from the Asilomar proceedings were scientific representatives from the ecological sciences as well as environmentalists. Yet once the results of Asilomar were delivered to NIH, important science policy decisions would follow, placing those who did participate in a very influential policy role.[9]

The scientists were very concerned that a general consensus emerge at Asilomar. With a greatly expanded list of participants, made up of scientists from fields only tangentially related to rDNA research, general agreement would have been much harder to reach. For a major convocation of scientists to fail to establish acceptable regulatory guidelines would alarm the public, undermining their confidence in the scientists and inciting them to take control of the issue away from the scientists altogether. Krimsky notes: "Concern about losing control over their research loomed heavily on the minds of those scientists who worked conscientiously to find lines of agreement."[10]

3. *Enforcement.* For enforcement of the research regulations, the scientists hoped to use a set of incentives that scientists would clearly recognize, even if participants from other decision making arenas might not. One of the groups working at Asilomar, for instance, urged that the editors of major science journals refuse to publish research results derived from studies that did not employ the guidelines. To outsiders, such a suggestion might seem quite harmless; but for those who live and work within the academic-professional arena, and who depend very heavily on publications for professional advancement, the threat of exclusion from the major science journals was thought by the Asilomar scientists as quite an effective penalty.

One sanction that was included in the guidelines was the threat of cutting off NIH funding for those who failed to abide by the guidelines in their research.

In the end, however, they relied heavily on the professionalism of the scientists and researchers, inasmuch as each scientist was ultimately responsible for implementing the research regulations. In other decision-making arenas, reliance upon professionalism might seem a rather toothless regulation, but among members of the academic-professional arena, professional standing and reputation are, indeed significant factors.

The NIH Guidelines   In 1974 NIH responded to the rDNA controversy, creating the Recombinant DNA Advisory Committee (RAC), commissioned to investigate the current state of knowledge and technology regarding rDNA research and to propose research guidelines. The first guidelines prepared by RAC were criticized as too weak, were revised during 1975, and finally promulgated in June 1976. They have been revised a number of times since then, as well. Although not regulatory, the NIH guidelines did contain several layers of rDNA research reviews, including reviews by RAC, and a mandated cutoff of NIH funding for any scientist who violated the guidelines.

While not all genetic scientists approved of every element of the rDNA guidelines, those regulations did represent a seemingly successful containment within the scientific community of a potentially highly divisive set of issues. Indeed, many within the scientific community felt quite proud that the original questioning of rDNA research had come from the very scientists involved   rather than from critical outsider groups—and the issue was promptly and responsibly resolved by those same scientists, confirming yet again that the scientific community could indeed police itself with no outside interference. However imperfect the NIH guidelines might be, they did allow rDNA research to resume under the control and direction of the scientists directly involved.

Breaking the Academic-Professional Arena's Control of rDNA Research
This tightly knit decision process was soon to come unraveled, though, as a variety of participants from other decision-making arenas made their concerns felt. The clearest proof that the efforts to contain the question of rDNA regulation within the scientific community had failed came when Cambridge, Massachusetts—the home of Harvard University and the Massachusetts Institute of Technology, both world leaders in genetic research—tried to impose its own moratorium on some forms of rDNA research within its borders.

The Cambridge controversy began when some Harvard University biologists objected to a proposed expansion of rDNA research facilities at Harvard because such experimentation would take place in a crowded city. Their objections were publicized by the local media, and the Cambridge City government responded by conducting public hearings on the issue. The city ordered a moratorium on all rDNA research within city boundaries until a special citizen commission could review the issue and give its recommendations.

In a truly remarkable experiment in nonexpert citizen decision making about a very complicated technical issue, the citizen commission recommended that rDNA research *should be permitted*, given the imposition of a small number of safeguards beyond those required in the NIH guidelines. The City of Cambridge eventually allowed such research to occur, within limitations most scientists found reasonable and bearable.

However, even before the Cambridge citizen commission issued its recommendations, several other communities around the country (see Table 10–1) expressed interest in the rDNA issue. What had at one point seemed a very successful effort to limit decision making about genetic engineering to the scientists closest to the research suddenly became the nightmare of dozens or hundreds of different communities imposing restrictions on the work of individual scientists. Scientific autonomy, many scientists believed, could never survive an onslaught of untutored politicians only too eager to fan the flames of unfounded public fears and then inflict unneeded and unrealistic curbs on scientists in their laboratories. Indeed, as Krimsky notes, a number of scientists who had originally criticized the NIH guidelines quickly endorsed them when it appeared that local governments might impose their own limits: "…many scientists put aside their technical disagreements

Table 10-1
Comparison of Provision in rDNA Legislation for Two States and Four Municipalities

Locale Provisions	Cambridge, Mass.	Berkeley, Calif.	Princeton, N.J.	Amherst, Mass.	New York, State	Maryland
Licensing or certification		X			X	X
Special officer			X		X	
Special committee	X		X			X
Citizen participation on IBCs	X		X	X		
Penalties	X			X	X	X
Liability			X			X
Health monitoring	X	X	X		X	
NIH containment requirement			X	X	X	X
Added containment requirements	X	X				
Preemption					X	
Enforcement provisions		X			X	X
Protection of proprietary information					X	

Source: Sheldon Krimsky, *Genetic Alchemy: The Social History of the Recombinant DNA Controversy* (Cambridge, Mass.: MIT Press, 1982), p. 308.

[about the quality of the NIH guidelines] to avoid what they perceived to be a greater threat—public intervention into decisions about scientific research.[11]

The Scientists Counterattack: The Fight Shifts to the Legislative Arena

Once it became clear that the scientific community could not maintain tight control over the rDNA issue, and that there might be dozens of other "Cambridges" all over the country, the scientists responded by bringing in a different group of decision participants—the U.S. Congress. While the scientists had never before welcomed Congressional involvement in this area, many concurred with Rockefeller University biologist Norton Zinder's gloomy prediction: "The proliferation of local option with different guidelines in different states and different cities can only lead to a situation of chaos, confusion, and ultimately to hypocrisy amongst the scientists involved."[12]

Facing the possibility of a bewildering array of multiple local regulations, the majority of microbiologists reluctantly agreed that federal legislation mandating preemptive, uniform federal standards was needed. Besides, the scientists had had numerous contacts with Congress over the years and were generally respected by the legislators. The scientists felt justifiably confident that in the cozy, familiar confines of committee hearing rooms, they would be able to bring the members of Congress around to their point of view on rDNA regulation.

This, too, is a typical technique used in technological decision making: If you cannot control a desired decision from within your own arena, or if the decision is occurring in an arena in which you have little influence, shift the locus of decision making into an arena where you have more influence than do your opponents.

However, the consumer and environmental participants could legitimately hope to influence Congress as effectively as the scientists. Indeed, the consumer and environmental participants have been particularly effective in recent years at manipulating the intensely constituent-oriented pressures that do work very well in the legislative arena. Members of Congress are not trained in the complexities of biotechnology, nor are they especially responsive to the pressures and demands that drive the academic-professional world. Activists associated with protecting the environment and the consumer should be much better at mobilizing voter concerns than academic or commercial scientists, especially since many of the environmental groups had their own scientists on staff to criticize the NIH guidelines.

By bringing Congress into the action, therefore, the contest between the environmentalists and the biologists over rDNA research regulation appeared much more evenly matched than it had been when the decisions remained in the hands of only the scientists.

Congress Tackles Biotechnology

All sides in this debate geared up their efforts to shape and influence the kinds of decisions emerging from the legislative arena and to get individual legislators to make specific, desired decisions about how much, if any, federal regulation should be imposed on researchers. From the late spring of 1977 until early 1980, more than a dozen separate bills governing rDNA research were debated in Congress (see Table 10-2). In this complex interplay of pressures and arguments, the scientific community showed itself to be a very capable player indeed.

Table 10-2
Key Events in the Legislative History of rDNA Research, 1977–80

1977

19 January	Representative Richard Ottinger introduces H. Res 131
4 February	Senator Dale Bumpers introduces S. 621
7–9 March	Academy Forum on Recombinant DNA Research, National Academy of Sciences
8 March	Senator Robert Metzenbaum introduces S. 945
9 March	Representative Paul Rogers introduces H.R. 4759
1 April	Senator Edward Kennedy introduces administration bill S. 1217
6 April	Representative Paul Rogers introduces H.R. 6158
12 April	Curtiss letter to Donald Federickson on safety of *E. coli*
26 April	Resolution of the National Academy of Sciences on legislation
8 May	Nine principles on rDNA legislation issued by the American Society for Microbiology
24 May	Representative Paul Rogers introduces H.R. 7418
20 June	Representative Paul Rogers introduces H.R. 7897
20–21 June	Falmouth Conference on the use of *E. coli* as a host for rDNA experiments
15 July	Gordon Conference letter on legislation
22 July	Senator Edward Kennedy introduces a substantially modified version of S. 1217
2 August	Senator Gaylord Nelson amends Kennedy's version of S. 1217 in the nature of a substitute (S. 754)
6 September	Stanley Cohen's letter to Donald Frederickson that eukaryote-to-prokaryote gene exchange occurs in nature
28 September	Senator Edward Kennedy withdraws support from S. 1217 and substitutes a new bill as an interim measure
1 November	Senator Harrison Schmitt introduces S. 2267, the National Science Policy Commission Act

1978

19 January	Representative Harley Staggers introduces a bill written by Harvard University, H.R. 10453
28 February	Representative Harley Staggers and Representative Paul Rogers introduce H.R. 11192

1980

29 January	Senator Adlai Stevenson introduces the Recombinant DNA Research and Development Notification Act of 1980, S. 2234

Source: Sheldon Krimsky, *Genetic Alchemy: The Social History of the Recombinant DNA Controversy* (Cambridge, Mass.: MIT Press, 1982), 323.

The bills introduced to regulate rDNA research contained a wide assortment of provisions. Most proposed that the secretary of health, education, and welfare (HEW; now health and human services HHS) regulate the research, including private research, although one bill urged the creation of an 11-member, free-standing commission to do the job. Several required that researchers obtain government licenses for their rDNA research, while some would impose stiff monetary penalties on those who violate NIH guidelines.

Federal preemption was a paramount issue for the academic-professional participants. Avoiding the confusion of multiple local regulations, after all, had been one of the chief reasons the microbiologists supported congressional involvement. And while some legislators were sensitive to the scientific community's demand that, if there must be regulations at all, they be standardized, national regulations, others believed that state and local governments have the right to set their own standards for protecting their citizens. The two major bills contained opposing positions on preemption, with Representative Paul Rogers' bill allowing for greater federal management and that proposed by Senator Edward Kennedy allowed for greater local control of rDNA research.

Scientists as Lobbyists   Harlyn O. Halvorson, a microbiologist with the American Society for Microbiology (ASM), orchestrated most of the scientists' lobbying efforts. Halvorson and his associates marshalled the scientific community into a lobbying program of considerable sophistication.

He publicized the scientists' worries about local regulations among other microbiologists, and among scientists in other fields who might fear that similar local restrictions might be placed upon their research if the federal preemption efforts failed for rDNA work. He contacted and recruited university administrators, pointing out the possible impacts of local restrictions on each university's ability to attract research dollars. The administrators joined microbiologists in directly lobbying with senators and representatives by visiting their offices in delegations led by Halvorson.

At one point in the congressional deliberations, Halvorson even led a telephone campaign from the microbiology department at Duke University, in which all 39 members of the House Committee on Interstate and Foreign Commerce were contacted concerning undesirable amendments to the Rogers bill that Halvorson wanted defeated. Krimsky tells us about Halvorson's tactics in the Senate:

> To mount an effective campaign against the Kennedy bill, Halvorson selected out individual senators for more intensive lobbying. He urged [Senator] Gaylord Nelson, reminding him of the benefits microbiology brought his own state of Wisconsin, to oppose the Kennedy bill. Nelson was persuaded and introduced his own legislation that met ASM objectives.[13]

Halvorson also matched ASM members with their representatives for home district pressures, arranging for direct lobbying contacts. Town and community officials in each congressional district were involved, each local official discussing the negative consequences for the regional economy if university research were impeded through unnecessary legislation.

Of course, the environmental and consumer groups were engaged in similar political machinations, activities in which they, too, have shown substantial acumen. Their goals were twofold: first, to impose necessary limitations upon what they saw as dangerous rDNA research and, second, to increase the level and significance of non-expert participation in decisions about this and other areas of scientific activity. Just as the microbiologists sought out sympathetic senators and representatives, the environmental/consumer participants looked for congenial members willing to introduce bills containing restrictive provisions or willing to obstruct the progress of bills supported by the scientists.

However, the consumer and environmentalist position weakened because the microbiologists were able to exert influence over some well-known scientists who served on the advisory boards of a number of environmental organizations. Concerns about the integrity and independence of science in general persuaded these scientists to oppose the legislative and judicial efforts of the environmentalists. Lewis Thomas, from the Sloan-Kettering Cancer Center and a member of the Friends of the Earth advisory board, Joshua Lederberg, past president of Rockefeller University and a trustee of the Natural Resources Defense Council, and biologist Paul Ehrlich, of Stanford University and associated with the Friends of the Earth, were among the more notable scientists to break with their environmental organizations over rDNA research restrictions.[14] Such defections led members of Congress to conclude that the consumer and environmental participants could no longer muster solid scientific reasons for their contention that rDNA research posed significant hazards to society.

Indeed, as the months rolled by and the debates continued on Capitol Hill, many members of both houses came to believe that the need for regulation of rDNA research was far less pressing than originally suggested. A prominent reason for the declining interest among legislators was the very effective use made by the academic-professional participants of new data and information generated since the Asilomar conference.

One of the chief conclusions of the Asilomar conference had been that the scientific community simply lacked sufficient data to know whether or not rDNA work posed significant public dangers. Since the conference, considerable, if scattered, work had been done to eliminate some of the fearsome unknowns. One particularly important development was the introduction of an weakened variety of E. coli, the K12 strain. This strain possesses a much lowered ability to survive outside the laboratory, thereby reducing the potential of genetically altered pathogens accidently escaping laboratory confinement and finding a successful niche in the general environment.

The development and use of the K12 strain led to one of the most telling reversals in the entire rDNA debate when the highly respected biologist Roy Curtiss, who had expressed early and very publicly his concerns about using a bacteria found in the human gut, just as publicly withdrew his previous support for regulation because of the availability of the K12 strain. After careful examination of the latest evidence, he asserted that the K12 strain "offers no danger whatsoever to any human being with the exception...that an extremely careless worker might under unique situations cause harm to him or herself."[15]

While the Curtiss statement was widely hailed in the scientific community, and had limited impact on policymakers, it did lead to a major conference, at Falmouth, Massachusetts, in June 1977, in which the issue of *E. coli* was the focus of attention. After the meeting, its chair, Sherwood L. Gorbach, chief of the infectious disease unit at Tufts University, issued a controversial public statement asserting the conference's unanimous opinion that the K12 strain of *E. coli* could not be converted into a human pathogen.

The Gorbach statement was reprinted in the *Federal Register* and in a variety of newspapers and journal editorials. The Falmouth conclusion was often cited as a reason for not only abandoning congressional legislation to regulate rDNA research, but also for relaxing the existing NIH guidelines. In addition, new experimental evidence appeared that suggested that the transfer of DNA materials may occur naturally outside the laboratory. Naturally, the academic-professional participants took great care to see that this new information circulated widely among members of Congress and their staffs. In combination with the Gorbach statement, these results convinced legislators that the K12 strain was truly safe and that the kinds of operations microbiologists were contemplating in the laboratory actually occur spontaneously in nature.

Throughout the congressional debate, the academic-professional participants displayed unexpected skill in politicking. Krimsky notes:

> The scientific lobby was the major reason for the change in congressional mood behind strong legislation. Scientists worked one on one with Senators and Representatives, created a major political force in the American Society for Microbiology, developed new coalitions among scientific societies, used scientific meetings as lobbying instruments, and applied the prestigious National Academy of Sciences as a persuasive force.[16]

Although many voices within the popular mobilization arena continued to express concerns about the potential dangers of genetically altered organisms, the wind gradually dissipated from the sails of the pro-regulation forces, as David Dickson summarizes:

> Public interest and environmentalist groups such as Friends of the Earth and the Environmental Defense Fund, along with their supporters in the scientific community, argued that the scientific uncertainties still surrounding the research demanded a conservative approach to safety and environmental precautions. Yet faced with the opposition, they found themselves with dwindling political support in Congress. Eventually this support evaporated completely, and all proposals for congressional action—whether requiring federal preemption or not—were dropped from the legislative agenda.[17]

Academic-Professional Control Restored Thus, in the end, the issue of controlling rDNA research, which had begun with the scientists directly involved, eventually returned to those same scientists, through the NIH guidelines, for management. Having lost control of the issue within the academic-professional arena, due in large measure to the actions of participants from the popular mobilization arena (along with a number of dissident scientists), the scientists accepted legislative arena involvement in preference to state and local regulations. Once the decision shifted to Congress, the scientists proved themselves more effective at manipulating the pressures within that arena in order to get the kinds of decisions they wanted than were the environmental or consumer groups that were arrayed against them. In the end, the scientists won back control of the issue within their own arena.

Relaxing the Guidelines After the issue of rDNA research regulation "came home" to the academic-professional arena, the scientists were able gradually to relax the restrictions imposed by the original NIH guidelines, based on emerging laboratory experience. Some of the techniques the scientists used to soften the guidelines, as Wade tells us, may well have departed a bit from the "scientific ethos":

> ...biologists put pressure on the NIH to reduce the stringency of the safety rules. Conferences would be held at which interested experts would pooh-pooh the possible risks of recombinant DNA. Typically there would be little new evidence beyond that which the NIH Recombinant DNA Committee had already considered in drawing up its rules. But the "consensus" of experts would be cited as proof that the rules should be rolled back in this area or that.[18]

However, when NIH scientists first discussed relaxing the guidelines, considerable public criticism of the lack of public participation in controlling rDNA research emerged. This led NIH Director Donald Frederickson to expand the size of the Recombinant DNA Advisory Committee by now including known critics of biotechnology and of RAC and NIH procedures. However, as Dickson relates, the inclusion of NIH critics on RAC served more to legitimize RAC's decisions than to significantly alter the general trend toward relaxing the guidelines:

> Scientists at NIH were even able to exercise considerable influence over the choice of public interest representatives, vetoing those they felt would be too troublesome.... In practice, therefore, the presence of public interest representatives on the RAC, many of whom were openly critical of the dominant role of scientists on the committee, did not slow the pace at which the guidelines were dismantled.[19]

In an effort to forestall public criticism of the tightly held decision process concerning rDNA by the scientific community, Fredrickson also allowed his Director's Advisory Committee (DAC) to be used as a sounding board for public comments on the NIH guidelines. Many people complained, however, that the expansion of DAC was no more than a token effort to include non-scientists in the decisions being made.

When the preliminary NIH guidelines were published in 1976, they were met by considerable public criticism from members of the popular mobilization arena. At the first open meeting of the director's Advisory Committee, several groups presented their critiques of the guidelines. Most of these criticisms and comments, however, had little impact on the NIH guidelines, and did not seriously threaten the scientific community's control of the issue. Dickson characterizes the DAC meeting as

> carefully structured to give more time to the critics of the research than to the supporters, since its purpose was not to develop a consensus—or even to discover what the critics had to say—but merely to be able to demonstrate, if later challenged, that in reaching its eventual conclusions on the guidelines, opposing points of view had been adequately listened to.[20]

Once again we see the political savvy of the academic-professional participants: Having averted local community meddling in rDNA research decision making by shifting the issue into the legislative arena and then restoring scientific control of the rDNA issue through their sophisticated congressional lobbying techniques, they moved to blunt criticism that the public was systematically excluded from rDNA decision making within NIH but without sacrificing their hard re-won control of the issue. Having successfully pacified most of their critics (at least those with the power to interfere with "scientific autonomy") the microbiologists could then move circumspectly to relax the NIH guidelines without inciting local groups or members of Congress. All told, it had been a rather successful effort by scientists to fend off attempts by participants from other arenas to interfere with their ability to make rDNA decisions exclusively according to the basic rules operating within the academic-professional arena.

The Second Fight over rDNA Regulation

The story of genetic research regulation does not end here. Ten years after the first attempt to frame regulative limitations on such research, people are once again concerned about safety and regulation.

The biotechnology industry has matured a great deal since the mid-1970s. Where the earlier issues had been how to regulate laboratory research, now the focus is on the problems of commercial applications that have grown out of that laboratory work, such as field testing genetically altered organisms by deliberately releasing them in the general environment, clinical tests of new pharmaceuticals, agricultural applications of genetically engineered hormones, and so on.

Once again, the academic-professional arena finds its exclusive control of this research domain being challenged, once more by members of consumer and environmental groups. And, once again, the legislative arena is drawn into the controversy. This time, however, both the judicial and the regulatory arenas have important roles in the controversy, adding new levels of complexity and unpredictability to the conflict. Also, the problems of public safety come almost entirely from nonscientists, unlike the first round that began with scientists. Indeed, most of the scientists involved do not believe that there are substantial public risks involved in the practical applications of genetic engineering, even though, given the experiences of a decade ago, they are very sensitive to even unsubstantiated public anxieties.

Practical Applications of Lab Results　Bioengineering techniques have matured considerably since the mid-1970s, when laboratory research was the focus of debate. Both the science and the technology have advanced to the point where large-scale deliberate release of bioengineered organisms into the general environment is advancing apace. This prospect raises considerably more complex problems for policymakers. Aroused public anxieties have generated renewed pressures for government regulation of these technologies and has produced a complex web of bureaucratic regulatory jurisdictions, "turf" fights, and litigation. Often, the new biotechnology industry and the government complain that complicated and unneeded regulations threaten to undermine the U.S. lead in this new and very promising technology.

Frost-Resistant Bacteria　The issue of deliberately releasing bioengineered organisms into the general environment came to a head in 1983–84, when two University of California scientists, Steven Lindow and Nickolas Panopoulos, requested permission from NIH to apply a genetically altered frost-resistant bacteria on a test site in northern California. The scientists had perfected a laboratory version of the bacteria, but now needed an actual test in the outside environment. RAC approved the experiment. Since the agriculture industry suffers $1–$3 billion in losses each year from frost damage, a successful experiment could mean significant savings in food loss.[21]

However, before the test could be conducted, a variety of environmental groups, led by Jeremy Rifkin, president of the Foundation on Economic Trends, brought suit in federal court, seeking to block the release of the microorganism. Thus, for the first time, the judicial arena became involved in a major biotechnology issue. Rifkin asserted that NIH had violated the National Environmental Policy Act in giving permission for the test, since no Environmental Impact Statement, required by NEPA, had been prepared. NIH declared that its own internal environmental assessment was sufficient, even if not matching NEPA guidelines.

Most biologists involved believed that the release of a bacterium virtually identical to that found naturally in the environment ran a nearly unmeasurable risk to humans, while promising substantial benefit. The environmentalists, on the other hand, rejected the biologists' easy optimism, arguing that the peril of ecological disaster from genetically altered organisms was beyond the ability of contemporary science to assess. They said that if the organism's safety could not be guaranteed, no release into the environment should be allowed.

The Judicial Arena's Impact　On May 16, 1984, Federal Judge John Sirica granted an injunction stopping the experiment, sending shock waves throughout NIH and the scientific community. The injunction would remain in force until NIH complied with the requirements of NEPA. Sirica explicitly exempted NIH approval of private, commercial deliberate release experiments on the grounds that both NEPA and the NIH guidelines on rDNA applied only to federally funded research. Private companies not receiving federal support could simply proceed with their deliberate release experiments because there was no federal legislation restricting their activities. Indeed, shortly after the Sirica decision, a different government agency, the Environmental Protection Agency, approved essentially the same frost-resistant bacteria experiment for a private biotechnology company, Advanced Genetic Sciences, Inc. (this release experiment, too, has been delayed because of law suits filed by members of the consumer/environmental arena).

Popular Mobilization Arena   Many scientists complained loudly that the decision created a double standard in the regulation of genetic engineering, one for federally funded university research and a different one for commercial work. The Sirica decision was described as opening a "gaping loophole" in the regulatory framework surrounding genetic engineering, and prompted demands from academic scientists and from the commercial biotechnology industry for more coherence and coordination among federal agencies responsible for overseeing genetic engineering.

The Coordinated Framework   To address these problems, the Reagan administration created a cabinet-level working group to decide if the existing array of regulations and agencies was adequate to deal with both federally sponsored university research and commercially based biotechnology, or if new organizations and new legislation might be needed. The working group issued in December 1984, and in revised form in November 1985, its recommendations for biotechnology regulations, entitled "Coordinated Framework for Regulation of Biotechnology." The "Coordinated Framework" sought to resolve agency jurisdiction problems over various aspects of biotechnology and to enhance regulatory coordination throughout the federal government.

Dividing the Regulatory Workload   Under the Coordinated Framework, various aspects of biotechnology would be parceled out to the four major agencies with regulatory jurisdiction. Federally sponsored university research, for instance, continues under the NIH guidelines. Responsibility for overseeing specific commercial applications is distributed in this way: The Occupational Safety and Health Administration after genetically engineered products used in manufacturing facilities; the Environmental Protection Agency regulates genetically altered microorganisms, under the Toxic Substances Control Act and the Federal Insecticide, Fungicide, and Rodenticide Act; the Department of Agriculture administers animal biologics, such as gene-altered animal vaccines, diseases, plant materials, and plant pests; and the Federal Drug Administration is responsible for animal drugs and human health care products derived through genetic engineering techniques.

A second tier of regulation was the Biotechnology Science Board (renamed the Biotechnology Science Coordinating Committee, BSCC), intended to oversee the other agencies and with substantial power to enforce coordination, consistency, and cooperation among the frontline agencies. However, scientists in both academic research and in commercial biotechnology complained about the duplication of having two levels of federal regulation to pass, and the working group stripped BSCC of most of its supervisory powers. At present, BSCC has four functions: to coordinate agency information sharing and problem solving, to promote the development of consistent procedures and techniques, to encourage agency cooperation, and to point out important gaps in scientific data.[22]

Responses to the Coordinated Framework   This new and complex array of agency relationships and responsibilities has now enmeshed biotechnology inside the decision-making environment of the regulatory arena, where pressures and constraints different from those found within the scientific community dominate the kinds of decisions that are made. One knowledgeable observer characterized the new arrangement as "a patchwork of conflicting regulatory policies."[23]

The arrangement leaves many within the corporate-managerial arena dissatisfied, including both biotechnology startups, such as Genentech, and giants like Monsanto and E. I. du Pont de Nemours & Company, that have bet heavily on the new science. They, too, find that important decisions that affect their investments are being made by people who respond to pressures and constraints different than those that operate within the corporate-managerial arena. Obtaining the kinds of regulatory decisions they want can be costly and time consuming, which are significant faults in a fast-changing industry like genetic engineering. The costs can be steep: years of clinical tests that can run from $20 million to $50 million. Regulatory delays may mean that one's competitors—whether American or, increasingly, foreign—that do not face such delays have great advantages in bringing new products and processes to market and in earning back in profits the hundreds of thousands of dollars of research investment needed to bring a product forward.

Corporate-Managerial Frustration   In at least two circumstances, biotechnology companies have shown their impatience with regulators by engaging in open release of bioengineered microorganisms without first getting regulatory clearance. Advanced Genetic Sciences, the company that had gained EPA approval for the release of the same genetically engineered frost-resistant bacteria that the University of California scientists had been prevented from using, actually conducted its own unauthorized field test some months before EPA acted. Monsanto also participated in an unauthorized environmental release of a microorganism it was developing prior to regulatory approval.

Both actions were a substantial setback for other members of the corporate-managerial arena involved in biotechnology. Surreptitious, unapproved experiments, when they become public, give very effective ammunition to biotechnology's opponents, adding substance to Jeremy Rifkin's criticism that such actions send "a message to the world that the industry is not to be trusted with the responsibility of policing itself."[24]

Academic-Professional Disappointments   Academic microbiologists were also unhappy with the complex and cumbersome regulatory framework created by the government. Many scientists object to the extensive documentation required by EPA before a biotechnology experiment can go forward. In effect, they assert, government regulators have bent over backward to provide excessively stringent safeguards lest they arouse the fears of the public or the legal specialists of the environmental groups. As the *Wall Street Journal* recently editorialized:

> ...it has become an established phenomenon of public life that if someone can generate an atmosphere of fearful controversy around some aspect of modern technology—genetic engineering, nuclear energy, research with animals—politicians and bureaucrats will tremble. Most often they respond by imprisoning the technology in additional regulations, and supposedly this makes the scary thing go away.[25]

The regulations have gotten so complex that, as one scholar noted, "Persons reading those documents would be confused, even if they were trying to do the right thing."[26]

At least one academic scientist has admitted to violating EPA rules about environmental release of genetically altered microorganisms, declaring his deed to be "an act of civil disobedience."[27] Gary Stobel, a plant pathologist at Montana State University, injected 13 American elm trees with a genetically altered bacterium intended to fight Dutch elm disease. What is more, Stobel admitted that during 1983 and 1984, he had released a different genetically altered bacterium in experiments in South Dakota, Montana, California, and Nebraska. The bacteria had been altered to enhance nitrogen fixation in plants. Stobel was reprimanded by his university and by EPA, with restrictions imposed upon future experiments. He was also required to cut down the elms, incinerate them, and treat the stumps with a powerful herbicide and the surrounding ground with a fumigant. However, after studying the case, NIH concluded, that Stobel had not violated its guidelines on biotechnology.

When word got out about Stobel's actions, and the relatively lenient treatment he received from other scientists, heated protests from environmental groups demanded that he be sanctioned more severely. Rifkin asserted Stobel had proved that "[w]e cannot expect the scientists to police themselves. They feel they are above the law."[28] It seems that Stobel's actions may have hurt the standing of microbiologists just as the unauthorized releases of Monsanto and AGS have hurt the standing of biotechnology corporations. This is all the more so in Stobel's case since he is an academic scientist supposedly under the discipline of that profession and under the watchful eye of scientific agencies.

Consumer and Environmental Complaints   On the other hand, members of consumer and environmental groups are not pleased with the new plan either. Their concerns are that the existing legislation under which the regulatory agencies will oversee biotechnology are not adequate to the job, especially the use of the Toxic Substances Control Act (TSCA) under which EPA will regulate genetically altered microbes.

According to the environmental groups, the problem is that TSCA was enacted before biotechnology techniques were perfected, and that "there is no evidence that Congress ever considered the possibility that the statute would regulate biotechnology."[29] According to TSCA, a manufacturer of any "chemical substance" (which EPA somewhat controversially interprets as including genetically engineered organisms) must notify EPA 90 days prior to the start of manufacturing. The Premanufacturing Notice (PMN) must identify the product and must include any health or environmental data in the manufacturer's possession. In response, EPA can delay the introduction of the new chemical until further tests are completed, or, if the EPA administrator finds that the new chemical presents an unreasonable risk to health or to the environment, the agency must either ban or closely regulate the product.

However, EPA has only 90 days to review the new chemical and the data provided by the manufacturer and reach its decision. If the agency fails to act within the 90 days, the manufacturer can proceed with the production and distribution of the product. This very short screening time is unrealistic when dealing with wholly new organisms and their potential impacts on the open environment. To meet this short time limit, environmentalists fear EPA will have to cut corners on testing, and thus an EPA clearance for a new microorganism will "create the undesirable presumption of release biotechnology's safety."[30]

Another objection to TSCA is that a manufacturer does not need to obtain a permit or license before beginning production, so long as the manufacturer submits a PMN to the Environmental Protection Agency. In fact, when dealing with new genetically altered microorganisms, EPA may not have enough information even to know if more information is needed to determine the risks involved in an environmental release of the organism. EPA must first show that the organism presents an unreasonable risk before it can require the manufacturer to develop more complete data. The point is that the burden of demonstrating that more information is needed rests with EPA, not with the manufacturer. As such, the manufacturer has no real incentive to develop data on the risks of the new rDNA product. In the end, we have a situation in which "[b]iotechnology companies eager to recapture their research investments through the commercialization of bioengineered products are pressing understaffed regulatory agencies to permit the release of microorganisms...into the environment."[31]

Environmental groups once again have resorted to legislation to correct these problems, with bills introduced into the Senate by Senator David Durenberger of Minnesota and in the House by Representative Don Fuqua of Florida. The scientific community is divided about this legislation, with some applauding its efforts to clear up the confusions of the existing arrangement and others complaining that the bills impose demands for absolute safety assurances for the release of microorganisms, something no scientist can supply. Thus divided, the scientific community is not in a position to mount the kind of coordinated lobbying effort that we saw in the 1970s.

Bovine Growth Hormone   Another contemporary environmental release controversy surrounds somatotropin, an animal growth hormone. This is not actually a genetically altered product, because the pituitary gland, in cows produces somatotropin naturally, in minute amounts. Rather, a number of biotechnology firms have found a way, using genetic engineering laboratory techniques, to mass-produce somatotropin, generally called bovine growth hormone (bGH). They then inject milk cows with bGH, thereby increasing the milk output of the cow by as much as forty percent. The struggle over this product pits members of the corporate-managerial arena against participants from the popular mobilization arena; the scientific community has not gotten deeply involved.

The development of bGH is dominated by four of the biggest American chemical and pharmaceutical companies: Monsanto, American Cyanamid, Upjohn, and Elanco Products (a division of Eli Lilly & Company). These members of the corporate-managerial arena are intensely competitive, and are working simultaneously on bGH, which, when marketed, is likely to be a major profit maker. And bGH is only the beginning, as a representative of American Cyanamid said: "It's not just BST [bovine somatotropin]. We're laying the groundwork for a whole series of products."[32]

However, demand for bGH within the dairy industry, while sizable, is not projected to be strong enough to support all four firms, meaning that developing the first usable bGH and getting it approved by the Food and Drug Administration is essentially a zero-sum proposition for these companies—only one company can win. Competitive pressures like this would be enough of a problem for members of the corporate-managerial arena to handle even if the decisions about bGH were being made entirely within that arena. With tens, perhaps hundreds, of millions of research and development dollars at risk, with personal careers staked on the success of this new product, individual technological decision makers within the corporate-managerial arena must navigate a mine field of potential disasters, if they are to bring the project to fruition. But the decisions about bGH will not be made only within the corporate-managerial arena. Other participants from other arenas, responding to different pressures and constraints, are also involved.

The environmental groups involved in these decisions, again led by the ubiquitous Jeremy Rifkin, are pursuing a three-prong strategy to obtain the kinds of decisions about bGH they want. As they have done in other biotechnology issues, they are attempting to get the corporations involved to alter their decisions to market biotechnical products by obtaining decisions from outside the corporate-managerial arena, such as the legislative, judicial, and regulatory arenas. Their use of lawsuits, appeals to regulators, and lobbying efforts in Congress are examples. In the case of bGH, Rifkin has filed suit in the federal courts to block the use of this product. They have also testified before congressional committees investigating the safety of bGH.

However, in the case of bGH, they have also tried to manipulate directly the pressures at work within the corporate-managerial arena. A second strategy they are using is to form alliances with potential users of bGH, with dairy farmers and dairy associations, including the Wisconsin Family Farm Defense Fund, Wisconsin's Secretary of State Doug LaFollette, and the Humane Society of the United States.

The alliance members point out the economic risks farmers face if they purchase and use bGH. They remind dairy farmers that there is already too much milk production in this country, without taking steps to increase the supply of milk. Making more milk available on the market will only push prices lower, driving small, family-run farms into bankruptcy. Moreover, they argue, bGH may be harmful to the cattle, damaging their health and shortening their productive lives while increasing output. They also encourage Congress to warn dairy farmers that they cannot hope for rescue from the government if they are reckless enough to use bGH. In the words of Representative Tony Coelho, "If they [the farmers] decide to go ahead and produce more [milk]...they're going to have to suffer the consequences."[33]

Their third strategy is to go after the farmers' customers. By publicly disputing the industry's claims that bGH is harmless, that it leaves no residues in the milk on the store shelves, and so on, they hope to create uncertainty and concern in the minds of people in dairy cooperatives, processors, retailers, and, ultimately, ordinary citizens. As Jonathan Rauch puts it: "Rifkin's coalition is planning to do everything possible to make BST a marketing problem for dairymen."[34] The strategy can be effective, as seen when dairymen in California hastily pulled milk from test herds using bGH from the market, and tried to get assurances from the chemical companies that such "tainted" milk would not again enter the milk supply. In the words of one member of the California Milk Advisory Board: "The word 'hormone' scares people; psychologically, the consumer is not ready for that."[35]

The corporate-managerial participants are cooperating in response to these tactics, despite their being fierce competitors. One of them has hired the country's largest public relations firm to plan strategy and keep watch over the actions of other participants. The corporations are also actively lobbying with Congress, and have put together a collective public information campaign to counter the program of the environmentalists. This poses some serious problems for them, though, because the more they tell the public about bGH, the more they tell each other. Competitors within the corporate-managerial arena are usually secretive about products and processes, lest they give away proprietary secrets or advantages to others. But, to overcome the alarm the environmentalists have created among the drug corporations' own customers, they must set aside their usual suspicions and work together. Rauch summarizes the situation: "Rifkin pledges that this will be just the beginning. It remains an open question whether he is right in his belief that it won't take much to turn consumers against bovine growth hormone, or whether the drug companies can swallow their secretiveness and hang together."[36]

Thus far, the opponents of bGH have had a number of successes: Wisconsin and Minnesota[37] have imposed moratoria on the sale of bGH-treated milk, while several companies, including Kraft USA, Borden, Inc., Dannon, Inc., Safeway Stores, Kroger Stores, and Ben and Jerry's Ice Cream[38] now refuse to sell or use treated milk products. There are international trade problems for the corporate-managerial side, too: the European Community has also banned bGH-treated milk.

In the face of such orchestrated opposition, corporate-managerial spokespersons have been reduced to public complaining: "Special-interest groups are using animal safety arguments as a Trojan cow for other agendas, which include stopping biotechnology and bashing big business."[39] And: "Why are the BST [bovine somatotropin] greens falling all over themselves to outlaw these healthy, environment-friendly products?" Another corporate-managerial representative asks, "Are we really dealing with a reflexive hostility to anything produced by technology, especially if produced for profit."[40] And from a representative of Upjohn, a major developer of bGH: "This country has got an excellent market for fear."[41] If other instances of popular mobilization arena-generated public health concerns are any guide, these grievances on the part of corporate-managerial decision makers will not assuage public fears. Recent studies show that the public is very leery of allowing corporate-managerial decision makers to choose when and how to release bioengineered products into the environment, preferring by a margin of 66 percent to 13 percent that such decisions be regulated by the government or some external scientific authority.[42] Others wonder why the biotechnology industry chose bGH as its first major product, when there is already an over-abundance of milk on the market.

The politics of environmental release has changed in more recent years, as Christopher Plein notes.[43] The biotechnology industry and its allies have been notably successful in altering the terms of the debate about this technology, shifting from public concerns about safety to worries about international competition. Those same companies actively petition Congress and the regulatory agencies for regulatory exemptions for various kinds of genetically engineered organisms.

What is even more worrisome for many observers of the biotechnology revolution is the tendency of many pharmaceutical and chemical companies to shift their laboratory research overseas, often to Third World countries where the strict regulations found in the United States and Europe are missing and where well-trained regulators are often not to be found.[44] Overseas testing places renewed pressure for streamlined regulatory procedures in the U.S. Chemical, pharmaceutical, and bioengineering firms can point to the rapid progress available to domestic or foreign manufacturers that test overseas, arguing that only if safety regulations in the United States are relaxed will American firms be able to compete. Betsy Hanson and Dorothy Nelkin quote some representative testimony before Congress:

> As Richard Godown, president of the Industrial Biotechnology Association has already pointed out, "A Japanese company has genetically engineered silkworms to produce a hepatitis vaccine," and "the United Kingdom and Ireland may be in the lead in animal biotechnology." Even China, "which we consider an under-developed country," said Dr. Thomas Wagner of Ohio University, is already test marketing low-fat pigs produced by growth hormone injection. "How are our farmers going to feel when that ham, which is 70 percent fat-free, comes here in cans, and is sold in the United States?"[45]

The picture of angry farmers waving cans of superior foreign hams will serve to marvelously concentrate the thinking of any member of Congress who desires to continue serving there. Certainly the first major breakthrough, such as an AIDS vaccine, attributable to relaxed or nonexistent regulations overseas will create a drumbeat of complaints against "excessive" safety precautions here.

CONCLUSIONS

What does this history tell us about how technological decisions are made in the United States? What lessons are there here for our understanding of technological politics?

For one thing, we can see that participants in the various technological decision-making arenas prefer, if possible, to maintain complete control of technological issues within their own arenas, where they are on familiar terrain and understand the normal practices, expectations, pressures, and limitations that characterize their decision making home. Permitting participants from other arenas to influence how issues are resolved increases the uncertainty and unpredictability that is always a part of technological decision making.

Allowing actual control over those decisions to shift into other arenas may mean that one's technological goals—toward which much effort may have already been expended, and upon which one's whole career may rest—are never reached. At a minimum, it would mean having to expend additional time and resources manipulating the technological decision makers in those other arenas to make the "correct," desired decisions.

We have also seen that it can be very difficult indeed for the participants of a single arena to maintain complete control over the technological decisions in which they are interested. The two examples we have seen here—the academic-professional arena's desire to control rDNA laboratory research and the corporate-managerial arena's goal of controlling the commercial introduction of bovine growth hormone—show how hard it can be to exclude participants from other arenas if those participants are determined to be included. The simple fact is that, for the important technological decisions in our society, decision makers in one arena must somehow obtain the cooperation of decision makers in other arenas in order to bring those decisions to completion.

We also see, in the first struggle over rDNA regulations, some of the techniques participants in one arena can use to get those desired decisions from participants in other arenas. Having lost exclusive control of the rDNA issue, and fearing that it might fall into the hands of state and local governments, the academic-professional participants deftly shifted the struggle into an arena, the legislative, where they could expect to have more influence. Once Congress got involved, the scientists mounted a sophisticated lobbying effort to ensure that whatever legislation might emerge was to their liking and to make sure that competing legislation designed by the popular-mobilization arena was delayed in committee hearings.

With the issue successfully shifted to the legislative arena, two strategies were pursued at the same time: If legislation finally came forth, it must have provisions desired by the scientists, most especially federal preemption of rDNA regulation. However, if the legislative process could be stretched out, and if new data on rDNA risks could be communicated to the legislators, they might avoid legislation altogether. This, in fact, is exactly what happened.

While the legislative consideration of the competing rDNA regulations dragged on, the scientists brought forth new evidence that the original concerns about DNA research were exaggerated, although, as Dickson tells us, some have questioned the validity of the new data:

> Objections that adequate risk assessment experiments...had not yet been completed were frequently answered with the claim that such experiments were no longer necessary. When caution was exercised in [relaxing the NIH guidelines], it was usually based on the fear that moving too fast would provoke a backlash from either Congress or local communities, rather than any conviction that the caution was necessary on scientific grounds.[46]

Once recombinant DNA technology matured adequately for commercialization, a new round of efforts to regulate rDNA work began.

Environmental groups once again appealed to the legislative, the regulatory, and especially, the judicial for decisions that would impede corporate-managerial decisions to bring genetically altered products to market. Judge Sirica's decision concerning the frost resistant bacteria experiments created enough dissatisfaction and pressure for the government to produce the "Coordinated Framework," parceling out responsibilities for regulation among several federal agencies.

This meant that the issue of regulating the environmental release of genetically altered organisms was now caught up in the pressures, constraints, and limitations that are found within the regulatory arena. No regulator wants to be responsible for a decision to grant a regulatory clearance for a product that might produce an environmental or public health catastrophe. Corporate-managerial decision makers found the array of steps and procedures imposed by federal agencies onerous and thought they would undermine the U.S. competitive lead in the new technology, while environmentalists complained that the restrictions were not strict enough. We also saw how disappointment and frustration with the maze of federal requirements and clearances led both corporate-managerial and academic-professional participants to conduct secret environmental release experiments in violation of federal guidelines.

In the case of bovine growth hormone, we see other techniques used by consumer and environmental groups to affect decisions about bGH made within the corporate-managerial arena. Jeremy Rifkin and other environmentalists are trying to affect the drug companies' customers: dairy farmers, milk processors and distributors, and citizens who buy milk at the grocery store. By raising health and safety concerns and potential economic problems, they hope to dissuade those customers from using bGH, thereby undermining the drug companies' expected profits.

This is an excellent example of how the members of one arena can try to pull the levers that work in another arena to obtain desired decisions from within that arena (in this case, to get the drug companies to reverse their previous decisions to introduce bGH into the marketplace). The corporate-managerial participants have mounted a countercampaign of their own, trying to allay customers' fears and prevent any legislative actions detrimental to their goals. However, the battle is occurring within the corporate-managerial arena, and the drug companies' endeavor is essentially defensive, while the initiative rests with the environmentalists.

Given the environmentalists' ideological motivation, the drug companies do not have much leverage inside consumer or environmental groups. Thus, the corporations must spend their time trying to convince members of the other involved arenas (legislative, regulatory, and judicial) not to accept the environmentalists' arguments. If they succeed, they usually leave the environmentalists with few techniques beyond public protest to influence the drug companies' decisions, a tactic the corporate-managerial arena has been rather efficient in blunting or simply ignoring.

For government decision makers, the choices are quite hard. They must find a balance between safety and profitability, between restrictions on new technologies and the worries many have that we are falling far behind our international competitors. How they eventually decide what kinds of limitations to impose or not to impose may hinge on fate as much as anything else. If a major medical breakthrough should emerge from the overseas laboratories of major chemical companies, there may be a rush to ease the regulations already in place. If, on the other hand, some kind of genetic catastrophe should follow upon some regulatory arena decision maker's approval of some particular environmental release project, the public is likely to demand even sterner and stricter regulations or perhaps outright prohibition. How should government decision makers approach a problem filled with such uncertainty? We address this question in Chapter 11.

ENDNOTES

1. EDWARD J. SYLVESTER and LYNN C. KLOTZ, *The Gene Age* (New York: Charles Schribner's Sons, 1983), p. 2 (emphasis in original).

2. MARTIN KENNEY, *Biotechnology: The University-Industrial Complex* (New Haven, Conn.: Yale University Press, 1986), p. 90, 94.

3. NICHOLAS WADE, *The Science Business: Report of the Twentieth Century Fund Task Force on the Commercialization of Scientific Research* (New York: Priority Press, 1984), p. 23.

4. KENNEY, op. cit., pp. 88–89.

5. DOROTHY NELKIN, *Science as Intellectual Property: Who Controls Research?* (New York: Macmillan, 1984), p. 24.

6. SHELDON KRIMSKY, "Regulating Recombinant DNA Research," in *Controversy: Politics of Technical Decisions*, 2nd ed., ed. Dorothy Nelkin (Beverly Hills, Calif.: Sage Publications, 1984), p. 261.

7. THOMAS O. MCGARITY, "Regulating Biotechnology," *Issues in Science and Technology*, 1, no. 3 (1985), 57–69.

8. KRIMSKY, "Regulating Recombinant DNA Research," pp., 256–257.

9. Ibid., p. 258.

10. Ibid.

11. Ibid., p. 265.

12. SHELDON KRIMSKY, "Research Under Community Standards: Three Case Studies," *Science, Technology, & Human Values*, 11, no. 3 (1986), 31.

13. SHELDON KRIMSKY, *Genetic Alchemy: The Social History of the Recombinant DNA Controversy* (Cambridge, Mass.: MIT Press, 1982), p. 329.

14. Ibid., pp. 330–331.

15. Ibid., p. 331.

16. Ibid., p. 327.

17. DAVID DICKSON, *The New Politics of Science* (New York: Pantheon Books, 1984), p. 251.

18. NICHOLAS WADE, " Biotechnology and Its Public," in *Biotechnology in Society: Private Initiatives and Public Oversight*, ed. Joseph G. Perpich et. al. (New York: Pergamon Press, 1986) p. 86.

19. DICKSON, *The New Politics*, p. 252.

20. Ibid., p. 246.

21. STEPHAN PENDORFF, "Regulating the Environmental Release of Genetically Engineered Organisms: *Foundation on Economic Trends v. Heckler*," *Florida State University Law Review*, 12 (1985), 891–921.

22. MICHAEL P. VANDENBERGH, "The Rutabaga That Ate Pittsburgh: Federal Regulation of Free Release Biotechnology," *Virginia Law Review*, 72 (1986), 1529–1568.

23. PENDORFF, "Regulating the Environmental Release," p. 921.

24. LAUREN WENZEL, "Congress Enters Biotech Regulatory Arena," *BioScience*, 36, no. 5 (1986), 306.

25. "Science Wins One," *Wall Street Journal*, January 14, 1987, 26.

26. MICHAEL LEMONICK, "Montana State's Troublesome Elms," *Time*, September 14, 1987, p. 67.

27. Ibid.

28. Ibid.

29. VANDENBERGH, "Rutabaga," p. 155.

30. RUTH E. HARLOW, "The EPA and Biotechnology Regulation: Coping with Scientific Uncertainty," *Yale Law Journal*, 95 (1986), 567.

31. VANDENBERGH, "The Rutabaga," p. 1592.

32. JONATHAN RAUCH, "Drug on the Market," *National Journal*, April 4, 1987, p. 818.

33. RAUCH, "Drug on the Market," p. 821.

34. Ibid., p. 820

35. Ibid.

36. Ibid.

37. PETER W. HUBBER, "In Praise of the Bionic Cow," *Forbes*, August 17, 1990, p. 108.

38. MARJORIE SUN, "Market Sours on Milk Hormone," *Science*, 246, November 17, 1989, pp. 876–877; Deborah Erickson, "Trojan Cow," *Scientific American*, November, 26, 1990, p. 26.

39. ERICKSON, op. cit., p. 26.

40. HUBBER, op. cit., p. 108.

41. SUN, op. cit., p. 877.

42. U.S. Congress, Office of Technology Assessment, *New Developments in Biotechnology—Field-Testing Engineered Organisms: Genetic and Ecological Issues.* OTA-BA-350 (Washington, D.C.: U.S. Government Printing Office, May 1988), p. 4.

43. CHRISTOPHER L. PLIEIN, "The Emergence of the Pro-Biotechnology Coalition: Issue Development and the Agenda Setting Process." (Paper presented at the annual meeting of the American Political Science Association, Atlanta, 1989).

44. PETER R. WHEALE and RUTH M. MCNALLY, *Genetic Engineering: Catastrophe or Utopia?* (New York: St. Martin's Press, 1988).

45. BETSY HANSON and DOROTHY NELKIN, "Public Responses to Genetic Engineering" *Society*, November/December 1989, p. 77.

46. DICKSON, *The New Politics of Science*, p. 252.

Chapter 11

Solving
the Problems
of Technological Politics

We have examined a number of examples of technological decision making within the American political system, and have reviewed problems of international economic competition, biotechnology, risk assessment, environmental degradation, and military technology. How are we to describe the common contours of technological politics in the United States?

Our first conclusion is that technological politics clearly resembles "politics as usual" in other policy domains, such as welfare, agriculture, or education policy. Science and technology-based policies share many of the same characteristics of any other policy sphere. Sci/tech policies go through similar policy cycles[1] and involve many of the same kinds of decision makers as other policies. Sci/tech policies must pass through the same maze of national (and often state and local) policymaking institutions—executive, legislative, judicial, and bureaucratic—and face all the contingencies and unpredictable influences common to those decisionmaking arenas. This is not surprising, as we did not expect sci/tech policies to be some kind of unique, one-of-a-kind policy realm.

We did find that we must give considerable attention to a number of non-government decision makers who play very important roles in technological politics. Thus, we have spent a considerable time exploring technological decision making within the corporate-managerial, academic-professional, labor, and popular mobilization arenas. This, too, fits the general pattern of American politics: Government policies always involve decision makers from outside the formal institutions and offices of the state. Indeed, we saw that sci/tech issues include considerable interest group pressures and bargaining, well within the dominant pluralist conception of American politics. We also observed that sci/tech issues can suffer from high levels of policy immobilism, exaggeration, sensationalism, stalemate, and gridlock, in large measure because of the intervention of nongovernment organizations and groups. This, too, is a characteristic many commentators generally find common in American politics.[2]

The Privileged Position
of the Corporate-Managerial Arena

Corporate-managerial decision makers are the most robust and powerful participants in American politics for the most part and, thus, in technological politics. As Charles Lindblom reminds us, corporate-managerial decision makers enjoy a preeminent degree of access to government officials and influence in shaping government policies: "Businessmen generally and corporate executives in particular take on a privileged role in government that is, it seems reasonable to say, unmatched by any leadership group other than government officials themselves."[3]

The Economic Role The basis of corporate-managerial dominance is the crucial role these decision makers play in promoting a healthy and vigorous national economy. Except for war and peace, no other issue is as critical for the nation and for its political leaders. Their status, positions, and careers ride on the state of the economy, and members of the corporate-managerial arena understand very well how dependent government decision makers are on the corporate community's willingness to perform its economic functions.

The president and Congress may be politically responsible for the state of the economy, but neither the president nor anyone else in either the executive or legislative arena can directly control how the economy performs. Decisions about the distribution of economic resources, investment plans, new product lines, allocation of labor, plant closings, production technologies—all are made within the corporate-managerial arena, not the government arenas. In the final analysis, the government cannot compel corporate-managerial decision makers to take the economic risks necessary for dynamic growth. Edward Herman reinforces the point, asserting that such dependence makes government "a hostage to the business community."[4]

Corporate-Managerial Leverage This places considerable policy leverage in the hands of corporate-managerial decision makers, who are often successful in demanding "inducements" from government as the price for economic decisions desired by the president and Congress. What sorts of inducements are needed?

> They are whatever businessmen need as a condition for performing the tasks that fall to them in a market system: income and wealth, deference, prestige, influence, power, and authority, among others.... If businessmen say, as they do, that they need tax offsets to induce investment, governments...seriously weigh the request, acknowledging that the tax concessions may indeed be necessary.... If corporation executives say that the chemical industries need help for research and development, governments will again acknowledge the probability that indeed they do and will commonly provide it. If corporate executives want to consult with government officials, including president or prime minister, they will be accommodated.... If corporate executives ask, as they frequently do, for veto power over government appointments to regulatory positions, it will again be acknowledged that such a concession may be necessary to induce business performance.[5]

Corporate representatives do not have to threaten politicians to get what they want. They need only point out the adverse economic consequences that will follow if their demands are not met. Any perceptive executive or legislative decision maker will take careful note of corporate policy demands, as a natural part of the business of governing.

Shared Powers

In a manner reminiscent of the shared powers of church and crown in the Middle Ages, Lindblom tells us that government decision makers in market-oriented, democratic societies *must* share important leadership duties with corporate-managerial decision makers. Corporations perform a wide array of economic policy roles that are, in effect, "delegated" to them by the government. They directly make, or strongly influence, a wide spectrum of economic policy decisions that affect the lives of everyone: "jobs, prices, production, growth, the standard of living, and the economic security of everyone all rest in their hands."[6] And corporate-managerial decision makers, of course, never have to stand for democratic election.

Instead of authoritative commands, executive and legislative arena decision makers must rely on market pressures and a variety of government fiscal and monetary policies, to stimulate corporate decision makers to increase investments, create jobs, open new factories and plants, and other steps desired by the government. Herman echoes Lindblom's assertion:

> The relationship between government and business has been obscured by a tendency to exaggerate both the degree of conflict between business and government and the scope and impact of government regulation. Contrary to the current cliché, government and business are not merely "adversaries," they are often allies and partners.[7]

An Uneasy Partnership

However, the "partnership" between the government and corporate-managerial decision makers is often uneasy, and not just because politicians worry about their electoral chances if corporate decision makers allow the economy to deteriorate. There are many other important constituencies making demands upon the executive and legislative decision makers and significant social and political problems that require responses by government. Solving those problems can be as imperative as pleasing corporate interests, and may put executive and legislative decision makers at odds with the desires of the corporate community.

What this array of conflicting pressures means is that corporate-managerial decision makers do not always get their way in every case. For one thing, corporate-managerial political influence rises and falls over time, rather than remaining constant, as Lindblom's comments seem to suggest. David Vogel[8] detects a pattern to the "fluctuating fortunes" of the corporate-managerial arena: When the economy performs well, the political clout of the business community tends to wane, as other groups and other agendas emerge from the general background of economic prosperity. However, when the economy stalls, corporate-managerial decision makers regain their political influence. A faltering economy tends to drown out demands for other political goals, as executive and legislative arena decision makers become more pliant to corporate policy demands.

Because their perspectives and vantage points differ, corporate-managerial decision makers do not always see all policy problems in the same way, nor do they support the same varieties of government decisions. As we noted in Chapter 3, corporations engaged in the mass production of standardized commodities face different decision environments than do companies engaged in new-product developments. But while the former is now the norm, the latter occurs relatively infrequently. Divisions within the corporate-managerial arena must be factored into assessments of how much political clout decision makers from this arena have at any particular time. As Vogel tells us: "When business is both mobilized and unified, its political power can be formidable."[9]

Thus, decision makers in Congress and in the executive branch are not simply at the beck and call of corporate-managerial decision makers. Government decisions on taxes, spending, patents, and regulation shape the economic environment for corporate-managerial decision makers. Moreover, despite vigorous corporate opposition, the popular mobilization and labor arenas have led Congress to enact a broad array of environmental and health and safety regulations and to empower regulatory agencies to impose important restraints on corporate-managerial decisions. Even during the "antiregulatory" 1980s, the Reagan administration was unable to get the legislative arena to make any important changes in environmental or health and safety legislation, even though executive decision makers did attempt to impose policy changes through personnel appointments and budgetary reductions.

While government and corporate decision makers cannot afford simply to ignore the demands of labor, judicial, regulatory, popular-mobilization, or academic-professional arena decision makers, the technological projects initiated by these other arenas most often are re-actions to corporate-managerial, executive and legislative decisions. Decision makers from these three arenas clearly have the initiative in technological politics, with corporate-managerial decision makers very often the first among equals. The other five technological decision-making arenas usually play secondary roles; they can either contribute to or obstruct the technological projects selected by decision makers in the three principal arenas.

The partnership and policy tensions between corporate leaders and governmental decision makers produce what Edward Woodhouse has called "a formidable problem-creating system of technological decision making."[10] Selected according to vastly different criteria, two sets of leaders (corporate and government) pursue agendas that sometimes coincide and sometimes diverge, each capable of impeding the other's plans, and thus each needing to be mollified if either agenda is to be completed. The relationship among decision makers in these three technological decision-making arenas is truly "where the action is" in technological politics.

SOME SOLUTIONS

Technological politics in the United States is often beset by three interlocked and interactive sets of problems: social, economic, and ecological problems, flexibility problems, and political decision-making problems. What can be done to rehape how we make decisions about technology that may relieve these difficulties? Several different kinds of programs are suggested for resolving these technology-induced challenges.

Use the Market

Many argue that the most efficient and effective way to alleviate the problems associated with technology is to rely on the free market to solve them. At its simplest, this means that if consumers want pollution-free air and water, they need only signal this desire to manufacturers through the market—purchasing only those products that are manufactured in nonpolluting ways or those from manufacturers that take effective steps to clean up unavoidable pollutants. Any business foolishly insensitive to this demand will be driven from the market.

More complex versions of this approach, recognizing that consumer demand does not always effectively transmit these kinds of demands, urge that existing regulatory agencies and programs adopt more market-oriented incentives as a substitute for inherently inefficient regulations. Thus, for example, some urge the imposition of various kinds of "pollution taxes," which would allow a manufacturer to create as much pollution as it desired, but must pay a, hopefully stiff, tax on pollutants emitted into the atmosphere. If the tax is sufficiently stiff, the manufacturer will have sufficient incentive to clean up and stop polluting. Some even urge the creation of "pollution markets," in which manufacturers can buy and sell pollution "rights" from each other. Those manufacturers whose processes are already pollution-free could then sell their pollution rights to manufacturers that use less efficient processes.

As to other technology-induced problems—for example, job displacement and community disruption from plant closings, layoffs, and the like—the market still offers the most efficient way of resolving such issues, supporters of market solutions assert. Because they assume that consumer demand independently drives technological change, any modifications in employment demand, skills, and so on, are not the "fault" of either the technology or of the corporations that manage it. The impersonal operations of the market demand adaptations and changes; workers and communities need to be as flexible as corporations.

Such reasoning, however, ignores the many ways that corporate-managerial decision makers manage the market, shaping consumer demand through sophisticated techniques of market analysis, advertising, and so on, to meet corporate requirements. Back in the 1960s, economist John Kenneth Galbraith[11] detailed the many ways in which modern corporations circumvent the marketplace, engage in long-term consumer demand manipulation, and attempt to establish and maintain effective control of their environments. It is difficult to assert, in the face of this evidence, that corporate-managerial decision makers are simply responding to market signals when they adopt job-eliminating or deskilling manufacturing technologies, or when they assert that shifting consumer demands require the closing of factories and plants. Corporate-managerial decision makers expend a lot of effort making sure that the market gives precisely the kinds of signals they want it to give.

Cancel the Market

Others take a diametrically opposed view: Since market forces create the many technological problems we face, we should take steps to neutralize those market forces. The most extreme versions espouse a wholesale replacement of our capitalist economy with one or another form of socialism, in which the government assumes the economic role currently delegated to corporate-managerial decision makers. However, the experience of several socialist economies in the world suggests that the government arenas are not particularly adept at managing the thousands of decisions that go into running a national economy.

Less extreme views urge the abandonment of certain features of the market, while maintaining the overall structure. One view urges that technology's problems derive primarily from the mass production, mass consumption ethos of modern society. The solution is to return to simpler, smaller-scale lifestyles that are not so damaging to the environment and to the quality of life. Thus, we see a scattering of groups propounding a "back to nature" lifestyle, using small-scale, low-tech approaches, especially in the area of energy consumption. Such groups recognize that their recommendations would require a major reorganization of society, but argue that environmental degradation and resource depletion make a "small is beautiful" orientation essential for survival.

Others reject such extensive restructuring of the economy as unnecessary or impractical. Instead, they encourage greater reliance on policies to regulate the normal operations of the marketplace. They explicitly reject the assertion that market pressures and market incentives can effectively curb the most egregious of technological problems, and that, indeed, more extensive economic intervention is needed to compensate for the market's less desirable features. Such intensive interference in the marketplace, however, would be hard to manage efficiently. It would involve substituting bureaucratic decision makers for corporate leadership, and it runs all of the risks attendant upon bureaucracies in general.

Technological Forecasting

Yet another approach to controlling the concrete problems posed by technology is the use of several different techniques for predicting what the consequences of specific technologies will be, so that steps can be taken ahead of time to eliminate, ameliorate, or correct the least desirable effects. If we can forecast the most likely problems that a new technology might present, perhaps we can take measures to avoid the negative consequences while enjoying the positive results of deploying and using the technical opportunity.

Several forecasting models and techniques exist for this purpose. We have already seen how the Office of Technology Assessment (OTA) serves precisely this function for the legislative arena. In the corporate-managerial arena, a variety of market forecasting, market analysis, and consumer preference techniques are employed to assess the acceptability of technological options. Within the regulatory arena, formalized techniques, such as cost-benefit and risk-benefit analyses, are used to anticipate the consequences of regulatory decisions. Regulatory arena utilization of these forecasting techniques came as a result of instructions to those agencies from both the executive and legislative arenas. Many people criticize these techniques, especially cost-benefit and risk-benefit analyses, for reliance on a pseudo-mathematical precision, neglecting to account for various intangible—and thus difficult to measure—impacts of technologies and for reducing technological analyses to those items measurable by dollars.

Aside from these problems, technological forecasting is also difficult and often unreliable simply because it is impossible to predict the future. No matter how many variables are included in complex computer models, it remains impossible to include all of the factors likely to affect a new technology, or all of the consequences that derive from its introduction. All forecasts are going to be wrong, to one degree or another, and the history of forecasting is littered with predictions that have been wildly off target.

Make Corrigible Decisions

Because returning to a pure marketplace, or socializing the economy, or using low-tech technologies, or applying sophisticated technology forecasting techniques are all ineffective in correcting the structural and political obstacles to satisfactory technological decision making—not to mention environmental and health and safety problems—what are we to do?

If we could clearly identify those technologies likely to engender significant public controversies, we could take steps to control their worst social consequences or forbid them outright. The problem is that it is exceptionally difficult to know which new technologies will be dangerous. This presents us with what might be called the "Collingridge dilemma" in the control of technology:

> ...attempting to control a technology is difficult, and not rarely impossible, because during its early stages, when it can be controlled, not enough can be known about its harmful social consequences to warrant controlling its development; but by the time these consequences are apparent, control has become costly and slow.[12]

Technologies still in their infancy can be managed or controlled with relative ease, David Collingridge tells us. However, with new technologies our capacity to predict even the short-term consequences, much less the long-term impacts, is so meager that any such controls would be arbitrary and capricious. On the other hand, by the time a technology has been used long and widely enough for us clearly to understand what sorts of negative consequences it produces, that technology may be so entrenched throughout society and the economy that imposing restrictions upon it may be prohibitively expensive.

A few policy analysts, such as David Collingridge, Joseph Morone, and Edward Woodhouse,[13] and Langdon Winner,[14] suggest some alternatives. If we cannot accurately predict the future, maybe we should approach these problems from the other end. We should find ways to make technological decisions that remain correctable after they are implemented. Then, at least, we will be able to amend those decisions that turn out to be mistaken or present unexpectedly negative consequences. This is what Collingridge means by *corrigible decisions*:

> A decision is easy to correct, or highly corrigible, when, if it is mistaken, the mistake can be discovered quickly and cheaply and when the mistake imposes only small costs which can be eliminated quickly and at little expense. The essence of decision making under ignorance is to place a premium on highly corrigible options.[15]

What we need, Collingridge argue, are decisions that resist the inflexibility of premature entrenchment, are sensitive to consumer, environmental, and labor concerns, and do not play so easily into political stalemate. Collingridge suggests that flexible, correctable technological decisions would

1. *Minimize lead time.* The shorter the lead time involved in implementing a decision, the quicker modifications or corrections can be introduced, if needed.
2. *Keep unit size small.* Small unit size preserves a greater degree of decision flexibility.
3. *Avoid high expenditure prior to performance.* Keeping investment costs low helps prevent rigidity and allows for changes as we learn from experience.
4. *Minimize infrastructure.* By keeping the number and extent of ancillary technologies likely to be affected by a specific technical choice, corrections are much easier to implement.

Try Simple Trial and Error

In the same spirit, Morone and Woodhouse assert that when faced with decisions with inherently unpredictable consequences, the only available decision-making strategy is some variation of trial and error: Allow the introduction of the new technology, carefully monitor its impacts, and then modify the initial decision as dictated by experience. Woodhouse lists the necessary preconditions for a successful trial-and-error strategy:

1. Errors must generate noticeable symptoms.
2. Someone must perceive these symptoms.
3. This feedback must be communicated to those with competence to interpret it.

4. Such interpretations must then be communicated to those with authority to take action.
5. The error must be correctable and/or compensable.[16]

Both Morone and Woodhouse, however, are skeptical about the efficacy of simple trial-and-error approaches for dealing with modern technology. This would be simple enough, if only technology would cooperate. Unfortunately, too often it does not. There are a number of real-world problems with a simple trial-and-error approach:

1. In many cases, there is a long lag time between the introduction of a technology and the feedback needed to detect errors. Many industrial chemicals and agricultural pesticides, while dangerous to humans, have such long latency periods that we are unable to detect symptoms for years or decades later. During this time, such products may have become deeply entrenched in the economy and thus be very difficult to remove once their dangers have become apparent.
2. Even if the appearance of symptoms of error is not delayed, the state of scientific knowledge may not allow for the feedback to be recognized: "the negative feedback may not be perceived due to the esoteric nature of many science-laden social problems. Unless a pollutant creates visible symptoms or has a distinctive smell or taste, normal human senses are usually unable to detect it."[17] If the pollutant is in wide use in the economy, it may be very difficult to remove or even to restrict, if it lacks unequivocal indicators of its danger.
3. Some technological decisions may be irreversible, even if symptoms of error appear quickly. The wholesale destruction of a nuclear war or the widespread contamination of water supplies are examples of technological decisions that are impossible or extremely difficult to reverse. In these, and other similarly catastrophic cases, detecting that "errors" had been made would be easy enough, assuming that any humans survived to raise the question. Remedial actions, however, might well be impossible because of the scale of the error. Woodhouse notes with wry understatement: "Because errors could have catastrophic consequences, merely waiting for errors to show up would appear to be an unpromising regulatory strategy."[18]

Try Sophisticated Trial and Error

These and similar problems make simple trial and error too risky a scheme in making decisions about technology. Yet something like a trial-and-error method seems the only practicable decision strategy. Thus Morone and Woodhouse urge that decision makers adopt a "sophisticated trial and error" method, in which decision makers consciously and intentionally seek to make decisions that are "forgiving of errors." Sophisticated trial and error takes the best elements of simple trial-and-error methods and makes them into explicit guidelines for decision makers. Woodhouse specifies five components to a sophisticated trial-and-error strategy:

1. Protect against those undesirable consequences that can be foreseen. Some risks are foreseeable, even if many are not. We should begin by protecting ourselves

against those negative impacts of technological decisions that we can clearly anticipate.

2. Err on the side of caution. As we begin gradually to introduce a new technology, we should move deliberately, allowing enough time for unexpected consequences to emerge at a pace we can handle. Overwhelming ourselves leaves no room for corrections.

3. Accelerate negative feedback from technological decisions by testing the risks. Rather than waiting for possibly severe negative impacts to appear, we should actively test for adverse consequences. The sooner we know about problems, the easier it is to adopt changes in the technology.

4. Prepare to learn from experience. We should energetically monitor new technologies, and be prepared to make modifications if evidence indicates the need. Passivity means only that undesirable impacts of new technologies catch us unawares and unprepared.

5. Set priorities of which risks to deal with first. Where the array of potentially troublesome technologies is large—as in our society—we must set reaction priorities. We cannot attend to every risk at once, and trying to will only waste resources and effort. We should attend to the greatest risks first.

Collingridge and Morone and Woodhouse thus argue that greater social control over the consequences and direction of technological change, including greater protection against the often unexpected negative impacts of technology, requires technological decisions that are more flexible and more correctable than those of the recent past.

INSTITUTIONAL AND PROCEDURAL REFORMS

How can we ensure that technological decision making embodies corrigible decisions guided by sophisticated trial and error? Education would surely help. If decision makers at all levels and in all arenas were fully imbued with the strictures laid out by Collingridge and Morone and Woodhouse, we would, at a minimum, expect to see fewer technological decision errors, and probably considerably less political gridlock, since there would be less need for invested decision makers to defend inflexible decisions. If more decision makers committed to these sensible principles took positions of power within the corporate-managerial, executive, and legislative arenas, we would still face a variety of technology-based problems, to be sure. However, we would be better prepared to deal with those problems in a technologically responsible and democratically responsive manner.

But is it enough to hope that decision makers can be found or trained, to overcome the three levels of problems in technological decision making we have seen repeatedly in earlier chapters? What about the existing array of pressures, constraints, and limitations that constitute the decision making environments in which those newly enlightened decision makers must operate? Won't those environmental forces ultimately overwhelm even the best trained and most dedicated individual technological decision maker? Can we make some institutional and procedural changes to enhance the probability that sophisticated trial and error is actually implemented and that technological decisions remain corrigible? Collingridge and Morone and Woodhouse do not specify the institutional and procedural changes needed to accomplish their purposes.

However, our technological decision-making arenas framework allows us to offer some suggestions along these lines. We will make a series of recommendations about how to alter the decision making environment of each technological decision-making arena to enhance the goals of corrigible decisions guided by sophisticated trial and error. Because of the central importance of corporate-managerial decision makers, the first focus of change must be the array of incentives, constraints, pressures, and goals found in this arena.

Corporate Social Responsibility

Some corporate observers reject the idea that any significant changes are needed. They echo A. A. Berle's assertion that professional corporate managers resemble "a professional civil service far more than a group of property-owning and property-minded entrepreneurs."[19] And, indeed, many well-known corporate leaders are on public record admitting that corporations have "social responsibilities" beyond generating profits, and point to the charitable, educational, and public service contributions of corporate resources as evidence that they are meeting their social obligations.

Nevertheless, the pressures and constraints found today in the corporate-managerial arena work against the development of much sensitivity to concerns unrelated to corporate profits. The large size and hierarchical, top-down authority system of the corporate-managerial arena seems to insulate individual decision makers from being overly sensitive to issues demonstrably unrelated to corporate profit and growth. John De Lorean, certainly no stranger to life in the corporate-managerial arena, clearly captures how personal perceptions of right and wrong can differ from corporate perceptions:

> The system has a different morality as a group than the people do as individuals, which permits it to willfully produce ineffective or dangerous products, deal dictatorially and often unfairly with suppliers, pay bribes for business, abrogate the rights of employees by demanding blind loyalty to management or tamper with the democratic process of government through illegal political contributions (quoted in Wright[20]).

Taking sensitivity to the impacts of plant closing decisions on workers and communities as one measure of "corporate conscience," Herman concludes that

> large managerial corporations may be taking advantage of their greater flexibility to abandon local communities and workers more readily than small local enterprises...large, profit-seeking companies under competitive pressure have a structural bias *toward* irresponsibility, in the sense of greater capability of externalization of social costs through abandonment.[21]

Corporate-managerial performance in a number of other areas also fails to substantiate corporate claims of "enlightened" social consciousness: indifference to environmental problems and recalcitrance in the face of pollution reduction measures, unsafe and illegal toxic waste disposal, disregard for community-wide impacts of plant closing decisions; unsafe working conditions, and so on.

Design Phase Intervention

One approach, consonant with the Collingridge-Morone-Woodhouse recommendations, is to interject consumer, environmental, and labor concerns much earlier in the corporate-managerial decision making process, during the design phase of new technologies. Entering the decision process early in the design phase significantly increases the leverage such social and political considerations can have on the final technical outcome. As Winner notes:

> ...a particular device or system that contains important social consequences does not first appear as a single, unambiguous, finished entity. In many cases there exists at the outset of a particular variety of technological development a spectrum of possibilities for the creation of devices and systems of possibilities of various kinds, technologies likely to have widely different kinds of social consequences. From that spectrum social actors eventually select the form of the device that eventually becomes an object in common use. One way in which such choices are expressed is in the design of both material objects and of the institutions that accompany them.[22]

Proponents of early design phase entry want to influence which options are ultimately chosen from the "spectrum of possibilities" presented by the technological project at issue. If corporate-managerial decisions included consumer, environmental, and labor concerns at the same time that traditional market issues were addressed, a number of advantages might be gained. First of all, the quality of the decisions themselves would improve, if by this we mean that traditional notions of economic efficiency would immediately expand to encompass a variety of issues usually left out of such decisions. An enhanced sensitivity to these concerns during the time a new technological product or process is being designed might well eliminate or greatly reduce expensive and time-consuming conflicts as the technology is introduced to the market. This would mean a quicker, more supple response to changing market demands and a shorter time from R&D investment to commercial payback for the corporation. It would also reduce the debilitating and wasteful procedural delays in the legislative, regulatory, and judicial arenas.

But how are environmental, consumer, and labor concerns to enter systematically into corporate-managerial decision making? What changes in that decision making environment are necessary? One good place to begin is by altering who gets to participate in corporate-managerial decision making.

Stockholder Activism

Because corporations are theoretically controlled by their stockholders, greater stockholder participation by groups and individuals concerned with environmental, health and safety, and labor issues might induce corporate decision makers to take closer account of these matters. David Vogel, reviewing efforts by concerned stockholders to influence corporate-managerial decision makers through stockholder resolutions and proxy fights, concludes:

> For the most part, corporations take citizen demands, particularly when expressed through stockholder resolutions, with increasing seriousness.... By any objective criteria—the willingness of management to voluntarily include public interest resolutions in their proxy statements, the number of resolutions withdrawn after satisfactory negotiations with politically oriented investors, and the frequency of meetings between chief executive officers and activists—the acceptance of citizen pressures by business has increased considerably.[23]

During the politically activist 1960s and 1970s, a number of popular mobilization arena groups, including those led by Ralph Nader, various church groups, and others, raised complaints about corporate behavior through stockholder meetings. However, their overall effectiveness is open to debate. Rarely do such groups ever accumulate significant stockholdings, and they always constitute small minority positions at stockholder meetings. They have never garnered enough stockholder votes to elect a sympathetic member to the board of directors.

Such groups sometimes threaten to sell off their stockholdings all at once, thereby depressing the market value of the stock, unless the corporation alters its decisions. More effective, however, have been public proxy fights, with all the attendant publicity focused on alleged corporate misbehavior. Labor union pension funds, now one of the most important investors in the stock exchange, have substantial potential to reshape corporate decision making. Recent campaigns opposing aggressive sales of powdered infant formula in the Third World, and demands for disinvestment in South Africa are examples of effective stockholder pressures on corporate-managerial decision makers. There are some brokerage firms that specialize specifically in investments in environmentally sensitive companies for private investors or groups.

Boards of Directors

Another step, placing consumer, environmental, and labor arena decision makers directly on the boards of directors of major corporations, might help to ensure that consumer, environmental, and labor concerns would find expression at the larger corporate policy level. Many countries, especially in Europe, require labor representatives among a corporation's directors, ensuring that labor interests are heard at the highest level of corporate-managerial decision making. The inclusion of popular mobilization arena decision makers also makes sense.

As useful as including consumer, environmental, and labor representatives on boards of directors might be, there are some problems that need to be addressed. Martin Carnoy and Derek Shearer detail these problems:

> Corporate boards—indeed, boards of directors as presently operated *no matter who sits on them*—are problematical in terms of enterprise decision making for fairly obvious reasons: 1) any group that meets so rarely and is so dependent upon others (i.e., management) for information and advice cannot hope to control in any real sense; 2) managers have authority within the firm, detailed knowledge and information, and large resources in terms of personnel; the exact opposite is the case with outside directors...; 3) to the extent that the board does make any real decisions, these are usually arrived at <u>in advance</u> through informal communications between like-minded directors; troublemakers—worker-directors, for example— are simply excluded from the process. Sometimes, committees of the board are formed and control can be maintained by excluding worker-directors from the key committees.[24]

The reality of corporate power is that management controls boards of directors and often has the biggest hand in selecting board members and control board agendas. It would be easy enough for corporate decision makers to allow token representatives without permitting them to actually influence corporate decisions. Indeed, having popular mobilization and labor participants on their boards might allow them to claim that consumer, environmental, and labor interests are a part of corporate-managerial decision making, even if those interests were, in fact, systematically ignored by the corporation: "The danger of worker-directors, as is clear from the European experience, is not that they constitute a subversive force, but that they may be simply irrelevant and a sham."[25] Popular mobilization and labor arena participants on corporate boards would need assured access to corporate accounts and guaranteed membership on all important board committees to ensure that their participation would be more than empty showcasing and their interests powerfully represented.

Other, more intrusive steps, might involve including labor, consumer, and environmental representatives on some of the operational committees within the corporation. For instance, planning committees considering closing specific plants or factories might include members of the local community. And new-product committees might involve outside participants representing workers, consumers, and public interest groups concerned about environmental impacts.

Federal Corporate Chartering

Urged for years by Ralph Nader and others is to have the federal government directly charter corporations. Under current law, corporations receive their charters from individual state governments, which Nader says leads to a competitive bidding-down of restraints on corporate behavior by states eager to attract business:

> Federal incorporation is necessary because state incorporation has failed its past missions and avoided even acknowledging its future responsibilities toward a fast-changing corporate society. And the reason why is clear: what good is it for fifty-one jurisdictions to have tough business codes if one is a coddler? With the states stooping to that lowest common denominator, corporations have conquered. The only remedy for this permissive structure is to have one chartering authority.[26]

Federal chartering would establish uniform standards, in place of the multiplicity of conditions presented by so many individual state governments. If consumer, environmental, and labor participation on corporate boards of directors is desired, federal chartering could establish consistent procedures for the selection of such directors, along with provisions guaranteeing such outside directors proper access to corporate information and to important board committees. Federal chartering would recognize the greatly enhanced power of the largest national and international corporations to overwhelm dependent state governments.

Workers' Control

A different, more extreme suggestion involves having labor arena decision makers directly involved in corporate-managerial decisions. This would entail a radical change in traditional labor-management relationships so characteristic of American industrial relations. Gone would be the carefully demarcated line between skilled and unskilled workers and supervisors and managers. Also gone would be management's exclusive control of the work process, the speed of work, the type of production, the kinds of manufacturing technologies used, new-product introduction and marketing, research and development priorities, and the like while workers in organized unions struggle with management over rates of pay, work rules, and benefits. There are several models of workers' involvement in management, ranging from American labor-management cooperation programs in which workers are allowed greater participation in managerial decisions but denied overall control of corporate decisions, to forms of true labor-management power sharing, as in Sweden and in German codetermination practices, to outright workers ownership of the corporation and its assets, as in Yugoslavia.

Workers' control allows for a more direct and aggressive assertion of labor arena concerns within the corporation. Labor worries about working conditions, the introduction of job-destroying technologies, plant closings, off-shore production, the deskilling of existing jobs, worker exposure to hazardous chemicals, and other health and safety issues would obtain greater corporate attention than provided through stock manipulations, proxy fights, or even participation on the board of directors. This does not mean that there would be no room for technical changes in the workplace, however. Rather, it means that, in addition to the accustomed corporate concern for marketability and bottom-line profits, changes affecting workers would have to be sensitive to the impacts they might have on those workers.

The other side of the coin, is that workers' control would require labor arena decision makers to face up to the very real problems corporate-managerial decision makers face in running business enterprises in a highly competitive world. Decisions about plant closings, layoffs, worker discipline and firings, new product development, foreign competition, and so on would rest at least as much on labor's shoulders as on management's. Short-sighted efforts to prevent technical change, to preserve inflexible but inefficient work rules, to obtain inflationary wage and benefit increases that are significantly higher than productivity, and other uneconomic labor demands would have to cease, and workers would have to begin identifying their material welfare more with the health of the company for which they work than with older class interests. Thus, while workers' control would incontrovertibly alter the decision-making environment of the corporate-managerial arena, it also would considerably alter the labor arena, perhaps to the benefit of both.

Not surprisingly, there is substantial opposition to workers' control in the corporate-managerial arena, where decision makers are loathe to see their entrenched prerogatives diluted by the inclusion of previously excluded decision makers. Independence to set the major policies of the corporation, determine product lines, create marketing systems, choose manufacturing technologies, and so on falls within the corporate-managerial domain, and must remain so, they argue. After all, they assert, their actions on behalf of the corporation are dictated by the marketplace, and they must retain the maximum degree of managerial flexibility if they are to survive in a competitive environment.

However, corporate-managerial decision makers realize that workers' demands for more say in decisions affecting them will not go away. And a number of studies document the beneficial impact of greater worker involvement in corporate decision making, especially in areas involving shop floor organization, but also including useful suggestions for improvements in product quality and overall corporate productivity and competitiveness. The shift away from authoritarian domination in favor of more cooperative interactions increases worker job satisfaction and directly contributes to labor stability and industrial peace, all of which contributes to corporate competitiveness.

To accommodate those demands, but without surrendering central managerial authority, some of the larger corporations have initiated cooperative programs in conjunction with labor unions. Sometimes called quality of work life (QWL) and employee involvement (EI) programs, these efforts attempt to enhance job satisfaction by encouraging greater worker involvement in day-to-day shop floor decisions, by redesigning production processes to allow greater team effort by workers, and by encouraging more worker suggestions to improve product quality and productivity.

Such programs are often modeled after European and Japanese systems, and are adopted largely because corporate decision makers are fearful of more efficient foreign competitors. These enhancement programs are often tied to management demands for wage and benefit rollbacks during contract negotiations. And, by and large, American unions have cooperated with management in many areas:

Newer auto-assembly plants now have fewer than five job classifications, compared with 200 or more at older plants, which gives management much greater flexibility in moving workers from job to job.... At Ford, executives credit blue-collar employees with the success of the company's popular Taurus sedan. During the planning phase, for instance, assembly-line workers were asked for advice and management was flooded with helpful suggestions.[27]

Other observers are not so sanguine about QWL programs. Too often, they complain, corporate calls for cooperative programs with union workers are actually intended to undermine union organizing efforts. Also, they point to repeated corporate-managerial decisions shifting investments and production away from regions of the country, and of the world, where unions are robust, all the while requesting more cooperation from organized workers:

> We believe there is a central contradiction in the current operation of U.S. industrial relations. Leaders from all parts of society, including many corporate executives, are calling for an expansion of cooperative efforts at the workplace. They are asking union leaders and members to support these cooperative efforts and to continue moderating their wage demands. At the same time, the dominant trend in strategic business and industrial relations decisionmaking within firms is to shift investments and jobs to nonunionized employment settings.... It is difficult to see how unions can continue to act cooperatively in an environment in which their basic security is being questioned and undermined.[28]

What is at first surprising is that a number of labor arena leaders oppose worker participation in managerial decisions. They worry that worker control will turn out to be a subtle form of co-optation, that workers engaged in management will abandon their loyalty to the labor movement, and that by implicating the labor movement in corporate decisions, management will actually restrict labor's flexibility and independence.

There is also some concern that a workers' control movement in the United States might undermine the power, position, and prestige of existing labor arena leaders. Continuing the tradition of labor-management antagonism and conflict preserves the jobs of labor leaders. Corporate efforts to improve job satisfaction outside the purview of union organizations, many fear, will undermine worker loyalty to unions as a vehicle for expressing labor demands. Better, union leaders say, to rely on collective bargaining and the threat of strikes to wrest concessions from management:

> We do not seek to be a partner in management, to be, most likely, the junior partner in success and the senior partner in failure. We do not want to blur in any way the distinction between the respective roles of labor and management in the plant. We guard our independence fiercely—independent of government, independent of any political party, and independent of management (quoted in Marshall[29]).

Other labor arena decision makers, skeptical of corporate-managerial promises, and pointing to alleged corporate efforts to break existing unions and undermine organizing campaigns, urge a great deal of caution before entering into cooperative arrangements with corporate-managerial decision makers:

> You can't ask unions to walk hand-in-hand into the unknown land of worker participation while going full-speed ahead with union-busting anti-labor programs. There has to be greater acceptance of unions in this country...management can't expect cooperation when the hand it puts around my shoulder also has a knife in it (quoted in Marshall[30]).

It may be the case that labor leaders no longer speak for average workers; with union membership under 20 percent of all laborers, leadership rejection of workers' control measures will affect only a small minority of all workers in this country.

Corporations as Political Institutions

The unifying theme of each of these proposed steps—stockholder activism, membership on corporate boards of directors, federal chartering, and various forms of workers' control—is that corporations are as much political as they are economic institutions. Thus, in addition to taking care of stockholders and creditors, corporations should also be sensitive to the interests of their other "constituent" groups, such as workers and their communities, consumers, and environmentalists. To ensure such sensitivity, the argument continues, such groups should have formal standing to participate in corporate decision making, rather than being restricted only to reacting to those decisions after they have been made by others. This is in effect a call for corporate and workplace democracy, with rights to participate accorded to all groups affected by corporate decisions.

Implicitly, and often quite explicitly, supporters of measures such as these reject as simply inadequate the traditional economic controls over corporate behavior. Economic theory asserts that control of corporate behavior resides with two groups: corporate stockholders and the company's consumers, all within the discipline of the marketplace. Consumers, through their free choices in the market, let the corporation's directors and managers know what kinds of products to produce. Should managers fail to respond to consumer demand, the board of directors will remove them; should the board fail to act, the stockholders will remove the board, and if stockholders fail to discipline the board of directors, the company will eventually go out of business. Thus, while corporate decision makers are accorded a significant amount of decision-making independence, they are not free simply to exploit their prerogatives. Their actions are restrained through the market and contribute to the general welfare whether they want to or not.

Indeed, it is marketplace discipline that justifies allowing corporate-managerial decision makers the privileged position in our political system documented earlier. Those who favor increasing the influence of consumer, environmental, and labor groups within corporate decision making assert that neither stockholders nor consumers really control corporate behavior, and that corporations have many tools for escaping from market discipline. Continued corporate emphasis on classical economic theory, even if it were at one time accurate, only serves to rationalize nearly unchecked corporate power. Classic democratic theory, an older and equally prestigious source of decision-making authority, requires that centers of concentrated power be controlled directly or indirectly by the people most affected by that power.

While workers' control would improve corporate responsiveness to labor arena concerns, it is not sure that it would also be responsive to the concerns of the other technological decision-making arenas. This may be particularly true for environmental issues. It is true that labor unions have a long history of support for environmental regulations, and we might expect this involvement to continue in the future.

There is no assurance, though, that, once faced with managerial decision making, labor arena decision makers will not sacrifice environmental values for corporate economic needs, much as current corporate-managerial aecision makers sometimes do. This is more likely to occur in worker-run firms that are only marginally competitive and thus very concerned about cutting operating costs. Labor arena decision makers may find themselves facing difficult trade-offs between, for instance, pollution abatement, on the one hand, and jobs, competitiveness, and economic survival, on the other.

CHANGES IN OTHER TECHNOLOGICAL DECISION-MAKING ARENAS

Assuming that we can make these recommended alterations in the decision-making environment of the corporate-managerial arena, it may still be useful to fine-tune the decision-making environments in other arenas as well.

Regulatory Reforms

As we have discussed in several chapters, one of the most difficult political problems surrounding science and technology is the prolonged administrative and procedural delays involved in setting, and challenging, regulatory decisions. The exercise of regulatory discretion satisfies virtually no one, and very often results in extended administrative challenges and judicial adjudication. Some, perhaps a great part, of the problem derives from the unclear, equivocal legislative charges often given to regulators from Congress. Legislative arena decision makers, unwilling for political purposes to make clear choices about dangerous technical risks, pass the buck to the regulatory arena in the hope that the issue will simply get lost in a bureaucratic maze. The political battle then shifts into the regulatory arena, where that arena's judicial, adversarial procedures are ready-made for delays and obstructions.

Including environmental, consumer, and labor concerns earlier in corporate-managerial decision making might alleviate some of these regulatory logjams, since many conflicts would be resolved within corporate decision making. However, such modifications of the corporate-managerial decision making environment cannot guarantee that environmental and consumer problems will no longer arise, and popular mobilization arena decision makers will not be willing to rely solely on participation in corporate-managerial decision making to protect their interests. Thus, some forms of regulatory struggles are sure to persist, even in the improved relationships between corporate interests and other coalitions we have suggested. But some alterations in regulatory decision making will also be necessary to avoid the time and resource-consuming inefficiencies of current practices.

One possible reform, described by Mark Rushefsky[31] and others[32-35] involves substituting a negotiation process for the current adversarial structure in rule making, which might reduce or eliminate the resort to obstructionist tactics by contending sides. Negotiated rule making involves

> a variety of approaches that allow the parties to meet face to face to reach a mutually acceptable resolution of the issues in a dispute or potentially controversial situation. Although there are differences among the approaches, all are voluntary processes that involve some form of consensus building, joint problem solving, or negotiation.[36]

The process brings together regulatory arena decision makers, corporate representatives, consumer, labor, and environmental groups, and other affected parties in a mutual exchange of views and information. The goal is a consensual resolution of the policy issue at stake in, it is hoped, less time and at less cost than through traditional adversarial rule-making procedures. Rushefsky summarizes:

> Negotiations should include all parties to a dispute (or at least representatives of all parties) under conditions in which each interest has some political power. With such a result, the expectation is that a rule recommended by the negotiation panel and adopted by an agency will have greater acceptance than one adopted through more traditional procedures.[37]

The negotiation process may be led by the regulatory decision makers or by an impartial mediator who is seen by all to be nonpartisan and serves at the pleasure of the negotiating parties. The mediator's job extends beyond simply hearing each side's views:

> A mediator is responsible not only for tending to the more mechanical aspects of negotiation such as scheduling meetings and keeping records, but also for more substantive functions such as ensuring a common understanding of technical points among all participants, suggesting courses of action for helping to resolve disputed points, and proposing alternative formulations of agreements.[38]

The mediated negotiations would allow each participant's values and goals a thorough airing in a context that avoids the defects of the traditional adversarial administrative process in which the parties "act as adversaries, presenting 'worst-case scenarios' and moving toward extremes."[39]

Other benefits of mediated negotiations include changing the attitudes of participants toward the generation and use of technical information. In an adversarial proceeding, the disputants see any information that is not supportive of their position as a threat, while in a mediated process they are encouraged to see information exchanges as leading to the possible reconciliation of their differences. In a mediated context, moreover, any efforts to squelch relevant data will undermine the credibility of the side hiding the information, the loss of which ultimately may outweigh any advantages gained by the suppression. Daniel Fiorino cites the reactions of several participants in environmental negotiations:

> ...parties to environmental disputes have found mediation and negotiation to be more satisfying, less expensive, and more constructive than an adversarial approach.... An environmental representative found it refreshing to be inside the policy process rather than on the outside looking in. A state official thought that he had far more influence than he would have had in a conventional rulemaking. An industry representative stressed the value of access to senior EPA program managers representing the Agency. Another appreciated the opportunity to make a case more than once and to bring the other parties around to a point of view.[40]

Proponents of mediated regulatory negotiation also hope that this technique may alleviate much of the procedural wrangling over which forecasting model to use in guiding decisions:

> When more than one forecasting model is possible, competing parties usually subscribe to the one that best supports their claims. Every modelling effort incorporates some value-bound assumption such as the specifications of sub-system boundaries, the level of sub-system complexity, the extent to which historical data can be used to describe future circumstances, and the relative importance of forces and factors external to the model. Mediation can provide a means of disengaging each party from its preferred models and encouraging a collaboration that forces a discussion of those assumptions. If the parties to a technical dispute can develop a model that incorporates key assumptions acceptable to all of them, they are more likely to produce a prediction that none can easily dismiss. The deceptive shield that technical analysis sometimes offers to affected interests wishing to disguise the self-serving nature of their position is torn away.[41]

Some observers, however, caution that the strongest supporters of negotiation overstate its value. Gail Bingham, for instance, in comparing negotiation to litigation in environmental disputes, cautions:

> A lawsuit that goes to trial may take a very long time, but few lawsuits go to trial. Some mediated environmental disputes may be resolved quickly, but voluntary dispute resolution processes are not necessarily fast if the issues are complex. In addition, although mediators generally charge less than attorneys, one is not necessarily a substitute for the other, and attorneys' and mediators' fees are not the only costs associated with resolving disputes. The costs of preparing for negotiation, for example, may be as high as or higher than the parallel costs of preparing for some kinds of litigation, particularly for public interest groups in cases requiring analysis of scientific information.[42]

Bingham goes on to argue that evidence that judicial arena actions are less efficient and more costly forms of regulatory dispute resolution, when compared to mediation, is unclear.

She also asks whether popular mobilization decision makers have much incentive to join in mediated negotiations, instead of existing adversarial procedures:

> Politically, the success of environmental organizations usually has been closely related to their ability to generate publicity for their efforts. Legislative and judicial campaigns often attract substantial media and public attention; mediation tends not to.... The use of adversarial strategies has resulted in significant success for environmentalists over the past 20 years, and they may be cautious about giving up such approaches unless the alternatives offer real promise of something better.[43]

Popular mobilization decision makers might resist negotiations because they lack the resources to participate effectively. Bingham cites an attorney with several years of experience litigating for environmental groups:

> ...the major obstacle to more negotiation (including mediation) and less litigation...is *not* the lack of mediation services but the lack of advocacy power (in the form of scientists, economists, and other technical resources) serving the "public interest."... Thus, I think if we had more resource power, we would be much more willing to negotiate; and our opponents would be more likely, also, to do so.... We lack the resources to stay out of court.[44]

We can conclude from these cautionary comments that some changes in the popular mobilization arena will be needed, if mediated negotiations can serve to relieve some of the political decision-making pathologies surrounding science and technology controversies.

Legislative Arena Reforms

Changing the legislative arena is more difficult than changing the regulatory arena, in large measure because of the intensely political nature of this decision-making environment. Ideally, when handling important scientific and technological issues, we would like to believe that legislative arena decision makers are well informed, comprehend both the immediate and the long-term consequences of their choices, and make decisions that are, at the same time, technologically responsible and democratically responsive.

As we have seen, however, there are several characteristics of Congress that work against comprehensive, long-term decision making. The lack of technical expertise among members is an important barrier, as is their highly constituent-centered operating style. Added to these must be the policy fragmentation produced by the committee system, in which issues are broken down into competing committee jurisdictions.

American electoral politics tends to select certain kinds of personal and professional backgrounds among congressional candidates, and there is rather little that can be done to increase the level of scientific and technical competency among members. Nor is there much likelihood of major alterations of the congressional committee system; there are simply too many diverse interests that benefit from the existing legislative structure to imagine that there would be more than a handful of supporters for changing the committee system specifically to enhance science and technology policymaking.

Suggestions for enhancing the legislative arena's ability to deal with scientific and technological issues usually focus on congressional staff support. Members' legislative aides, committee and subcommittee staff members, and the four congressional staff agencies (OTA, CBO, GAO, and LRS-LOC) are central to the legislative process:

> They develop information concerning potential legislation; they write the legislation; they prepare talking points concerning it. If there are hearings, the staffers are present, and they coach the Congressmen, feeding questions or comments to them. The staff interacts with staffs of other Congressmen, gathering intelligence about prospects for passage and negotiating support for the legislation. When bills have passed in both houses, the legislative aides have important roles in the conference that adjusts differences in the bills of each body and in preparing the final language.[45]

While legislative assistants are quite skilled in the political processes on Capitol Hill, the number who are also acquainted with science and technology remains small. To remedy this, a number of professional associations from the academic-professional arena, under the general direction of the American Association for the Advancement of Science (AAAS), operate a Congressional Science and Engineering Fellows Program, which places scientists and engineers in congressional offices as one-year staff aides. Some of the associations participating in this program include the American Society of Mechanical Engineers (ASME), Institute of Electrical and Electronics Engineers (IEEE), American Physical Society (APS), American Chemical Society, and American Geophysical Union.[46]

In the 15 years that the program has been operating, nearly 400 fellows have worked on Capitol Hill, in congressional offices, for committees, and for staff agencies. A number of fellows have stayed on as permanent staffers after their year's tenure ended. In addition to contributing their scientific and technical expertise to Congress, the fellows also serve as representatives of the academic-professional arena to Congress:

> Fellows provide technical expertise and judgment to their members and committees, helping them deal more effectively with technically based issues. Their knowledge and contacts also help the Fellows bring to the surface issues of scientific and technical interest and get these issues on the Congressional agenda. Fellows have served as points of contact in members' offices for scientific institutions in the members' states or districts, and have participated in developing initiatives that serve scientific ends as well as constituent needs.[47]

Another recommendation through which academic-professional decision makers might contribute to enhancing legislative arena scientific and technical expertise comes from James Everett Katz: the formation of committees of "informal science advisers" for members of Congress:

> Scientists on an independent, local basis could form small volunteer advisory committees (of perhaps three to seven experts) for their members of Congress, operating closely with members and their staffs in a *confidential*, informal manner. These committees would be drawn from each member's district—from industry, academia, and the public sector.[48]

Such advisory committees combine scientific and technical expertise with a familiarity with the unique circumstances of the member's home district, while confidentiality would allow freedom of comment by the volunteer scientists. Interactions between such an advisory committee and the member's staff would bring together concerns about scientific and technological responsibility and issues of democratic responsiveness, pushing those most concerned with politics to face up to the realistic demands of science and technology and requiring those unconcerned with pleasing constituents to recognize the pressures of real-world politics.

The core of both recommendations is the value of bringing members of the academic-professional arena into more regular contact with members of the legislative arena, especially with legislative staffers. Programs such as the AAAS Fellows could be substantially expanded, if funding can be found. The ideal situation would have at least one technically trained staff member in each member's office, along with service on committee staffs. In fact, a year's service advising Congress, either directly in Washington as a staffer or on a voluntary advisory committee back in the home district, might be introduced as a career advancement criterion among academic-professional decision makers. The experience would surely improve legislative arena understanding of the scientific and technological complexities of many policies, while exposing academic-professional arena decision makers at least briefly to the world of policymaking.

Executive Arena Reforms

Most criticisms of how the executive arena deals with science and technology focus on the need for greater coherence and coordination in national policymaking, based on more effective presidential leadership. Actually, these concerns have been voiced many times in recent decades; what has varied has been the specific range of scientific and technological problems needing more coherent, coordinated, presidential initiative. In each case, there was a cry for more centralized executive arena leadership to marshal the nation's scientific and technical talent to overcome the current crisis.

Suggestions for achieving greater executive arena leadership in science and technology involve increasing and enhancing the kinds of scientific or technical advice available to administration decision makers. Thus, the Office of Science and Technology Policy in the Executive Office of the President serves to provide focused scientific advice to the president, as science offices within the various executive branch departments offer science advice within each agency. Commentators from within the academic-professional arena and elsewhere assert that the existing science advisory mechanism is still too weak and too far away from the center of executive arena decision making:

> Since the demise of the President's Science Advisory Committee, the function of the President's Science Advisor has gradually become more akin to that of an individual member of the White House staff, rather than that of the head of a major policy office in the Executive Office of the President which Congress intended for the Office of Science and Technology Policy.[49]

The declining significance of the President's Science Advisor within the EOP may be partially attributable to the personal chemistry between individual advisors and individual presidents and in part to the pulling and hauling of bureaucratic politics. Whatever the case, many believe that rapid steps should be taken to reestablish the science advisor's role.

An even more ambitious way to upgrade science and technology advice in the executive arena is to create a formal cabinet-level Department of Science and Technology, which would consolidate most of the scattered civilian R&D efforts of the federal government under a single organizational structure. While several variations on this theme have been heard in the United States since the mid-1800s, the most recent recommendation for a Department of Science and Technology (DST) comes from the 1984 President's Commission on Industrial Competitiveness,[50] a group composed predominantly of leaders of successful American industries.

The DST would be made up of OSTP and the Science Advisor, plus the National Science Foundation, the major R&D functions of the Department of Energy, the National Bureau of Standards, the National Oceanic and Atmospheric Administration, the nonmilitary elements of the National Aeronautics and Space Administration, and the National Institutes of Health, among others. Supporters of a DST, such as Reagan administration Science Advisor George Keyworth, assert that it would have important impacts on Washington: "We should not underestimate the importance of having a Cabinet-level presence for science and technology, a presence that is backed up by what would turn out to be one of the largest *discretionary* budgets among all the departments."[51]

A cabinet-level Department of Science and Technology, according to some, would provide greater efficiency in the use of federal R&D money, make better use of federal laboratories, help science-based agencies defend their budgets before the Office of Management and Budget and the committees of Congress, increase the political clout of the scientific community through greatly enhanced public visibility, enhance the effectiveness of the President's Science Advisor, and give impetus to new policy directions that redefine the federal role in science and technology.[52] These improvements would be of special help, supporters assert, in reinvigorating American international economic competitiveness.

Perhaps surprisingly, many academic-professional decision makers oppose the notion of collecting the scattered federal civilian R&D programs under a single administrative unit, even one with the visibility and political standing of a cabinet department. Many fear that the centralization of federal science and technology support would sacrifice the beneficial, if admittedly often messy, pluralism of the existing system, without obtaining any sustained and useful advantages. The multiple, scattered sources of federal funding for science from the federal government allow researchers many opportunities to obtain support, while a centralized support system might mean that new, creative ideas might be smothered in a bureaucratic orthodoxy. Some point to the continued successes of U.S. science as proof that the existing system works well, and, as the saying goes, "If it ain't broke, don't fix it."

There also would be problems in organizing a Department of Science and Technology, since the mission-agencies would resist surrendering their R&D components to a new bureaucracy, and Congress might well resist the new department since its creation would require the legislature to reorganize some of its committees. Many echo Richard Barke's criticism of the DST idea:

> Fragmentation, duplication, and conflict are not entirely flaws in the system. Science and innnovation appear to flourish when they are somewhat unplanned. Individual initiative and creativity need the opportunities of serendipity. Although better communication and cooperation would reduce the problems that plague risk assessment, cost-benefit analysis, and the ranking of research priorities, the virtues of pluralism—especially the opportunities for lay citizens to participate—in science and technology policy could be retained while the specific vices are addressed.[53]

Barke touches here on some of the pathologies of technological politics mentioned earlier. One of the problems contributing to the bureaucratic delays found in risk assessment is the lack of coherent and consistent standards for determining how to measure and evaluate risk. Given the legislative arena's tendency toward fragmented policymaking, it is not surprising that the specification of risk standards in legislation has been often inconsistent, as we saw in earlier chapters.

However, a single agency, even one that contained relatively independent subunits as most versions of a Department of Science and Technology include, might bring greater coherence and guidance to risk standards throughout the government. What is more, a more intelligible executive arena posture on risk problems might help the legislative arena to overcome its aptitude for creating ad hoc standards in different pieces of legislation. Some steps were taken by the executive arena's Office of Management and Budget to create cancer standards applicable across agencies, but with limited success. Clear, consistent standards might reduce the procedural hassles and delays in regulatory agencies, as well as the number of judicial challenges by those unhappy with regulatory arena decisions.

A Department of Science and Technology might also contribute to more effective communication among specialists in different disciplines, which might, in turn, directly help the system's ability to learn from technological mistakes, a central component of the Collingridge-Morone-Woodhouse recommendations. All three analysts emphasize the critical need to test potential risks and to monitor technological decisions after they have been made. It would not be necessary for a DST actually to take over the testing and monitoring duties from existing agencies, such as EPA and OSHA, although DST management of federal laboratories might be used to augment the overextended resources of these organizations. Rather, DST could serve as a clearinghouse of information, verification, and publicity aimed at detecting and correcting technological decision-making errors.

Popular Mobilization Arena

If the changes in corporate-managerial and regulatory arena decision making already described were put in place, there would have to be some corresponding changes in popular mobilization arena decision making, too.

The political situation of consumer and environmental groups would vary dramatically if these other changes are implemented. Rather than being policy outsiders who must bulldoze their way into decision making dominated by other technological decision-making arenas, consumer and environmental interests would be direct participants in those decisions, whether as members of boards of directors, participants in product design committees, or in regulatory negotiations. Consumer and environmental decision makers would have to change their political strategies considerably as we mentioned earlier when discussing regulatory negotiations. Giving up previously useful political strategies, even if the alternative promises better regulatory outcomes, can be difficult for some organizations to do.

Also, much greater attention to the intricacies of corporate organization and operations, product design, marketing, manufacturing, and so on would be necessary; effective participation in corporate-managerial decision making requires an intimate familiarity with all of these areas. Some consumer groups, such as Ralph Nader's Conference on Corporate Accountability, have attempted to master the problems of corporate management in order to establish their competence to join corporate boards of directors. Environmental groups also will need to establish their ability to deal with the intricate realities of corporate management in an environment of intense national and international competition, if they are to join in collective decision making aimed at preserving environmental values, economic competitiveness, and jobs.

Academic-Professional Arena

In addition to continuing the congressional fellows program to provide technical expertise to the legislative arena, there are other useful steps that academic-professional decision makers could take to improve society's ability to deal with science and technology.

According to the Collingridge-Morone-Woodhouse thesis, the ability to monitor for and correct errors in the application of technology is critical to maintaining control over technical change, and getting reliable feedback is essential for that monitoring. However, often those decision makers most committed to a technology are most reluctant to have problems aired, and they treat anyone who discloses those problems as an enemy, as a traitor. Even if labor, consumer, and environmental groups participate directly in corporate-managerial decision making, we have no guarantee that, under intense pressure, those groups would not agree to hide evidence of problems with the technologies they employ.

However, the professional status of scientists, engineers, and technicians raises them above that of ordinary employees, in that they owe a loyalty to standards beyond those of their employers and are bound by professional codes of ethics to put public safety and well-being above the welfare of the specific corporation or government agency for which they work. For example, the Code of Ethics of the National Society of Professional Engineers stipulates:

> Engineers shall at all times recognize that their primary obligation is to protect the safety, health, property, and welfare of the public. If their professional judgment is overruled under circumstances where the safety, health, property, or welfare of the public are endangered, they shall notify their employer or client and other such authority as may be appropriate (cited in Lowrance[54]).

A number of scientists and engineers have tried to live up to this injunction, and similar ones contained in the codes of ethics of other professional societies, pointing out safety problems associated with civilian nuclear reactors, commercial airliner designs, and biomedical misconduct in research laboratories. Yet to become a whistleblower can bring many difficulties for any courageous enough to live up to their professional obligations:

> Professionally, it can cost an employee not only his or her job but also a career. Personally, it can cost much grief—disrupted sleep, strained friendships, and diminished fortunes. Those who decide to dissent publicly should recognize that they are gambling, and the odds are against them. [Whistleblowers] should realize that it is a lonely lot they are choosing, and they will receive little help from others. The stigma of being called a "whistleblower" ostracizes the individual from colleagues at work and other members of their professions. And even though they may be treated unfairly, they will typically find that they have little recourse through institutional channels like the courts, Congress, or professional associations.[55]

Academic-professional decision makers should take firm steps actively to support scientists and engineers who take the career risks of exposing the errors, misjudgments, and malfeasance of corporate and government authorities. In a few cases, such as the Institute of Electrical and Electronics Engineers, steps have been taken to support members who expose corporate or governmental technical malfeasance. However, as the Professional Ethics Project of the American Association for the Advancement of Science concluded: "Members who seriously seek to comply with their society's ethical rules can expect very little in the form of support activities."[56]

Professional associations should follow Rosemary Chalk and Frank von Hippel's advice to "require that employment contracts for their members include provision for the resolution of employer-employee disputes through hearing and appeal processes."[57] Additional measures include using the prestige of the association to conduct public investigations of alleged misbehavior reported by its members and making the findings known. The associations could also set standards for whistleblowers in order to avoid frivolous or unsubstantiated charges.

While there are a number of laws, including many environmental, health and safety statutes, which offer legal protection to those who expose violations of the law, professional associations should provide vigorous, organized legal support for those of their members who suffer retaliation from their employers for blowing the whistle. In fact, professional associations might publish lists of corporations and government agencies that take relatiatory actions against their members and make public recommendations against working for them until they correct the problems. They might also organize a placement service that would give assistance to conscientious members whose employment situations have become intolerable because of management hostility. As Ralph Nader notes:

> Corporate employees are among the first to know about industrial dumping of mercury or fluoride sludge into waterways, defectively designed automobiles, or undisclosed adverse effects of prescription drugs and pesticides. They are the first to grasp the technical capabilities to prevent existing product or pollution hazards. But they are very often the last to speak out.[58]

Scientists and engineers serve as "early warning" signals of impending problems with modern technology, an acutely important feedback mechanism in modern, technological society. However, only when members of the technical professions are sure that they can come forward with the prestige and support of their fellow professionals will they willingly take on the critical task of exposing from within the errors and problems with technologies that others, in order to preserve investments and profits, would hide.

CONCLUSIONS

We began this discussion with a description of American politics in which corporate-managerial decision makers enjoy a privileged position in the give-and-take of interest group bargaining. The corporate-managerial arena's importance to the national economy translates into preeminence in technological politics, as well. Also centrally important to technological politics are the executive and legislative arenas, with the other five technological decision-making arenas playing important, but essentially re-active, secondary roles.

The normal operation of technological politics in the United States results in at least three levels of interacting difficulties: material social, environmental, and ecological consequences of using modern technologies, extended structural difficulties in the selection and use of inflexible technologies, and political decision-making pathologies. Of various proposed solutions, all seem to fall short of providing us with the ability to control these difficulties.

An approach that offers some promise for dealing with both the structural and the political problems of technological decision making begins by recognizing that we cannot accurately predict the direction of technical change or the future consequences of technology, whether positive or negative. Rather than trying to do the impossible, we should instead reshape technological decision-making in order to maintain control flexibility after decisions are made, thereby allowing us to correct errors once they appear. Following this lead, we outlined several specific modifications in technological decision making environments intended to perfect the whole system's capacity to detect and monitor the effects of technological change and to take appropriate measures to correct decisions after they are implemented.

Because we recognize the centrality of corporate-managerial decision makers in technological politics, we do not pursue the unrealistic and counter-productive goal of eliminating market incentives and market discipline. Rather, we attempt to include more effectively within market-oriented corporate decision making a sensitivity to the health and safety of workers, the enrichment and security of their jobs, and concerns about what the production and use of modern technologies do to the natural environment and to the health and safety of consumers. We do this by including individual technological decision makers who are concerned about these neglected issues directly in corporate-managerial decision making.

By the same token, we hope to increase sensitivity to corporate concerns, maintaining corporate profitability, economic efficiency, and reinvigorating American competitiveness in national and international markets, among labor and popular mobilization arena decision makers. Such increased sensitivity would help to preclude unreasonable demands for wage and benefit increases wholly divorced from their impact on the corporation or on the larger economy. It would also preclude environmental and consumer demands that ignore their impacts on the ability of businesses to earn reasonable profits.

The mechanism we suggest for enhancing such sensitivity on the part of labor, environmental, and consumer decision makers is precisely the same one we recommend for increasing corporate-managerial sensitivity to labor, consumer, and environmental problems: include labor and popular mobilization arena decision makers directly in corporate-managerial decision making. As they bear the burden of making decisions for corporations, they will have to develop a deeper understanding of the conditions and problems facing corporate-managerial decision makers.

By involving different decision makers in the internal processes of the most important arenas, we hope to eliminate an unnecessary and futile over-specialization of goals found in the current array of technological decision-making arenas. A major source of the exasperating and endless administrative and procedural delays, exaggerations and sensationalism, cynical manipulation of inevitably limited technical information, and the intense polarization of debate is the tendency of decision makers in each participating technological decision-making arena to take responsibility for only their portion of the consequences of introducing new technologies.

Thus, corporate-managerial decision makers, in the traditional role of profit maximizers, assume that this is the extent and scope of their obligation; other decision makers have to attend to external concerns. Instead of corporate-managerial decision makers who neglect labor, environmental, and consumer concerns, we seek to have those concerns integrated into corporate-managerial decision making as early as possible in the design phase of new technologies. In like manner, labor arena decision makers, believing that their responsibility extends only to defending the interests of workers, often left to corporate and government leaders the problems of managing competitive, profit-making corporations. So also, consumer and environmental decision makers consider the representation of environmental and consumer concerns as the full scope of their responsibility. For both groups, the problems of running competitive, profit-making companies were essentially someone else's problem.

Since none of these arenas takes the burden of the full range of consequences involved in technological politics, they look upon each other as competitors and press their separate demands all the harder. In this competitive environment, the sensible Collingridge-Morone-Woodhouse recommendations simply get lost in regulatory wranglings, bureaucratic challenges, judicial reviews, and so on. In effect, steps to deal with the structural problems of technology are overwhelmed by the political pathologies of technological politics.

Integrating all of these concerns—running a profitable company and protecting workers, consumers, and the environment—is viewed as the government's job. Unfortunately, American politics, as we have seen time and again, is not very adept at such integration. Even when the complex processes of interest group bargaining generate what appears to be a definitive assessment of social and economic values, as seen in such enactments as the Clean Air Act, the Clean Water Act, and other important environmental programs, we have seen how too-often imprecise legislative language can easily be manipulated, how limitations and restrictions can be evaded, and how the skillful use of administrative procedures can endlessly delay unwanted decisions.

The recommendations made here—to include decision makers from different arenas in corporate-managerial decision making, to use regulatory negotiations instead of confrontation, to augment legislative arena technical competence and enhance executive arena science management—seek to shift the timing and location of that integration further back into the technological decision making process. Under current conditions, by the time compromise and integration are supposed to occur within the government arenas, the investments, commitments, and political positions of decision makers in the relevant arenas have already hardened. By this time, compromise and integration are very difficult, or impossible, which is precisely why integration must occur much earlier in the entire process.

Lamentably, even if these various steps do help resolve both the structural and the political problems surrounding technological decision making, we have no assurance that we will succeed in resolving the concrete problems of labor, of environmental degradation, acid rain, the greenhouse effect, toxic wastes, dangerous pesticides, unsafe consumer products, and so on, that threaten the quality of our lives. What is clear, however, is that if we fail to resolve the structural and political problems afflicting technological politics, we guarantee that we will also fail to face up to these threats.

ENDNOTES

1. JOHN KINGDON, *Agendas, Alternatives, and Public Policies* (Boston: Little, Brown, 1984).

2. MANCUR OLSON, *The Rise and Decline of Nations: Economic Growth, Stagflation, and Social Rigidities* (New Haven, Conn.: Yale University Press, 1982).

3. CHARLES E. LINDBLOM, *Politics and Markets: The World's Political-Economic Systems* (New York: Basic Books, 1977), p. 172.

4. EDWARD S. HERMAN, *Corporate Control, Corporate Power: A Twentieth Century Fund Study* (London: Cambridge University Press, 1981), p. 295.

5. LINDBLOM, *Politics and Markets*, p. 174.

6. Ibid., p. 172.

7. HERMAN, *Corporate Control*, p. 244 (emphasis in original).

8. DAVID VOGEL, *Fluctuating Fortunes: The Political Power of Business in America* (New York: Basic Books, 1989).

9. Ibid., p. 291.

10. EDWARD J. WOODHOUSE, "Decision Theory and the Governance of Technology," *Teaching Political Science: Politics in Perspective*, 14, no. 4 (1987), 176.

11. JOHN KENNETH GALBRAITH, *The New Industrial State* (Boston: Houghton Mifflin, 1967).

12. DAVID COLLINGRIDGE, *The Social Control of Technology* (New York: St. Martin's Press, 1980), pp. 17–18.

13. JOSEPH MORONE and EDWARD WOODHOUSE, *Averting Catastrophe: Strategies for Regulating Risky Technologies* (Berkeley: University of California Press, 1986).

14. LANGDON WINNER, "Political Ergonomics: Three Traditions of Design," paper presented at the annual meeting of the American Political Science Association, Chicago, September 3–6, 1987.

15. COLLINGRIDGE, *Social Control of Technology*, p. 32.

16. EDWARD WOODHOUSE, "Sophisticated Trial and Error in Decision Making About Risk," *Technology and Politics*, ed. Michael E. Kraft and Norman J. Vig (Durham, N.C.: Duke University Press, 1988), p. 212.

17. WOODHOUSE, "Decision Theory," p. 175.
18. Ibid.
19. A. A. BERLE, JR., *Power Without Property* (New York: Harcourt Brace, 1959), p. 110.
20. PATRICK J. WRIGHT, *On a Clear Day One Can See General Motors* (Grosse Point, Mich.: Wright Enterprises, 1979), p. 110.
21. HERMAN, *Corporate Control*, p. 261.
22. WINNER, "Political Ergonomics," p. 2.
23. DAVID VOGEL, *Lobbying the Corporation: Citizen Challenges to Business Authority* (New York: Basic Books, 1978), pp. 203–204.
24. MARTIN CARNOY and DEREK SHEARER, *Economic Democracy: The Challenge of the 1980s* (Armonk, N.Y.: M. E. Sharpe, 1980), p. 252 (emphasis in orginal).
25. Ibid., p. 256.
26. RALPH NADER, "The Case for Federal Chartering," in *Corporate Power in America*, ed. Ralph Nader and Mark J. Green (New York: Grossman, 1973), p. 79.
27. KENNETH SHEETS, "America's Blue Collars Get Down to Business," *U.S. News & World Report*, February 29, 1988, pp. 52–53.
28. THOMAS A. KOCHAN, ROBERT B. MCKERSIE, and HARRY C. KATZ, "U.S. Industrial Relations in Transition," *Monthly Labor Review*, 108, no. 5 (1985), 28.
29. RAY MARSHALL, *Unheard Voices: Labor and Economic Policy in a Competitive World* (New York: Basic Books, 1987), p. 165.
30. Ibid., p. 164.
31. MARK RUSHEVSKY, "Reducing Risk Conflict by Regulatory Negotiation: A Preliminary Evaluation," paper presented at the annual meeting of the American Political Science Association, Washington, D.C. August 28–31, 1986.
32. CONNIE P. OZAWA and LAWRENCE SUSSKIND, "Mediating Science-Intensive Policy Disputes," *Journal of Policy Analysis and Management*, 5, no. 1 (1985), 23–39.
33. JOHN MENDELOFF, "Regulatory Reform and OSHA Policy," *Journal of Policy Analysis and Management*, 5, no. 3 (1986), 440–468.
34. HENRY H. PERRITT, JR., "Negotiated Rulemaking in Practice," *Journal of Policy Analysis and Management*, 5, no. 3 (1986), 482–495.
35. DANIEL J. FIORINO, "Regulatory Negotiation as a Policy Process," *Public Administration Review* (July/August 1988).
36. GAIL BINGHAM, *Resolving Environmental Disputes: A Decade of Experience* (Washington, D.C.: Conservation Foundation, 1986), p. xv.
37. RUSHEVSKY, "Reducing Risk Conflict," p. 5.
38. OZAWA and SUSSKIND, "Mediating Science-Intensive Policy Disputes," p. 32.
39. RUSHEVSKY, "Reducing Risk Conflict," p. 5.
40. FIORINO, "Regulatory Negotiation," pp. 764, 768.
41. OZAWA and SUSSKIND, "Mediating Science-Intensive Policy Disputes," p. 33.
42. BINGHAM, *Resolving Environmental Disputes*, pp. 128–129.
43. Ibid., p. 159.
44. Ibid., p. 160 (emphasis in original).

45. PHILIP H. ABELSON, "Scientific Advice to the Congress," in *Science and Technology Advice to the President, Congress, and Judiciary*, ed. William T. Golden (New York: Pergamon Press, 1988), p. 396.

46. MICHAEL L. TELSON and ALBERT H. TEICH, "Science Advice to the Congress: The Congressional Science and Engineering Fellows Program," in *Science and Technology Advice to the President, Congress, and Judiciary*, ed. William T. Golden (New York: Pergamon Press, 1988), p. 448.

47. Ibid., p. 451.

48. JAMES EVERETT KATZ, "Congress Needs Informal Science Advisors: A Proposal for a New Advisory Mechanism," in *Science and Technology Advice to the President, Congress, and Judiciary*, ed. William T. Golden (New York: Pergamon Press, 1988), p. 428 (emphasis in original).

49. DAVID Z. BECKLER, "Science and Technology in Presidential Policy-Making: A New Dimension and Structure," in *Science and Technology Advice to the President, Congress, and Judiciary*, ed. William T. Golden (New York: Pergamon Press, 1988), p. 33.

50. President's Commission on Industrial Competitiveness, *Global Competition: The New Reality*, vol. 2 (Washington, D.C.: U.S. Government Printing Office, January 1985).

51. G. A. KEYWORTH, and BRUCE ABELL, "Priority for Science and Technology," *Technology in Society*, 8, no. 1/2 (1986), 13–14 (emphasis in original).

52. LEWIS M. BRANSCOMB, "A Federal Department of Science and Technology: The Case For and Against," *Technology in Society*, 8, no. 1/2, 65–69.

53. RICHARD BARKE, *Science, Technology, and Public Policy* (Washington, D.C.: CQ Press, 1986), p. 90.

54. WILLIAM W. LOWRANCE, *Modern Science and Human Values* (New York: Oxford University Press, 1985), p. 187.

55. FREDERICK ELLISTON, JOHN KEENAN, PAULA LOCKHART, and JANE VAN SCHNICK, *Whistleblowing: Managing Dissent in the Workplace* (New York: Praeger, 1985), p. 133.

56. ROSEMARY CHALK, MARK S. FRANKEL, and SALLIE B. CHAFER, *AAAS Professional Ethics Project: Professional Ethics Activities in the Scientific and Engineering Societies* (Washington, D.C.: American Association for the Advancement of Science, 1980), p. 103.

57. ROSEMARY CHALK and FRANK VON HIPPEL, "Due Process for Dissenting Whistle-Blowers," *Technology Review*, June/July 1979, p. 52.

58. RALPH NADER, "An Anatomy of Whistle Blowing," in Ralph Nader, et al., eds. *Whistle Blowing: The Report of the Conference on Professional Responsibility* (New York: Grossman Publishers, 1972), p. 4.

Index

Abernathy, William, 23–27, 31, 83, 85
Academe, 60, 61, 134
Academic-professional arena, 11, 15, 21, 29,
  37, 38, 41, 52, 59, 60, 63, 68, 69, 76,
  107–9, 115, 119, 134, 135, 147, 156,
  158, 166, 171, 174, 176, 182, 184–87,
  194, 195, 204, 212, 231–33, 235
Accommodations, 18, 73, 98, 100, 103, 113
Acid rain, 131, 139, 145, 151, 240
Adams, Gordon, 102, 103, 113
Ad hoc groups, 15
Administration, 60, 68, 116, 118–19, 121,
  130, 136–38, 140, 141–48, 150, 162,
  167–68, 170–73, 183, 197, 201
Administrative procedures, 5, 158, 166, 239
Administrative Procedures Act, 55, 161
Administrative rule making, 161
Administrators, 39–40, 143, 160, 181–82, 191
Adversarial techniques, 47
Advisory committees, 103–4, 232
Aeronautical and astronautical engineers, 60
Agriculture, 13, 178, 183, 196–97, 209
Agriculture, Department of, 34, 130
Alar (Daminozide), 148
Alliances, 75, 201
Allison, Graham, 115
American Association for the Advancement of
  Science (AAAS), 62, 231, 237
American corporations, 3, 82, 86, 90
American leadership, 79
American manufacturers, 79, 82, 84
American scientific and technological
  dominance, 81
Animal rights movement, 69
  animal experiments, 157
  animals in laboratory research, 69
  animal research, 69, 74

animal rights, 64, 69, 74
animal suffering, 69
  maimed or injured animals, 69
  small cages, 69
Anti-ballistic missile, 37, 117
Anti-environmental forces, 132
Anti-Vivisectionists, 69
Appealable questions, 56
Applied research, 61, 119
Architectural phase innovation, 26
Armed forces, 98, 103
Armed services, 105–6, 116
Artificial satellite, 36
Asbestos, 47, 168
Asilomar conference, 184–85, 192
Atkinson, Rick, 120
Atomic bomb, 35, 108
Authorities, 236
Automation, 28, 71–72, 80, 92–94
Automobile, 3, 27, 66, 71, 82, 92, 131, 145
Autonomy, 185, 188, 195

B-1 bomber, 106, 112
B-2 bomber, 9
Barke, Richard, 42, 50, 234
Basic research, 61–62
Benzene, 47
Berle, A.A., 219
bGH, 201–3, 205
bGH-treated milk, 202
Bingham, Gail, 229
Bioassays, 168–69
Bioengineered materials, 16
Biologists, 60, 184, 187, 189, 196
Biomedical research, 13
Biotechnology, 9, 83, 178–84, 189, 194–203,
  209

243